UNDERSTANDING THE LEISURE AND SPORT INDUSTRY

UNDERSTANDING THE LEISURE AND SPORT INDUSTRY

Chris Wolsey and Jeff Abrams (Editors)

Peter Bramham
Angela Green
Dominic Irvine
Sue Minten
Geoff Nichols
Leigh Robinson
Stephen Robson
John Spink
Peter Taylor
Mel Welch
Helen Whitrod Brown

Pearson Education Limited
Edinburgh Gate
Harlow
Essex CM20 2JE, England
and Associated Companies throughout the world

ISBN 0 582 38165 7

British Library Cataloguing-in-Publication Data
A catalogue record for this book is available from the British Library.

Set by 35 in 9.5/12pt Garamond Light
Printed and bound by CPI Antony Rowe, Eastbourne

Contents

Preface

Understanding the Leisure and Sport Industry provides a contemporary, applied and critical look at this important and rapidly expanding area of public, commercial and voluntary sector provision. The book is specifically aimed at those with a degree of prior knowledge in this area and seeks to apply received wisdom to the leisure and sport context. By adopting an applied look at contemporary issues, the reader is encouraged to draw both direct and indirect linkages between generic theory and the current challenges facing managers within the leisure and sport sector.

The leisure and sport industry is changing at a quickening pace. What was once relatively straightforward is becoming increasing difficult to rationalise. *Understanding the Leisure and Sport Industry* is intended to provide students, professionals and academics, with a text that is both interesting and informative. Existing managers should find it a useful resource text, helping to contribute towards a more informed understanding of existing challenges and subsequent decisions. For students, it will demonstrate how generic models and theories can be applied to the many contemporary leisure examples that are regularly reported in the literature that surrounds this area.

The book is divided into three sections, as below:

One – The Leisure Providers

Two – The Leisure and Sport Markets

Three – The Management of Leisure and Sport Organisations

An introduction is provided to each of the three sections. This provides the *rationale for the grouping of topics* and allows individual sections to be viewed as a whole and not simply a collection of unrelated chapters.

Individual chapters provide an up-to-date look at one aspect of the leisure and sport industry. However, it would be impossible to deal with all areas and all examples within the confines of a single chapter. Given the potential breadth and expressed aims of this book, the chapters focus on a more limited number of issues, reflecting the author's own areas of interest and expertise. In this way, each chapter reflects the individual style of the authors and provides varying mixtures of breadth and depth, applied to a specific leisure or management context. For example, Chapter 1 looks at the public sector through the lens of sports development, whilst Chapter 3 deals with the voluntary sector by taking a critical look at research based around the Guide Association. Although there are a range of different examples used throughout the book, each chapter is not burdened with the impossible task of attempting to be all things to all people. Given this approach, the reader should gain a deeper insight into the topics covered. This can then be transferred to areas of more personal interest.

Each chapter is capable of being read outside of the natural structure of the book. The Chapter Content is listed in order to provide the reader with *an indication of the areas covered.* More information is provided by the Abstract, which provides a *summary of the main issues* to be addressed by the chapter. Readers can dip in and out of the book, depending upon their particular area of interest. However, appropriate linkages with other chapters have been made in order to promote a wider and deeper understanding of the various topics that cumulatively constitute the full text. These are covered in the Related Chapters section and provide an indicative look at the *other related areas that lie outside of the section* in which the chapter is located. This is not meant to provide an exhaustive list, but merely make suggestions vis-à-vis areas of commonality and/or further development. The intention is to promote the multi-disciplinary nature of the literature available in this field. Indeed, it would be possible for all chapters to be linked in this way, if this was taken to its logical conclusion. Learning Outcomes are then listed in order to give an *indication of the chapter's objectives.* Readers are encouraged to critically engage with the subject matter in a way that *encourages the further development of ideas* by enabling rhetoric to be actively separated from reality. This is further promoted by providing a series of Suggested Tasks for Further Study.

As we move into the new millennium, there is a need for both managers and students to be reflective and reflexive in their approach to work, leisure and life in general. This requires the development of both knowledge and understanding in a way that is empathetic to individual goals and those of significant others. *Understanding the Leisure and Sport Industry* is designed to facilitate a deeper understanding of a selection of issues that have relevance to this area. A critical understanding of both theory and its application to practice should lead to better decisions and more considered approaches to existing challenges.

Section One

The Leisure Providers

The first section of the book deals with an area traditionally covered by most texts of this nature, i.e. the public, voluntary and commercial leisure sectors. This section provides an updated look at these areas by providing a commentary on the recent research and events that shape their contemporary development.

Chapter 1, written by *Stephen Robson*, discusses the impact of Compulsory Competitive Tendering on the public leisure sector. The chapter goes on to more recent developments by addressing the current issue of Best Value and how this is impacting on the sector in general and sports development in particular. Underpinning the chapter is the use of organisation theory to evaluate and critique these recent developments. The chapter sets out not merely to evaluate these issues from the position of managers, but also from the perspective of all relevant stakeholders such as politicians, users and non-users.

Chapter 2 deals with the UK commercial sector. The authors, *Dominic Irvine* and *Peter Taylor*, begin by defining the concept of the commercial sector and by covering four main areas: the nature of markets; the importance of branding; the use of strategic alliances; and, the role of technology within the sector. These areas are supported by recent research completed by the authors that reinforces the nature of the changes within the sector. The chapter also identifies cultural issues as being key in how the UK commercial sector responds to the four themes developed within the chapter. The complexity of the sector and therefore management within the sector is also discussed. The chapter provides an analysis of the commercial sector's impact on leisure provision and the pervasive challenges of consumerism and with it, the increasing commodification of global leisure experiences.

Chapter 3, written by *Geoff Nichols* discusses the nature, size and importance of the UK voluntary sector. This is done by firstly defining the sector, then by discussing the relationship between the public, commercial and voluntary sectors. The focus of the chapter is on sport and, therefore, covers the impact that the UK Sports Council has on voluntary sporting organisations. Problems facing the voluntary sector are identified and discussed.

The chapter also provides recent research regarding the Guide Association to reinforce the discussion in previous sections. The voluntary leisure sector is having to adapt to a variety of external pressures. Increasingly there has been a move towards greater accountability and a need to professionalise within the sector. Despite the fact that vast numbers participate in this area, external pressures are changing the very fabric of their existence. The chapter explores this problem.

Chapter 4 brings together many of the themes developed in the previous chapters and provides a natural coherency to the opening section dealing with The Leisure Providers. *Mel Welch* provides an overview of changes within each sector with a particular focus on sport. This is done from a UK national, regional and local level, but also from a global and international perspective. The chapter provides an historical overview of the development of sport within the various sectors. This is followed by a discussion of the range of sport providers and the impact of the market and professionalisation on sport. The chapter provides a source of coherence for the previous chapters in this section by applying relevant themes to the specific UK and international sports context.

Chapter 1

The Public Sector, Best Value and Local Authority Sports Development

Stephen Robson
Leeds Metropolitan University

Chapter Content

Abstract

The purpose of this chapter is twofold – to give the reader an appreciation of key recent developments in the field of public sector leisure and sport provision, and to illustrate how the application of relevant organisation theory can foster an enhanced and more critical understanding of the organisations and structures involved. It would, of course, be impossible within the scope of the chapter to deal, in any meaningful way, with the full range of organisations and the provision they make. Thus, the relatively new profession of sports development will provide the main focus. By engaging with selected principles of organisation theory, as they apply to this particular field, the reader will gain a deeper understanding of their wider use.

A brief review of the role of the public sector in sport provision will be presented. The influence of central governmental politics will be a particular focus. Contemporary examples will illustrate how the changing political landscape has affected the UK public sector. Critical comment on the impact of Compulsory Competitive Tendering (CCT) will be offered (from the viewpoint of the sports development process). The onset and implications of the current Best Value initiative will be considered in depth by means of a case study.

Organisation theory will be presented, with reference to the implementation of Best Value. This relates to the structure and function of bodies with responsibility for sports development, particularly within local authorities. The effects of organisational culture will be considered and environmental analysis will highlight the vital role that partnerships have to play in the sports development process.

Related Chapters

Chapter 6: Strategy, Competition and the Commercial Leisure Markets: The two chapters review different approaches to understanding various strategic aspects of contemporary leisure markets. Approaches are transferable across the public and commercial sectors. For example, the 'cultural web' section could be applied to any commercial leisure organisation. Similarly, this approach could be contrasted with the section dealing with Strategic HRM in Chapter 6.

Chapter 7: Access and Leisure Policy: This provides a case study dealing with issues of access to the countryside. Such issues could, usefully, provide a frame of reference to discuss the access to sporting facilities and further explore the managerial implications of leisure/public policy, as applied to sport development.

Chapter 11: Service Quality and the Public Leisure Industry: The need for accountability is a key characteristic of approaches to the quality assurance of public sector service delivery levels. The quality literature could be contrasted with the actualities of operating in a Beckett Park-on-Sea SDU, in which accountability rules and the means seem to justify the ends!

Learning Outcomes

- to provide an overview of the range and historical context of public sector organisations engaged in the provision of sporting opportunities
- to illustrate the impact of governmental policy on sports development service delivery
- to provide an appreciation of the potential impact of Best Value for sports development professionals
- to provide an appreciation of how organisation theory can be applied to the sports development context

Introduction

This chapter deals with both the sports development process and the sports development profession. Eady (1993:10) posits that sports development should seek to promote positive change 'in the context of sporting structures and opportunities'. This will take place through a combination of both direct and indirect provision. However, sports development provides far more than a purely provisional remit. It also acts as a critical and creative advocate for this area by challenging traditions, removing barriers to participation and influencing the political and structural forces which direct UK sport. In order to establish the appropriate context, it is useful to briefly consider the historical backdrop of this relatively young profession, although for a fuller discussion of the history and development of the public leisure sector see Haywood *et al.* (1995).

The notion and language of the 'sports development' process and profession were established in the early 1980s. This followed the initiation, during the preceding 20 years, of key national agencies concerned with sport management. Following the Great War of 1914–1918, the Forestry Commission became the first governmental body with a statutory responsibility for recreation. Notable legislation between the wars (e.g. the Physical Recreation and Training Act, 1937) sought to impose structure to people's leisure behaviour. In 1957 the Wolfenden Committee was formed, tasked to develop proposals for greater cohesion and clarity in sport management. Lord Wolfenden's principal recommendation was for the instigation of a Sports Council, which was finally constituted in 1965 by Wilson's Labour government. In 1972, Heath's Conservative government conferred *quango* (quasi-autonomous non-governmental organisation) status upon the Council. It has since been the subject of lively debate which questions the degree of autonomy it enjoys from central government (see Henry 1993:73).

The onset of the Thatcher Conservative government in 1979 led to a new political and economic environment. Building upon the Sports Council's 'Sport For All' initiative of the mid to late 1970s, funding was identified for the establishment of *Action Sport* projects, with the expressed intention of providing free daytime, publicly funded, sports activities. Following the inner-city riots of the early 1980s, this could be cynically viewed as a politically motivated decision as the government grappled with increasing levels of unemployment and disillusionment among the nation's youth. However, the decision to house the schemes within local authorities proved instrumental to the subsequent establishment of the sports development function within the public sector.

Throughout the 1980s, the notion of sports development became increasingly internalised by local authority managers and politicians. Many of those who had been temporarily employed in the Action Sport scheme were rewarded with more substantive and permanent roles. Thus, at the end of the decade, local authorities were well placed to take advantage of the positive benefits of sports development. Unfortunately, with the onset of Compulsory Competitive Tendering (CCT), the potential to fully exploit this position was mitigated by a number of factors.

Compulsory Competitive Tendering

The term Compulsory Competitive Tendering (CCT) was the ultimate expression of the Conservatives' desire to reduce the scope of local government and to foster a market environment for the provision of public services. While the sports development service was not directly subjected to the rigours of tendering, the implications were clear. Local authorities were required to open up the management of a vast range of their services to the marketplace. From refuse collection to landscaping, private sector organisations were invited to bid for the right to manage these activities more efficiently than their public sector counterparts.

In most areas of the country, with the notable exception of the south-east, most leisure contracts were won by the 'in-house' bid. A number of factors may have contributed to this situation:

- Certain facilities (e.g. swimming pools, municipal golf courses) are subject to high operating costs and subsequently difficult to run at a profit.
- Local authority leisure managers were often shrewd in the way in which they structured specification documents, packaging heavily subsidised facilities together with those more desirable to interested private concerns.
- Similarly, leisure managers used the flexibility of the tendering process to insist upon stringent (and often expensive) health, safety and quality regimes.

Paradoxically, a 1993 Sports Council study concluded that CCT had engendered increased management innovation, but that the sports development activity in public leisure facilities had diminished. One of the principal reasons for this seems to have been that sports development was seen as a form of discrete provision. Specification documents, in many instances, marginalised the role of sports development, with reductions in facility access and the number of joint initiatives. However, in a significant number of areas, far-sighted managers seized the opportunity CCT presented to ensure that sports development was fully supported. Managers recognised that development is a process in which all those with a role to play in sport should be engaged. As a consequence, some sports development professionals were able to lay claim to premium facility time, full engagement in projects by facility staff and, crucially, a voice in important decision-making mechanisms.

No sooner were local authorities becoming accustomed to the rigours and practicalities of tendering and managing services under the umbrella of CCT, than the change of government to Labour in May 1997 precipitated a move to an arguably more exacting accountability measure – Best Value.

Best Value

This section reviews the implications of Best Value in the context of organisation theory. The environmental analysis aspect of this serves to illustrate the disparate range of both individuals and organisations that impact on the sports development arena.

Principles of Best Value

Best Value is here for the foreseeable future and is the expression of the Labour government's manifesto commitment to the modernisation of public services (Labour Party website 2000). Following the 1997 election victory, a number of 'Best Value authorities' were designated. Selected areas of expenditure acted as the test bed for the eventual across-the-board enforcement of the initiative. The 1999 Local Government Act cemented Best Value in the statute books and set out the requirements to which all local authorities in England would ultimately have to conform. The guidance circular distributed by the Department of the Environment, Transport and the Regions (DETR) in 1999 outlined the scope of the modernisation exercise:

> *Best Value authorities (should) make arrangements to secure continuous improvement in the way in which they exercise their functions, having regard to a combination of economy, efficiency and effectiveness.* (DETR 1999:3)

Intriguingly, the document, whilst dealing with the imposition of Best Value through legislation, 'recognises local government as an equal partner with central government' in the initiative. However, if local authorities fail to meet the requirements of the Act, the Secretary of State may implement 'last resort powers' of intervention (DETR 1999:4).

The key demands of Best Value are that local authorities:

- Undertake a leadership role in the form of a *community strategy*, designed to 'improve the social, economic and environmental well-being of their areas' (DETR 1999:4), following appropriate consultation with the local community.
- As a consequence of this exercise, *determine strategic objectives and corporate priorities.*
- Develop a *performance management framework*, incorporating targets for desired performance levels which will be subject to independent auditing.

At the local level, the notion of the 4Cs has attained virtual mantra status, as senior managers are required to:

- *Challenge* purpose
- *Compare* performance
- *Consult* community
- *Compete* with others (DETR 1999:4)

All members of the community should be involved in the process. This includes the 'hard-to-reach', for example, those for whom English is not their first language. This principle is already imbued in the psychological contract that governs the actions of sports development professionals. Multi-agency, cross-sectoral *partnership* working is at the heart of all Best Value programmes. Again, the growth of sub-regional sports development consortia, combined with the need for collaborative ventures to access National Lottery funding (Sport England website 2000) ensures that the profession is already accustomed to working in this manner.

Best Value and local authority sports development

In its document outlining generic performance indicators for 2000–2001, the government acknowledges the contribution that *cultural* services (including sport) make to the quality of life (DETR 1999a: ch10). Crucially, for those attempting to secure long-term funding for such activities, the document recognises the positive role they play in several of the government's wider priority areas, such as social inclusion, healthier lifestyles and life-long learning. It also concedes that, due to the essentially qualitative nature of cultural and related services, it is difficult to develop concrete performance indicators. After all, how does one measure fun?

In keeping with the themes summarised above, all local authorities in England were expected to have a *local cultural strategy* in place by 2002. Unsurprisingly, in outlining performance measures applicable to sport and recreation, the document only makes reference to facility visits and the scale of facility provision. No specific indicators for developmental activity are attempted.

Organisations, such as the Institute of Sport and Recreation Management (ISRM) and Sport England, have undertaken to present the most sophisticated argument yet for the value of sport at all levels in the community. This exercise is driven, in part, by a concern that Best Value may pose a very real threat to public sector sport, given its non-mandatory status in England and Wales. This support mechanism may prove instrumental in securing the continuation of this function within local authorities – particularly those who are less comfortable with this intangible and often politicised service strand.

With this in mind, Sport England (1999) produced a report entitled *The Value of Sport*. Similarly, ISRM argued that the role of sport in the well-being of the nation is incontrovertible and commenced a comprehensive evidence-gathering exercise to that effect. Sport contributes around £10bn/annum to the UK economy and adds kudos to the national and, thus, government profile (ISRM website 1999). The ISRM action plan includes gathering further evidence 'extolling the virtues of sport'. This includes collating information on Best Value good practice and producing specific guidelines on how sport managers should tackle the strategic and evaluative demands discussed above. ISRM also aims to 'form an alliance to push the case of sport and recreation', and to instigate a lobbying campaign. (For further details, see the ISRM website.)

Having examined national priorities and issues, we will now focus on a case study of an existing local authority sports development team, whose role and function shall be subjected to analysis through the lens of relevant organisation theory.

A Case Study of Beckett Park-on-Sea

An interview was conducted with a sports development officer based in an English local authority. In order to highlight issues of interest, an organisation experiencing significant difficulties was selected. For anonymity's sake, the local authority shall be referred to as Beckett Park-on-Sea. The Sports Development Unit (SDU), having previously survived the waves of financial restrictions experienced across the public sector in the 1990s, entered the new century in a mood of uncertainty, as successive council restructuring exercises had resulted in a gradual downsizing of the team. The officer concerned was experiencing an escalating workload in terms of quantity and responsibility, with no additional remuneration and limited support from equally pressurised middle management.

The research focused upon the SDU's likely future in a Best Value environment. This is considered, with specific reference to partnership working, while applied organisation theory provides 'abstract images of what an organization is, how it functions, and how its members and other interested parties interact with and within it' (Hatch 1997:7). The study of partnerships is readily accommodated, particularly in terms of scrutinising *interactions* between organisations and people. Branches of theory include the design and structure of organisations, management of organisations, decision-making, conflict and managing change. The chapter considers the *environmental* and *cultural* dimensions of organisations. However, although these topics will be dealt with discretely, they are indelibly linked to a host of other factors.

Environmental perspective

Organisations are located in an environmental context which is shared with 'other organizations and people with whom transactions have to take place' (Pugh and Hickson 1996:52). The organisational environment for a sporting body incorporates an *interorganisational network* of national and regional governing bodies, government and other political concerns, the public, commercial and voluntary sectors, current and potential sports participants, suppliers and so on. It is apparent that all the inhabitants of the environment are potential Best Value partners.

A *network analysis* 'presents the interorganizational network as a complex web of relationships in which a group of organizations is embedded' (Hatch 1997:65). This enables the manager or student to make a critical assessment of the organisation's wider role. Whilst a full-blown analysis is not within the scope of this chapter, it is necessary to make an assessment of both the key players and the boundaries of the interorganisational network. This will be taken to extend as far as national bodies with an interest in sports development. Figure 1.1 depicts that network. The Beckett Park SDU is placed at the centre of the network for convenience and should not be thought of as occupying that actual position in 'real world' terms.

At the national level, the government, Sport England and other organisations provide a legislative and regulatory framework within which the SDU must function. This relationship creates a dependence upon these bodies for resources of various kinds.

What is perhaps of greatest interest is the interplay between competitors, customers and partners. In the context of Best Value, certain actors in the environment can be placed in all three categories. For instance, the 'in-house' facility management team, is ostensibly an

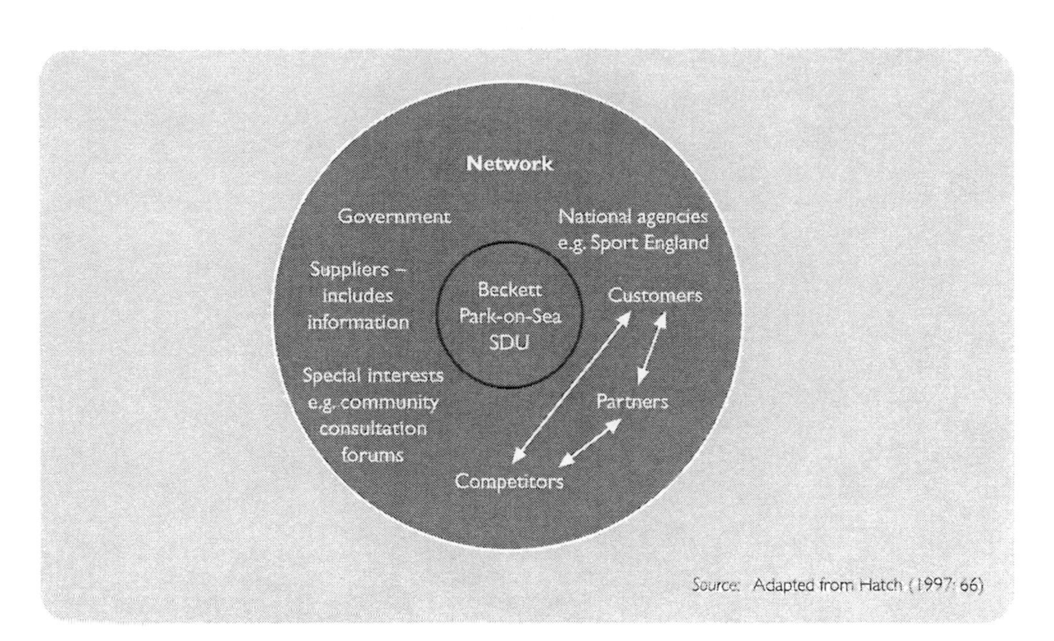

Figure 1.1 Beckett Park-on-Sea sports development team at the centre of its network

internal partner and ally, particularly with reference to health-related initiatives. However, the facilities are also competitors in that they are vying for the time and money of the citizens of the area and customers, in that the SDU occasionally provides technical support on projects. So, in terms of the Best Value requirement to 'compete with others', it is a perplexing task facing the manager who must determine how the competitive relationships *within* the organisation will be handled.

Beyond the confines of the local authority, there are a number of agencies, each pursuing multiple roles, within the interorganisational network. Extensive links exist with the local health authority, as patients are encouraged to become physically active. The healthcare providers are both partners and customers. This is equally true of the patients, as under the 4Cs, the SDU needs to demonstrate that meaningful *consultation* has occurred. Already, it is apparent that organisation theory presents managers and students with an opportunity to shed new light on convoluted scenarios.

All actors in the interorganisational network are subject to changes (demographic, technological, political, technological etc.) to which the organisation needs to be able to respond. These have been classified by Hatch (1997:67) as the *general environment*, as demonstrated by Figure 1.2.

In this context, it is useful to pursue an *environmental analysis* (see for instance Johnson and Scholes 1999: ch3). This identifies the forces that impact on the organisation, but remain outside its direct control (Table 1.1)

A full environmental analysis would clearly involve all elements and necessitate much greater depth. You are encouraged to attempt this in relation to your own organisation or one with which you are familiar. Developing these notions further, we shall now consider the organisation's *interaction* with the environment.

Organisation-environment relations

Early writers on *contingency theory* made an assertion that we today take for granted – that managers should organise as a response to the demands of the environment. This is particularly apropos in the Best Value climate, as aspects of the environment make

Figure 1.2 Sectors of the general environment

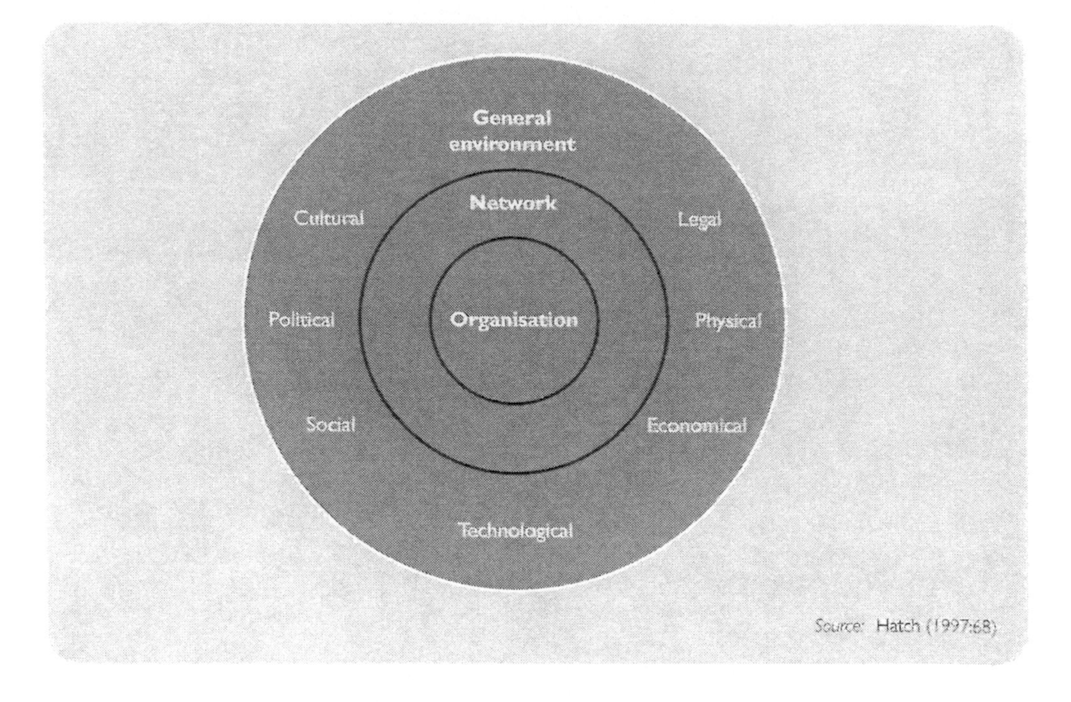

Table 1.1 Sample from an environmental analysis relating to Beckett Park-on-Sea SDU

Category	*Issue*	*Implication for SDU under Best Value*
Cultural	'Footballisation'/ marginalisation of minority sports.	Demonstrate that all reasonable measures are taken to promote wider sport participation.
	Growth of sedentary activities.	Increased efforts to promote physical activity, tying into wider government health agendas.
Political	Government modernising agenda.	Modern approach to service delivery, in line with government priorities.
	'A Sporting Future For All' – government strategy for sport (DCMS 2000).	Demonstrate alignment with key principles.
Social	Some sections of society continue to be socially excluded.	Explicitly address social exclusion through sport. Encourage partner agencies working in this area to embrace sport.
Technological	Internet as a resource for sports organisations.	Gear up to support local voluntary and education sectors in maximising use of the Internet.
	Escalation of computer 'sports participation'.	Address social exclusion and health issues through promoting the benefits of sport.
etc	etc	etc

demands which are disregarded at the SDU's peril. Contingency theory incorporates three key perspectives.

The first of these is *resource dependence*, which assumes that organisations are controlled by their environments, due to the need for resources like knowledge, labour, equipment, customers, political support and so on. A resource dependence analysis begins by tracing each of the needed resources back to its source in order to categorise the levels of dependence (Pfeffer and Salancik cited in Pugh and Hickson 1996). According to the officer, Beckett Park SDU fails to address pure sports development issues, because managerial priorities are skewed towards attracting external finance – 'any initiative accompanied by money is embraced'.

This prevents the SDU from devoting more of its attention to creating a 'counter-dependency' in the environment. Pfeffer and Salancik determined that an organisation should endeavour to render elements of the environment dependent upon it. Ironically, one of the tactics they propose, is to work in partnership with other organisations. The SDU officer felt that partnerships were vital, particularly as prescribed under Best Value, but was concerned about the ability of partners/customers (the distinction is deliberately blurred in Best Value) to articulate the benefits of working with sports development. Schools, who paid a fee to receive coaching sessions in a variety of sports, were 'not the most discerning customer', displaying apathy or inexperience of consuming the service. Many members of the general public, meanwhile, would find it difficult to articulate the esoteric nature of the role and functions of sports development.

Thus, from the *resource dependence* perspective, the SDU officer was uncertain whether key actors in the environment would be in a position to act as advocates for the service, and in so doing, enunciate the counter-dependence that may be critical in Best Value terms.

The second strand of contingency theory, *population ecology*, starts from the same standpoint as resource dependence theory. The difference is that population ecology uses the perspective of the relative success and failure of all the organisations competing in a given 'resource pool' (Hatch 1997:81). The environment has the ability to select from all of the organisations competing for its resources. Writers such as Hannan and Freeman (cited in Pugh and Hickson 1996) see the world of organisations from a Darwinesque 'survival of the fittest' standpoint. Specific areas within the environment, called *ecological niches* create resource pools on which groups of organisations are mutually dependent.

Beckett Park SDU can be said to be dependent on an *ecological niche* in which it is competing with internal and external competitors for public funds. In addition to this, most of its work is currently conducted in partnership with healthcare providers and schools. Thus, the SDU is in pursuit of resources from a wider set of niches and, in certain cases, is in competition with schools and healthcare practitioners for the same resources. Some schools are paying for the same services year-on-year, with seemingly no commitment towards the training of teachers to lead activities as part of an on-going strategy for PE provision. This, it would appear, suits the local authority managers' financial imperative.

Population ecology focuses on patterns of survival, and not on the links between organisations and their environments. Maintaining the Darwinian theme, population ecologists are interested in the evolutionary processes of *variation* (the entry of new organisations into the population, or the adaptation of existing ones), *selection* (by the environment on the basis of fitness) and *retention* (equals survival). Under Best Value, variation implies changing the focus of Beckett Park SDUs work to accommodate the government's requirements. From a partnerships perspective, this will involve consolidating existing links and developing new ones, while demonstrating their effectiveness in order to ensure selection and retention. The SDU officer was sceptical about the likely worth of Best Value performance indicators in terms of measuring qualitative factors, presumably including the quality of partnerships. However, Eady (2000) is optimistic that 'subsidiary indicators' can be developed for facets of sports development work such as partnerships. This may be necessary for selection and retention under the population ecology model, as the Best Value 'competition' theme allows for other organisations to be considered for the sports development delivery role.

The third contingency theory perspective is *institutional theory*. Here, environments force organisations to play specified roles and maintain desired outward appearances by placing social and cultural demands on them. The *institutional environment* represents the shared values of a society to which certain organisations are expected to conform (Hatch 1997:87).

It could be argued that Best Value will result in local authority sport and recreation providers becoming obsessed with harmonising their image to suit the government criteria for quality. In a partnerships sense, this could lead to the inherent problems associated with *enforced* joint working. This runs counter to the SDU officer's assertion that 'the customer will decide what constitutes Best Value', as the organisation, under the institutional model, may invest more in its outward aspect than in meaningful service improvements.

The greatest benefit to the manager or student is to scrutinise the organisation from each of the perspectives and to be prepared for unexpected findings that may result from their triangulation. In the Beckett Park example, the three perspectives all indicate that managers give priority to activities that can be easily monitored and evaluated. In some cases, this will be to the detriment of 'pure development' activities. More optimistically, the performance indicators used to measure sports development may obviate this need. However, this can only be achieved by emphasising initiatives that make a genuine difference.

Dealing with complexity and uncertainty

Finally for this section, we will consider those branches of organisation theory which allow managers to protect their organisations from 'shocks' in the environment. Hatch (1997:88–9) characterises the environment as having properties of complexity (number and diversity of elements) and being subject to constant change. These factors lead to uncertainty in the minds of managers, who lack the information they need to make robust decisions (known as the *information perspective*). Brooks (1999:124) states that 'complete knowledge is unattainable'. The environment for Beckett Park SDU, is clearly complex and contains an array of local, regional and national organisations, across all sectors, at all levels of sport and other services. The SDU officer felt that the 'comparison' aspect of Best Value is therefore problematic, due to the large number of variables at play. The ultimate in uncertainty occurs when, far from having the required information, the manager does not even know what type of information is needed. This may be a reality as Best Value is rolled out across the UK.

Isomorphism

Organisations who adopt a strategy based on isomorphism attempt to match themselves with the complexity of the environment. Two techniques used to achieve this involve *structural differentiation*, i.e. re-ordering aspects of the organisation to deal with specific aspects of the environment (see W. Richard Scott, cited in Hatch 1997:91).

The first of these is known as *buffering*, which is usually applicable to manufacturing organisations. This involves assigning certain personnel to insulate the remainder of the workforce from fluctuations in the environment. Typically, this may include resource shortages or increased demand (Slack 1997). In the partnerships context, Beckett Park SDU is part of an Active Sports consortium. The partnership manager's task is to interpret decisions emanating from Sport England and to disseminate the information to other partners in a way that minimises the disruption to programme delivery.

The second isomorphism technique is *boundary spanning*. This role is the personification of inter-agency working. Bedeian and Zammuto (1991:334) assert that organisations often 'reduce uncertainty by coordinating their activities with other organizations'. Boundary spanners conduct the transfer of information between the organisation and the environment. In the Beckett Park SDU, because of the nature of sports development work, any member of staff engaged in partnership working is fulfilling this function. The duality of the role is central to partnership as the boundary spanner provides decision makers with important information relating to the environment. The information can be taken from a range of diverse activities, from individual sessions to strategy meetings. The image of the SDU and Beckett Park-on-Sea Council is dependent upon the boundary spanners' dealings with outside agencies. This makes a pivotal contribution to matters such as counter-dependence in the environment, as well as the institutional perception of the organisation in the environment. As we have already seen, the SDU officer felt that a limited span of initiatives was being engaged in. As a consequence, the potential of boundary spanning, with respect to Best Value accreditation, was not being maximised.

The above paints a fascinating picture of how one organisation interfaces with its environment. As well as drawing conclusions about Beckett Park SDU, the commentary also reviews the usefulness of a particular theoretical perspective. However, it is also valuable to briefly consider how organisation theory can provide insight into the dynamics of human interaction.

Cultural perspective

Organisational culture can be considered to be 'the way of life in an organization' (Hatch 1997:204), or the meanings and norms shared between individuals within the workplace. Johnson and Scholes (1999) regard it in terms of the taken-for-granted (tacit) assumptions and routines of an organisation. Put another way, culture is 'how things are done around here' (Brown 1998:8).

There are numerous sources of cultural direction, or 'cultural frames of reference'. This section will focus upon those at organisational, functional and divisional levels, as they relate to Beckett Park SDU, and investigates the cultural paradigm, or common set of assumptions (Johnson and Scholes 1999:59) which exists between them. The coherency and nature of the paradigm throughout the intra/inter organisational framework has important implications for the implementation of Best Value.

As part of the research within Beckett Park SDU, an investigation of cultural issues was undertaken, and the findings analysed in the form of the cultural web provided by Johnson and Scholes (1999). This is predicated on the assumption that both physical and verbal clues can provide insight into the assumptions that underpin the organisational paradigm. The cultural web was constructed on the basis of information provided by Beckett Park SDU staff and is shown in Figure 1.3.

Examination of the SDU cultural web supplies new insights and reinforces the findings discussed in the previous section. The cultural condition of the SDU reveals many negative perceptions about the organisation (e.g. lack of prospects, poor managerial support

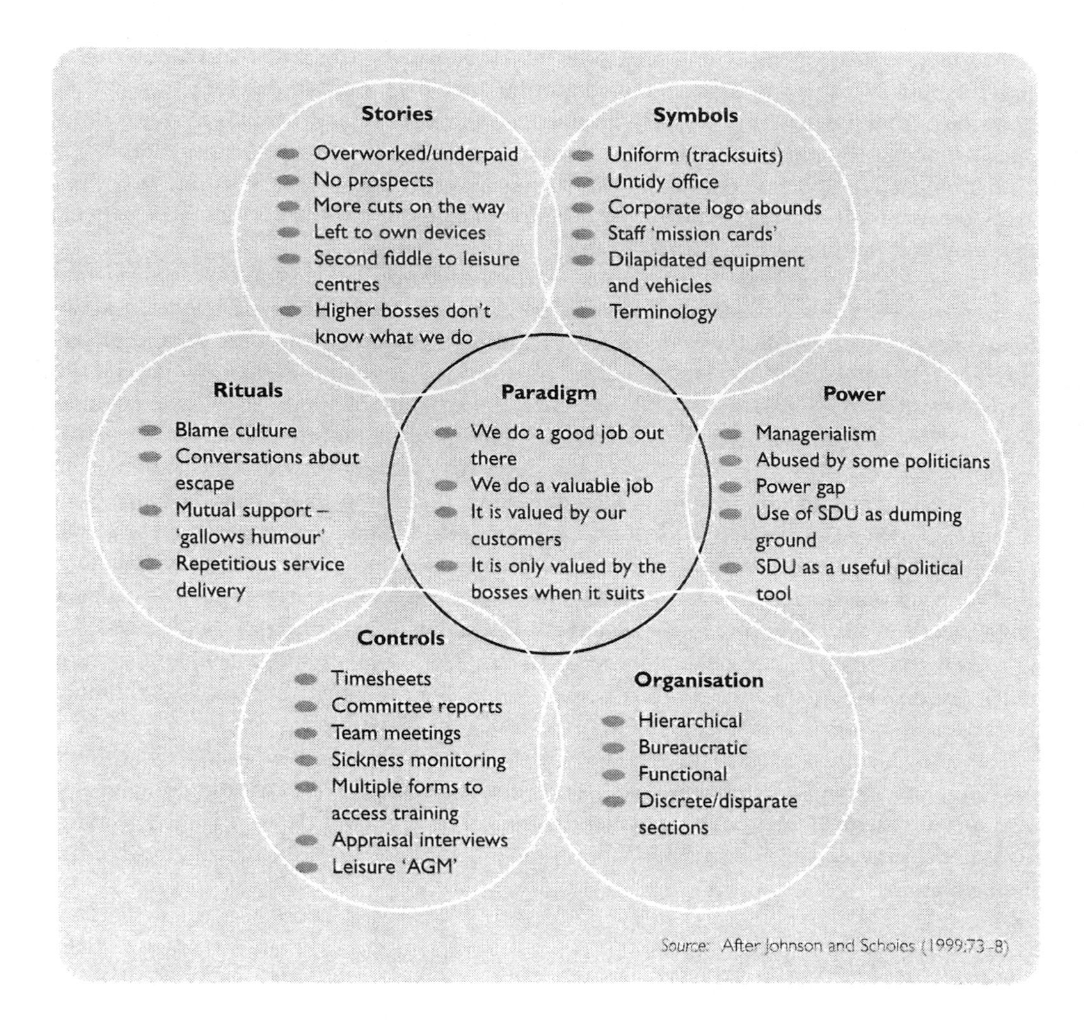

Figure 1.3 Cultural web of Beckett Park-on-Sea SDU

etc.). If this pattern applied across the organisation, this would be evidence of a *thin culture*, i.e. the employees do not subscribe to management values (Slack 1997:276). However, in Best Value terms, it is essential for employees, managers, partners and customers to be 'singing from the same hymn sheet' (thick culture) when service quality is evaluated.

Of course, without a wider study of the entire local authority, it is not possible to determine whether these attitudes are reflective of all staff, or merely a sub-culture at functional (SDU) level (Johnson and Scholes 1999:237). Regardless, the findings are still of great interest and will have a direct bearing on the SDU's performance under Best Value. The key issues from the SDU cultural web and their relevance to Best Value, are considered below.

Morale – this is clearly at a low ebb, as indicated by the stories and rituals in evidence. There is a feeling of being under-valued. Despite the efforts of staff to provide a high quality service, there is no extrinsic motivation to do this in the form of promotional prospects. Unless the SDU is especially isolated and unsupported, it is likely that these experiences are shared by other council staff, thus providing an insight into the cultural frame of reference within the organisation. When the organisation itself, either actively or passively, fails to offer a satisfactory level of support, the council may struggle to justify the existence of the SDU under the 'challenge purpose' ethic, espoused by Best Value.

Functional autonomy v individual accountability – there is a perception among SDU staff that they are often left to fend for themselves in carrying out the sports development function ('stories' section) and that their superiors are largely indifferent to their contribution. Conversely, there appears to be a number of bureaucratic procedures, such as that which governs access to training opportunities ('controls'). Once again, this hints at an organisational culture which undermines staff autonomy through the excessive policing of their activities. If this perceived preoccupation with accountability and protocol is mirrored across the authority, then boundary spanning staff are likely to (in)directly communicate this through their dealings with outside agencies. This has a clear and detrimental impact upon the potential for data collection within Best Value.

Symbols of decline – senior managers, and thus the organisation, can benefit from *managing* organisational culture (Hatch 1997:234). They would ideally like to instil values which are not merely words on paper (e.g. mission statements), but which are subscribed to by all employees. The cultural investigations highlight that, while staff are alert to the value of applying the corporate logo to all published material, they are cynical about initiatives such as the 'mission statement cards' they are asked to carry with them. Of greater relevance to them, in symbolic terms, is the dilapidated condition of their key equipment and transport, which communicates the listlessness of the organisation to their customers and partners. Again, the ramifications for Best Value are distinct.

Summary and Conclusions

Although the analysis of the cultural web has been brief, taken together with the previous environmental analysis, a revealing picture emerges. We have evidence of a service strand in decline (human resource attrition and decreasing financial support). However, despite the perception of managerial apathy, staff retain their pride in a service that is valued by all key stakeholders. As SDU representatives interact within an increasingly complex and resource-hungry environment, they have a growing responsibility to effectively manage the two-way flow of information. This ensures a positive representation within the Best Value framework. The SDU is perhaps best viewed from a *resource dependence* perspective. Although this is not independent from the population ecology and institutional standpoints, it most vividly depicts the constant battle to balance the dependence/counter-dependence equation in its exchanges with the environment. It is a battle the team cannot afford to lose!

Suggested Tasks for Further Study

As has been emphasised throughout the chapter, you are advised to embark upon independent study activities to enhance your understanding of the main issues. If all of the following tasks are addressed, you will have approached the material from a number of perspectives and thus nurtured skills which will have a wide range of managerial and academic applications.

1. Obtain copies of current local authority sports development strategies, and compare the different approaches to partnership evidenced within them.

Suggested Tasks for Further Study continued

Environmental analysis will sharpen your understanding of the organisations' motives for interacting with their partners.

2. Utilising sources such as the ISRM website and the Sport England *Value of Sport* document, prepare the ultimate case for a minority sport of your choice, to convince a resource-pressurised local authority to begin/continue supporting it under Best Value conditions.
3. Obtain and maintain up-to-date information in terms of the progress of Best Value and other government policy initiatives. Compare the responses and performance of several local authorities (utilising the above sports strategies).
4. Develop and review the cultural web relating to a sports organisation with which you are familiar.
5. Trace the history of sports development in the public sector in more detail and, based on historical lessons and the current position, try to make inferences about what the future holds (environmental analysis will also assist with this).
6. With reference to all of your reading about sports development, sports strategies, the current political and social contexts in sport and organisation theory, identify and justify all the factors that contribute to successful partnerships in sport.
7. Read about other branches of organisation theory (as mentioned in this chapter) and experiment with their application to the sports development context.

References

- Bedeian A and Zammuto F 1991 *Organizations: Theory and Design* The Dryden Press, Orlando
- Brooks I 1999 *Organisational Behaviour: Individuals, Groups and the Organisation* Financial Times/Pitman Publishing, London
- Brown A 1998 *Organisational Culture* (2nd Ed) Financial Times/Pitman Publishing, London
- DCMS website at www.culture.gov.uk
- Department for Culture, Media and Sport 2000 *A Sporting Future For All* DCMS, London
- Department for Environment, Transport and the Regions 1999 *Implementing Best Value: A Consultation Paper on Draft Guidance* Downloaded from www.local-regions.detr.gov.uk/bestvalue/bvindex.htm on 25 April 2000
- DETR 1999a *Best Value and Audit Commission Performance Indicators for 2000–2001* ch.10 Downloaded from www.local-regions.detr.gov.uk/bestvalue/indicators/html/10.htm on 25 April 2000
- Drennan D 1992 *Transforming Company Culture* McGraw-Hill, London
- Eady J 1993 *Practical Sports Development* Pitman, Harlow
- Eady J 2000 *Performance Indicators for Best Value* Paper delivered at ILAM Chester 2000 conference 'Contemporary Issues In The Development Of Sport' on 13 April 2000 © Knight, Kavanagh and Page
- Hatch M J 1997 *Organization Theory: Modern, Symbolic and Postmodern Perspectives* Oxford University Press, Oxford
- Haywood L *et al.* 1995 *Understanding Leisure* (2nd Ed) Stanley Thornes, London
- Henry I 1993 *The Politics of Leisure Policy* Macmillan, London
- Institute of Leisure and Amenity Management website at www.ilam.org.uk

- Institute of Sport and Recreation Management 2000 *Best Value – A Position Statement* Downloaded from ISRM website at www.isrm.co.uk/I-bv6.htm on 25 April 2000
- Johnson G and Scholes K 1999 *Exploring Corporate Strategy* (5th Ed) Prentice Hall Europe, Hemel Hempstead
- Labour Party *Manifesto 1997: Because Britain Deserves Better* Downloaded from Labour Party website at www.labour.org.uk on 25 April 2000
- Mullins L 1999 *Management and Organisational Behaviour* (5th Ed) Pitman, London
- Pugh D and Hickson D 1996 *Writers on Organizations* (5th Ed) Penguin, London
- Slack T 1997 *Understanding Sports Organizations* Human Kinetics, Champaign, IL
- Sport England 1999 *The Value of Sport* Sport England, London
- Sport England website at www.english.sports.gov.uk

Chapter 2

Commercial Leisure – an International Perspective

Dominic Irvine
Epiphanies Ltd
Peter Taylor
The University of Sheffield

Chapter Content

Abstract

Following a brief exploration of what is meant by the concept of commercial leisure, this chapter focuses on four main areas: the nature of markets; the importance of branding; the use of strategic alliances; and, the role of technology. Whilst many issues could be included in an analysis of commercial leisure these emerged as the most significant from research undertaken at the University of Sheffield. Any commercial leisure business needs to be aware of the milieu of the market in order to ensure that the offering will not conflict with the market culture. The significance of technology varies from one organisation to another. Whether it is simply the acquisition of a fax machine, or the use of a photocopier, or more sophisticated electronic point of sale (EPOS) systems, technology affects the way in which business is conducted. Whilst competitive advantage may not exclusively depend upon technology, at some point in the process of conducting business it will have played a part. Technology influences whether or not a business engages in strategic alliances and the nature of those strategic alliances. It makes them easier to establish and maintain because of the developments in communication technology. Through strategic alliances it is possible for smaller firms to gain access to the 'well-known name' and brand equity of a larger strategic partner in return for access to niche markets.

Related Chapters

Chapter 6: Strategy, Competition and the Commercial Leisure Markets: The realities facing the commercial leisure sector have a direct link to both the theory and practice of competitive strategy. New markets and market trends create significant challenges for strategic planners. This is particularly true of emerging technologies, which are discussed by both chapters.

Chapter 8: Globalisation: The ability and need for the commercial leisure sector to operate in global markets is further explored by this chapter. Globalisation has opened up new markets and trends as well as new consumer expectations. The chapters complement each other in a number of areas. Approaches to the concept of 'culture', for example, could be compared/contrasted and further explored by the reader.

Learning Outcomes

- to understand what is meant by commercial leisure
- to realise the value of the analysis of commercial leisure
- to appreciate the complexity of issues facing the commercial leisure manager
- to provide insight into the significance of the way markets are defined, the importance of branding, the role of strategic alliances and the influence technology has on commercial leisure

Introduction

At 17.5 per cent of Gross Domestic Product (GDP) (Irvine and Taylor 1998) commercial leisure is unquestionably a significant factor in the UK economy. Yet for many years it has remained an area little analysed other than in a few select areas such as tourism, hospitality and the airline industry.

> *This is worrying because many of the issues of leisure participation and provision can be better explained and understood by a fully informed appreciation of the differences and similarities between public, voluntary and commercial sectors. To do this it is necessary to identify and analyse commercial leisure as a perspective in its own right.* (Irvine and Taylor 1998:158)

The purpose of this chapter is not to explain the lack of research, but to illustrate the range and complexity of the challenges facing commercial leisure managers. Consider the example of attending a football match. The journey to the match might be in a Japanese car, the football clothes designed in Britain but manufactured in Asia, with refreshments at half-time brewed in the UK under licence from an American company and snack food in the interval whose component ingredients have come from across the globe. The complexity of variables in such a scenario in terms of the global interconnectedness (Golblatt *et al.* 1998) gives some idea of the challenge of interpreting the inter-relationships that may exist in contemporary commercial business.

The chapter begins by defining what is meant by commercial leisure and proceeds to examine four major considerations emerging from our research. While a broad range of issues could have been considered: the nature of markets; the role of technology; the use of strategic alliances; and, the importance of branding; emerged as the most significant. The chapter concludes by illustrating the interconnectedness of the variables. These areas are those which emerged as significant following research undertaken at the University of Sheffield, part of an ongoing research project investigating commercial leisure. In-depth interviews were conducted with 23 managing directors, directors and senior managers in 22 commercial leisure companies, ranging in size from multinationals to small limited companies, representing seven sectors of the commercial leisure industry (see Table 2.1). This chapter reports some of the findings from this research and continues the results presented by the authors previously (Irvine and Taylor 1998). For reasons of confidentiality it is not possible to cite the names of the companies or the people interviewed during the research.

Table 2.1 Sample of companies and persons interviewed

	Sector	*Person interviewed*	*Size of company*[1]
1	Airlines and airports (n=3)	Commercial Director	L
2		Commercial Director	M
3		Marketing Director	L
4	Brewers (n=4)	Marketing Director	L
5		Sales Manager	S
6		Strategic Director[2]	L
7	Film and television (n=5)	Assistant Director	L
8		Managing Director	L
9		Managing Director	M
10		Marketing Director	L
11		Marketing Manager	M
12	Gambling (n=2)	Managing Director	L
13		Strategic Director	L
14	Hotels and leisure centres (n=5)	Managing Director	L
15		Managing Director	S
16		Marketing Director	L
17		Marketing Director	L
18		Marketing Director	S
19	Sports equipment manufacturers (n=2)	Managing Director	M
20		Managing Director	M
21	Travel agents and tour operators (n=2)	Managing Director	L
22		Managing Director	S

[1] Size of company as defined by the Commission of the European Communities (1992). The total number of companies examined by size was: Large 13, Medium 5, Small 4. The definition of each, according to the Commission of the European Communities (1992) is as follows. The definition of a small enterprise is: it has no more than 50 employees and either an annual turnover not exceeding ECU 5 million (£6,000,000), or a balance sheet total not exceeding ECU 2 million, and is not more than 25 per cent owned by one or more companies not falling within this definition, except public investment corporations, venture capital companies or, provided no control is exercised, institutional investors. The definition of a medium-sized enterprise is: it has no more than 250 employees and either an annual turnover not exceeding ECU 20 million (£24,000,000), or a balance sheet total not exceeding ECU 10 million, and is not more than 25 per cent owned by one or more companies falling within this definition, except public investment corporations, venture capital companies or provided no control is exercised, institutional investors. Any enterprises exceeding these criteria can be considered large (Commission of the European Communities 1992:5).
[2] The person interviewed had recently moved post from a senior position within one of the subsidiaries to head office. As a consequence the person was interviewed twice, once from the perspective of the former role and once in the new capacity.

What is Commercial Leisure?

In order to be able to discuss commercial leisure it is first necessary to have a common understanding as to what is meant by the terms commercial and leisure. As Barrett (1989:9) noted:

> *Of all concepts that of leisure is the most intractable. Like the concept of time, in the words of St Augustine, we know what it is when no-one asks us, but when they ask we are hard put to find an answer.*

Commercial leisure is subject to the same conceptual difficulties as general definitions of leisure (e.g. see Barrett 1989; Glyptis 1989; Kelly 1990; Rojek 1989). As Kelly and Godbey (1992:13) show, each definition of leisure:

> *. . . is valid according to its own premises. Each of these perspectives is a metaphor that says, 'Viewed from this perspective, leisure is essentially like this'. This metaphorical approach takes the variety of definitions as complementary rather than competing. Each metaphor focuses on one or more aspects of the complex whole, not denying the others but stressing one. Metaphors of leisure, then, can begin with a stated premise. For example, a psychologist may begin, 'Viewed as experience, leisure is . . .'.*

The conceptual issue of what is commercial leisure depends on the paradigm adopted which in turn is dependent upon the ideas and opinions of the researcher and not on facts alone (Guba 1990). In this instance, the ideas and issues discussed in this chapter reflect the post positivist approach taken by researchers at the University of Sheffield. The post positivist perspective accepts that reality exists but recognises the difficulty of its comprehension (see Guba 1990 for a more detailed explanation).

In our earlier work (Irvine and Taylor 1998:159) it was argued that:

> *A commercial leisure organisation is primarily concerned with generating profit from leisure. Given that a profit is generated by businesses through the provision of products or services, commercial leisure refers to those leisure activities which depend on goods and services commercially provided. In accepting activities as the basis for defining leisure the well documented ambiguities detailed in sociological texts have some relevance.*

Thus commercial leisure refers to activities undertaken for profit. Issues of whether sponsorship/patronage ought to be included in the concept and the distinction between primary and secondary activities are addressed in full in Irvine and Taylor (1998). In essence, for the purpose of this chapter, the activities outlined in Table 2.2 are those that constitute commercial leisure. Table 2.2 is divided into two sections, *areas* and *fields*. The areas are the broad sectors of commercial leisure activities, while the fields represent the various activities that make up each area. The list is not exhaustive as new activities will emerge which will need to be classified.

In adopting this approach the following assumptions have been made:

- *Obligated activities are excluded*: The extent to which an activity is obligated is a moot point. By implication the examples in Table 2.2 are non obligated but in many cases it is not clear cut.
- *Illegal activities are excluded*: This removes from the analysis issues such as drug taking and prostitution.
- *Commercial leisure activities*: exclude other activities which may be undertaken in order to make the event possible. For example, when going to play a game of tennis, the travelling to and from the facility would be excluded.

Table 2.2 Summary of the commercial leisure market

Area	Examples
Arts	Reading material
	Brown goods
	CDs/Records/Tapes
	Radio relay services
	Musical instruments
	Museums and galleries
	Theatre and concerts
	Cinema
	Television relay services
	Photography/films/processing
	Music, video tapes
Sports	Participation
	Equipment
	Clothing and footwear
	Spectating
Attractions	Country houses
	Historic attractions
	Zoos
	Amusement parks
	Wildlife parks
	Theme parks
Travel	Travel agents
	Tour operators
Transport	To and from participating in leisure activities, or as a leisure activity in its own right, e.g. motoring for pleasure, rail or boat trips
Accommodation	Hotels
	Leisure villages
	Boats
	Second homes
	Holiday camps
	Caravanning
	Camping
Eating	Restaurants
	Fast food
	Take away
	Hotels
	Public houses
	Eating as occasion
	Snack bars
	Clubs
	Contract catering
Alcohol	Off licence
	Home brewing
	Licensed premises
Gambling	Amusement arcades
	Bingo
	Gaming
	Pools
	Betting
	Lotteries
	Casinos
Dancing	Dance schools
	Discos
	Night clubs
	Dance halls
Tobacco	All tobacco products
Home environment	Home computers
	Gardening
	Toys
	Car maintenance
	Art and antiques
	Games
	Hobbies
	DIY
	Pets and pet foods

Conceptually another clarification is needed between the following:

- *the commercial leisure industry*
- *the commercial leisure market*

. . . The commercial leisure market refers to those leisure activities which require a financial transaction to have taken place either between the participant (or on behalf of the participant) and a commercial organisation. Whilst the commercial organisation supplying the goods or services is part of the leisure market, it may well be that the leisure related aspect of their business is a minor part of their operation. A focus on the commercial leisure industry would be on those organisations whose

> core business *is the provision of goods and/or services for the leisure market. As such, the leisure industry may not represent the whole of the leisure market. Therefore to understand fully commercial leisure, it is necessary to adopt both a market and an industry based focus.* (Irvine and Taylor 1998:159)

Perception of Markets

The nature of commercial leisure necessitates viewing the markets from which goods/services are supplied and those to which they are provided in the widest sense. The view that a commercial leisure firm is often too small to be concerned about the bigger global picture is myopic.

> *. . . even firms which have no intention of entering other international markets are likely to find themselves in competition with international firms which have already entered, or are about to enter, their domestic market. This will change the basis of competition within domestic markets irrespective of the prevailing strategies of individual firms.* (Segal-Horn 1994:41–2)

Aside from the economic issues which merit separate consideration, understanding the international commercial leisure market requires an appreciation of two main factors, cultural and political issues. While these affect international trade in terms of the difference between nationalities, there are even greater variations intra-nation than inter-nation (Roth 1995).

Cultural variables

Despite the arguments propounded by Levitt (1983), Leontiades (1986), Turner and Hodges (1992) and others, on the shift towards increasing homogeneity of markets, no evidence was found in support of these claims. The evidence from the research undertaken at the University of Sheffield is that the nation state and the region remain significant defining variables of a leisure market. Primarily, this appears to be because of cultural variations within and between each nation state.

To take an example from our research, consider a student wishing to travel. According to the director of a travel agency for students, the French student does not wish to purchase products that overtly associate them with being a student, whilst a Greek student prefers to purchase travel services from an agency run by Greeks. In contrast, the British student requires the most competitive price regardless of whether this means being identified as a student or whether the service provider is British or otherwise. While a somewhat stereotypical image, it nonetheless illustrates how, according to the perception of those who run the business, student travel services are varied depending which country in Europe the service is being offered. The variations globally will be greater still. These factors are not limited to leisure. The medical care of students is similarly affected by the cultural background of the student (Irvine 1998). Cultural variables not only dictate the type of offering made to the customer but also the way in which business is conducted between businesses from one country and another.

As noted in 1968 (Buzzell 1968:104), and still seems to be the case today, over 30 years on '. . . a company should offer products, as well as packages, advertisements, and other marketing elements which are tailored to that country's distinctive needs and desires'. Other cultural factors that need to be considered include colour: for Northern Europe black has associations of premium quality products whereas in Southern Europe it has associations '. . . more mortuary than luxury' (Gander 1996:59). One of the key cultural differences is language. When cultural variations in language are ignored, the consequences can be serious, if not a little amusing:

> *Brand names with potency in one language have unfortunate connotations in another. Classic cases are two soft drinks, France's Pshitt and Japan's Pocari Sweat – both of which have unfortunate connotations in English. The attempt to sell a deodorant called 'Silver Mist' in Germany was hindered by the fact that 'mist' is the German for manure, while Coca Cola's carbonated beverage 'Mellow Yellow' had to be renamed in Thailand because in Thai 'yellow' means 'pus'.*
>
> (Turner and Hodges 1992:38)

Brown (1997:52) in an article asking 'What's in a name?' provides several more examples:

> *Plopp chocolate may go down well in Scandinavia but it is hardly likely to catch on here. The same is true for . . . France's 'Dribly' lemonade, and 'Kräpp' toilet paper from Sweden . . . Toyota's 'MR2' which sounds fine except in French, when it is pronounced 'M-er-deux'.*

Such examples are a warning that product naming, particularly when the name is designed for world-wide use, can be problematic.

> *In so far as the languages of cultures are not simply different, but in some instances are 'other in nature and radically so', then interlocution between cultures will continue to be subject to interference, to misunderstandings and misinterpretations, no matter how 'universal' our assumptions might be, or rather, particularly when we assume the existence of universality.* (Smart 1994:155–6)

Roth (1995) argues that strategies should be developed on a regional or even city-wide level and evidence was found from the research of such an approach within the brewing industry. This reflects the fact that there are often greater cultural differences *intra-nationally* than *inter-nationally*. Irrespective of where the differences lie '. . . cultural values rather than . . . material and structural conditions, are ultimate determinants of human organisation and behaviour, and thus determinants of economic growth' (Franke, Hofstede and Bond 1991:165–6) and hence are a topic for serious consideration by those working within the commercial leisure sector. Markets are more than just those groups of customers who are prepared to purchase a particular product or service as often seen by leisure academics. Successfully understanding cultural issues may mean it is possible to expand the market and/or achieve greater sales to an existing market which has implications for the effectiveness of commercial leisure in meeting social needs. Cultural variables are not the only critical factor in distinguishing markets. Political variables can also affect how markets are perceived.

Political variables

According to Grosse and Behrman (1992:94), the main distinction '. . . between domestic and international business is the existence of interventions by Governments of home and host countries in inter-country business activity'. Rugman and Verbeke (1991:66) define government interventions as 'shelter' barriers, where the word 'shelter' refers to '. . . an entry barrier which imposes artificial costs on rival firms. Government protection in the form of a tariff is an example of shelter'. In terms of identifying political issues that face leisure companies, Yong Kim and Olsen suggest:

the multinational firm faces many of the same events in the political environment as do other multinational industries. Limits on convertibility of local currency into foreign currency, restrictions on repatriation of capital, profit and management fees, restrictive labour laws, unique taxation policies and licensing agreements appear to have impacts on all businesses. (Yong Kim and Olsen 1993:171)

Yong Kim and Olsen (1993) provide an indication of the sort of barriers that hotel chains, for example, ought to expect to have to manage. These include, the minimum standards that are required in order to satisfy government rating schemes, restrictions in opening hours for restaurants and restrictions on the type of events that can be held in restaurants, the latter may be a result of religious restrictions. The point being made is that any company wishing to expand, must avail itself of as much information on restrictions that exist. This is in order to make the most informed decision possible especially as Poynter argues that most government interventions are costly to international business:

Government regulation and intervention has always been an important factor in international business operations. The impact of government's role varies from country to country, and in the same country from industry to industry and even from firm to firm. While some form of government intervention such as financial support and trade protection are often sought by international firms, most government intervention is costly to them. (Poynter 1985:1)

A manufacturer of climbing equipment reported that the European rules and regulations relating to safety equipment are perhaps one of the most effective shelter barriers preventing US companies entering the European market. A UK brewer identified the German regulations that restrict the ingredients in beer as being effective in protecting German brewers. Similarly, the Scandinavian requirements in terms of packaging of beers provide an effective shelter barrier by virtue of the fact that the costs associated with producing the required packaging and meeting the recycling regulations are prohibitive for a regional brewer in the UK looking to expand into other markets.

Major changes in the political leadership of a country can affect the trade that is possible. The failure of Communism and the increasing ethnic fragmentation in the Balkans have affected the nature and extent of trade. With the demise of apartheid in South Africa changes in legislation affecting the gaming industry necessitated some companies such as Sun International having to review their strategies. In as much as shelter barriers affect the format and distribution of the offering so too do issues of branding.

Branding

'Whether it's a well-known manufacturer's brand or a commodity group's trademark, branding represents an accumulation of quality imagery and goodwill that makes an indelible impression on the customer's mind' (Scarpa 1996:8). The significance of a well-known name or brand should not be underestimated. For example, Turner and Hodges (1992:34) argue that brand identity is a crucial variable in global trade.

What is happening in today's triad world is that the brand-driven giants – firms like Proctor & Gamble, Unilever, Levi Strauss, Mars, Kellogg's, Phillip Morris, Coca-Cola, Pepsi-Cola, Nestlé, Grand Metropolitan, LVMH (Louis Vuitton-Moët-Hennessey), Shiseido et al. *– are making a once and for all grab to fill the branding vacuums exposed by the lowering of barriers of national markets and the increasing internationalization of business.*

Such is the significance of a global brand name, that Turner and Hodges (1992:35) argue that 'whoever can establish their brands as leaders around the globe today will go a long way to establishing a lead position for years to come . . .'. Shocker, Srivastava and Ruekert (1994:150) would seem to agree, in order for brands to survive locally, it is necessary that they must '. . . thrive globally'. Given that this is the case, ownership of a brand with substantial value is a distinct advantage. According to Kahan (1996), a well-known name is a company's most valuable asset. A brand is the one item that is likely to last beyond the life span of most products, chief executives, and even beyond that of the company itself.

> *As companies merge and downsize, as CEOs come and go each time a corporation reinvents itself, brands may be the only thing to remain intact. The Pan Am brand for example, continues to live on and continues to attract buyer interest, even though the airline itself is long gone. Brands are becoming more important than ever, more important than the products themselves. Product can be duplicated quickly and easily. Brands cannot. Not surprisingly when all is said and done, leading global brands have become among the most valuable assets a company owns.*
> (Kahan 1996:142)

Companies such as Nike and Levi Strauss are no longer in the business of manufacturing, they are in the business of marketing. As Donaghu and Barff (1990:542) noted in their research into the athletic footwear industry and in particular Nike: '. . . virtually 100 per cent of the company's product is manufactured by production "subcontractors".' Given that brands have such value, as Saunders and Guoqun (1996:29) suggest:

> *. . . the way a company uses its portfolio of brands is a top management decision. It is somewhat ironic that the confidence of customers is maintained through the most intangible part of the offering.* (Saunders and Guoqun 1996)

Branding is a key issue for some commercial leisure companies. The subtlety of the process is such that whilst prima facie a company's brand is seemingly consistent globally, the reality is that not only are the offerings varied from one market to another but the essence of the brand varies from market to market. Thus, while a hotel company may operate in the two star market across Europe, the concept of what a two star hotel means varies from country to country. The breakfast served in France will differ from that served in the UK, and in Paris no breakfast may be served at all.

The link between culture and branding is such that in the brewing industry: 'there are differing expectations in terms of price, product mix, facilities, etc. from region to region. These differences all serve to make the development of a coherent national or even regional brand more difficult . . .' (Lincoln and Elwood 1995:13). Branding may not be a significant issue for all leisure companies, for example the sole trader operating a boat hire service in the Lake District. However, even for such a small operator, image, presentation and quality of service – constituent elements of branding – will affect the success of the business. Whilst small companies may not have substantial brand equity, it is possible to access a well-known name through a strategic alliance partner.

Strategic Alliances

A strategic alliance is, according to Daniels and Radebaugh (1995:18):

> *. . . an agreement between companies that is of strategic importance to the competitive viability of one or both. The alliance may involve a variety of operational*

> *forms such as joint ventures, licensing, management agreements, minority ownership in each other's company, or long-term contractual arrangements.*

A strategic alliance may be little more than an agreement between two companies, possibly little more than a verbal agreement. Examples of strategic alliances are those in which Nestlé are involved. Nestlé have agreements with Coca-Cola, General Mills, Baxter Healthcare, Disney (for food in Euro Disney) and BNS (Gugler 1992). In the case of the athletic footwear market, strategic alliances have gone so far that 'No athletic footwear firm now wholly owns integrated production facilities: athletic footwear production in general is presently typified by the large-scale vertical disintegration of functions and a high level of subcontracting activity' (Donaghu and Barff 1990:539). A major player in the leisure industry, Arthur Rank, formerly of the Rank Organisation PLC, was, according to Mirabile (1990:157) '. . . a lover of intricate corporate strategy'.

> *Strategic transnational alliances have become an important part of international trade. Leading companies are establishing complex webs of formal and informal alliances: they are networking. New forms of industrial structures are being created. The old oligopolistic markets are being replaced by more complex oligopolistic structures composed of several inter-firm clusters. The managers are confronted with new challenges. Their ability to resolve these new problems will have an increasing impact on their company's competitiveness. In fact . . . the competitive advantages of the firms reside more and more in their ability to create, acquire and co-ordinate the use of resources across national boundaries, rather than in the exclusive appropriation of strategic assets.* (Gugler 1992:99)

What Gugler (1992) appears to be suggesting is that strategic alliances may be more significant than the growth of the firm along the more traditional lines described by Daniels and Radebaugh (1995), namely: importing/exporting, leading to sales subsidiary, and subsequently international division. Given that the research undertaken previously (Irvine and Taylor 1998) has shown that the industry consists of a series of oligopolies within each of the sectors examined, the interesting issue is whether the use of strategic alliances serves to reinforce existing oligopolies or whether it serves to weaken the prevailing hierarchy with the emergence of new powers. The measure of industrial structure used previously did not take into account strategic alliances in determining industry structure. This issue merits further research.

According to Goldblatt *et al.* (1998) it is technology that is helping to shape the increased use of strategic alliances.

> *What is new about the modern global system is the stretching of social relations in and through new dimensions of activity – technological, organisational, administrative and legal, among others – and the chronic intensification of patterns of interconnectedness mediated by such phenomena as modern communication networks and new information technology.* (Goldblatt *et al.* 1998)

Thus technology helps in increasing responsiveness to the various markets and assists in developing relationships with other key stakeholders on a global scale. Evidence for this is, according to Goldblatt *et al.* (1998), the massive increase in telephone traffic and transnational cable links.

Strategic alliances in the commercial leisure industry are undertaken for a variety of purposes. Some companies use them as a source of finance. The costs which prohibit one company from undertaking a project are offset with the involvement of other companies. Such strategies are common in the film and television industry where the cost of producing a film or television programme and its subsequent distribution are beyond the capability of small and medium-sized firms necessitating the formation of alliances between those with the ability to produce, and those with the ability to distribute. The latter funds the former in return for a share of distribution rights.

Strategic alliances are undertaken in order to access expertise. One partner provides the resources and the other the skills and expertise. In some instances one company provides the brand and the other the resources. A contemporary exponent of such a strategy is Richard Branson's 'Virgin' brand. British Airways have entered into a number of agreements with smaller airlines in order to access niche markets in return for the smaller companies being able to trade under the British Airways brand.

Similarly, strategic alliances can be used to overcome regulatory hurdles such as the shelter barriers described earlier. Through forming an alliance with a local company it may be possible to circumvent the requirements imposed by the host nation. An example of this is the regulations relating to trading in Nepal. Legislation is such that it is necessary to establish a local company in Nepal before commencing trade. This creates a range of management difficulties for the small UK tour operator specialising in trekking holidays. An alliance partner in Nepal helps overcome many of the potential difficulties. The increased prevalence of strategic alliances has been made possible in part through the exploitation of technology. It is technology which is perhaps the single biggest variable influencing change in business today.

Technology

The exploitation of technology is one of the major challenges facing the commercial leisure industry. The manifestation of technology is threefold. First, in terms of the product offered, second, in terms of the process leading to the product/service offered and third, the use of technology as part of a management information system (MIS) (Capon and Glazer 1987).

Whilst technology has developed at an exponential rate, the effect is not new. In the fifteenth and sixteenth centuries, improvements in navigation technology led to greater sea exploration and ultimately the formation of joint stock companies. Part of the difficulty in assessing the effect of technology is identifying the significant technological developments, not because they are few but because often they are taken for granted. An example of this is the fax machine: whilst seemingly insignificant, the fax has enabled communication and hence trade overseas on an unprecedented scale. Technology that becomes common in its use becomes overlooked in terms of its significance. Yet technology such as the fax machine and telephone systems increase the interaction between strategic alliance partners enabling a faster response in order to maximise opportunities. For one small British tour operator specialising in trekking holidays in Nepal, the introduction of satellite communication has meant it is possible to manage the business from the United Kingdom whereas the manual exchange system which existed pre 1983 meant telephone calls had to be routed via India. The cumbersome nature of the phone calls meant managing a business remotely was a challenging task. Today, the telephone is taken for granted. With the arrival of the railways and the telegraph in the late nineteenth century '. . . companies appeared which were able to look upon the entire country as their sphere of operation' (Leontiades 1986:97). The late twentieth century may have seen an acceleration in the speed of transport and the development of greater communication networks but it was a process of development that was already well established. However, to conclude as Levitt (1983) does, that improved communication will result in a metamorphosis of markets leading to standardisation of products, is erroneous, not only in committing the error of underestimating the power of cultural variables, but also in assuming that better communication resolves differences. Thus, the evolution of communication may simply shift understanding of other markets from 'incoherent homogeneity to coherent heterogeneity' (Spencer 1862) and not necessarily an increase in trade. The rate of change through the exploitation of technology is greater than it ever has been and, according to Capon and Glazer (1987:3):

> *. . . the implications for firm decision making are perhaps more pervasive now than at any other time and involve numerous key areas of corporate strategy and structure: changing product life cycles, changing definition of marketing segments, changing definitions of industries/new sources of competition, changing employee relations, and increased globalization of markets.*

An example of the impact of technology is the impact the Global Reservation Systems (GRS) has had on the travel industry. The GRS refers collectively to the various online computer networks hosted by a number of organisations. Firms can register their services on these networks. Via travel agents and other organisations linked to the systems, customers can book the services registered. Thus the GRS is a distribution system. In one example a hotel group runs a reservation centre in London through which bookings are taken for hotels throughout the UK and Ireland. This reservation centre is in turn linked to a central reservation base in the United States run by a strategic alliance partner. Thus a customer in New York wishing to make a booking in the North of England would be routed through to the central reservation system, onto London and to the hotel, the confirmation route following in reverse. Whilst seemingly complex, a reservation can be made and confirmed within approximately eight seconds. The exploitation of such technology is not applicable to all sections of the commercial leisure market. To the adventurous tourist, the notion of pre-booking all accommodation prior to departure may be anathema. Neither are they appropriate for the small bed and breakfast establishment. Similarly such systems are not truly global in that not all parts of the world are linked to such systems. However, the examples given illustrate the way in which the potential market can be viewed as stretching ever further afield through the exploitation of technology.

The effect on corporate strategy of technology such as the GRS is significant, particularly within the airline sector. The significant factor being who owns or controls the technology. For example, if Gallileo is the preferred choice, British Airways which hosts the system predominates in terms of functionality and positioning on the travel agent's computer monitor. The significance of position on the screen is that 80 per cent of bookings are made from the top three selections on the screen. In addition, if only British Airways flights are requested then only British Airways flights will appear on the screen. Thus a flight which KLM might be operating, which may well be cheaper will not appear, purely because the information sought was limited to British Airways, hence the advantage of a well-known and significant branding. These are just a few examples of the way in which technology can affect strategy.

The outcome of this is an increase in the extent of strategic alliances made possible through the exploitation of technology. In this instance, the companies with whom strategic alliances are formed are determined by the manner in which the GRS functions. Technology thus alters the perception of markets and the way the industry is structured.

Changes such as the development of the GRS can have a profound effect on the commercial leisure industry and it is therefore necessary that firms develop a strategy that incorporates technology. Not embracing technology can be as risky as embracing technology and the implications in terms of cost and research and development:

> *Firms that choose to approach the technological frontier place themselves at risk, for technology research, development and exploitation are by definition uncertain. However, though remaining in familiar product-market situations reduces current uncertainty and may ensure profits, the avoidance of technological risk today may lead to considerable market risk tomorrow.* (Capon and Glazer 1987)

Thus technology is an asset and as such requires that the maximum return be obtained from that asset, recognising that over time technologies will change requiring new strategies and resources (Capon and Glazer 1987). Exploitation of technology may not be the best solution for a commercial leisure company but in some instances it is an effective strategy and in all instances it has a role, albeit a small one in some cases.

Summary and Conclusions

Technology and culture (which affects the way markets are perceived) are the most significant variables in terms of changing the way contemporary commercial leisure business is conducted. Cultural variables provide the direction of change towards an increasing heterogeneity of commercial leisure markets, made possible in part because of exploitation of technological advances. It is technology that most affects the way commercial leisure business is conducted, because it is within the capability of the firm. While changing cultural variables can be affected by the actions of a commercial leisure organisation, the process is infinitely more complex and success is elusive. Turner and Hodges (1992) use the extreme example of Nestlé attempting to convert the Japanese diet from raw fish and rice to breakfast cereal as an example of how difficult changing cultural variables can be.

As with cultural variables, the significance of technology varies from one commercial leisure organisation to another. Whether it is simply the acquisition of a fax machine, or the use of a photocopier, or more sophisticated EPOS systems, technology affects the way in which commercial leisure business is conducted. While competitive advantage may not exclusively depend upon technology, at some point in the process of conducting commercial leisure business it will have played a part.

Technology influences whether or not a business engages in strategic alliances and the nature of those strategic alliances. It makes them easier to establish and maintain because of the developments in communication technology. Technology affects the influence of size in that the increased opportunity for strategic alliances made possible through technology may reduce the dependence solely on the organic or acquisitive growth of the commercial leisure firm. Technology influences the way in which products are offered. It has enabled increased sensitivity of the offering.

Another of the major themes – branding – illustrates not only the power of identity but also the milieu of the market and the importance of ensuring that the offering will not conflict with the values, beliefs, language, colour and taste of the customer. The relationship is complex and involves a two-way interaction in which new ideas and products can become accepted and indigenised into the culture. As with technology, the significance of these variables varies from business to business. They seem to be particularly important to those commercial leisure firms trading internationally and seemingly irrelevant to those businesses operating in the domestic market. The evidence suggests that the shift towards heterogeneity is resulting in increasing fragmentation of commercial leisure markets within cultures. What is clear, is that the power of cultural variables affects all aspects of the business process, from the way commercial leisure business is conducted, through to branding and the product itself.

The complexity of issues outlined above illustrates the importance of furthering the research into commercial leisure. It is a rich vein and its exploitation will enhance our understanding of leisure overall.

Suggested Tasks for Further Study

1. Obtain the company reports of large multinationals to obtain a snapshot of the variety of product offerings tailored to different markets.
2. When travelling abroad, observe how products seemingly the same across the globe are packaged and delivered in different ways depending on the requirements of a particular market.
3. Follow the fortunes of leisure companies in the business press as they divest, acquire, are taken over, or take over other companies. Try and interpret their actions in terms of the significance of their actions internationally.
4. Watch for ways in which products and services in the leisure industry are increasingly becoming more tailored to individual requirements.

References

- Barrett C 'The concept of leisure: Idea and Ideal' in Barrett C and Winnifrith T 1989 *The Philosophy of Leisure*
- Brown 1997 'What's in a Name?' *Livewire* Dec/Jan The Illustrated London Newsgroup, London SE1 9PF
- Buzzell R D 1968 'Can you standardise multinational marketing?' *Harvard Business Review* Vol.46 Part 5 pp.102–113
- Capon N and Glazer R July 1987 'Marketing and Technology: A Strategic Coalignment' *Journal of European Marketing* Vol.51 pp.1–14
- Commission of the European Communities May 1992 *Community Guidelines on State Aid for Small and Medium-Sized Enterprises*
- Daniels J D and Radebaugh L H 1995 *International Business. Environments and Operations* (7th Ed) Addison Wesley, Wokingham
- Donaghu M T and Barff R 1990 'Nike Just Did It: International Subcontracting and Flexibility in Athletic Footwear Production' *Regional Studies* Vol.24 No.6 pp.537–552
- Franke R H, Hofstede G and Bond M H 1991 'Cultural roots of economic performance: A research note' *Strategic Management Journal* Vol.12 pp.165–173
- Gander P 1996 'Home and Away' *Marketing Week* Vol.19 Part 31 pp.55–59
- Glyptis S 1989 *Leisure and Unemployment* Oxford University Press, Milton Keynes
- Goldblatt D, Held D, McGrew A and Perraton J 1998 *Global Flows, Global Transformations, Evidence and Arguments* Polits Press, Cambridge
- Grosse R and Behrman J N Feb 1992 'Theory in International Business' *Transnational Corporations* Vol.1 No.1 pp.93–126

- Guba E G (Ed) 1990 *The Paradigm Dialog* Sage Publications, Newbury Park, Ca.
- Gugler P 1992 'Building Transnational Alliances to Create Competitive Advantage' *Long Range Planning* Vol.25 No.1 pp.90–99
- Irvine D and Taylor P 1998 'Value and Structure of Commercial Leisure' in Collins M F and Cooper I S 1998 *Leisure Management: Issues and Applications* CAB International, Wallingford
- Irvine D 1998 'The Management of Cross Cultural Issues in Student Health Service' *British Association of Health Services in Higher Education* 50th Annual Conference, King's College, Cambridge 5–11 July 1998
- Kahan K 1996 'How Fit is Fittest?' *Changing Business Dynamics: The Challenge to Marketing Research* 49th ESOMAR Congress, Istanbul Sept 1996
- Kelly J R 1990 *Leisure* (2nd Ed) Prentice Hall International Editions, Englewood Cliffs, N.J.
- Kelly J R and Godbey G 1992 *The Sociology of Leisure* Venture Publishing Inc, State College, PA
- Leontiades J 1986 'Going Global – Global Strategies vs National Strategies' *Long Range Planning* Vol.19 No.6 pp.96–104
- Levitt T May/June 1983 'The Globalization of Markets' *Harvard Business Review* pp.92–102
- Lincoln Y S 1990 'The Making of a Constructivist: A Remembrance of Transformations Past' in Guba E G (Ed) 1990 *The Paradigm Dialog* Sage Publications, Newbury Park, Ca.
- Mirabile L (Ed) 1990 *International Directory of Company Histories* Vol.II St James Press, London
- Poynter T A 1985 *Multinational Enterprises and Government Intervention* Croom Helm, London
- Rojek C 1989 *Leisure for Leisure* Macmillan, London
- Roth M S May 1995 'The Effects of Culture and Socioeconomics on the Performance of Global Brand Image Strategies' *Journal of Marketing Research* Vol.32 Part 2 pp.163–175
- Rugman A M and Verbeke A June 1991 'Trade Barriers and Corporate Strategy in International Companies – The Canadian Experience' *Long Range Planning* Vol.24 pp.66–72
- Saunders J and Guoqun F 1996 'Dual branding: how corporate names add value' *Marketing Intelligence and Planning* Vol.14 No.7 pp.29–34
- Scarpa J (Ed) 1996 'Why Brand?' *Restaurant Business* Vol.95 Part 5 pp.8–10
- Schocker A D, Srivastava R K and Ruekert R W May 1994 'Challenges and Opportunities Facing Brand Management: An Introduction to the Special Issue' *Journal of Marketing Research* Vol.31 pp.149–158
- Segal-Horn S (Ed) 1994 *The Challenge of International Business* Kogan Page Ltd, London
- Smart B June 1994 'Society, Globalisation and Postmodernity' *International Sociology* Vol.9 No.2 pp.149–159
- Spencer H 1862 'First Principles' cited in *Complex for Windows* Version 2.1 1993 Oxford University Press, Oxford
- Turner L and Hodges M 1992 *Global Shakeout* Century Business, London
- Yong Kim O and Olsen M D 1993 'A Framework for the Identification of Political Environmental Issues Faced by Multinational Hotel Chains in Newly Industrialised Countries in Asia' *International Journal of Hospitality Management* Vol.12 No.2 pp.163–174

Chapter 3

The UK Voluntary Sector

Geoff Nichols
The University of Sheffield

Chapter Content

Abstract

Texts on the leisure and sport industry typically attempt to divide it into the commercial, public and voluntary sectors. However, this distinction is not always easily made. In the UK the voluntary sector has a particular and peculiar significance for sport, being the provider (outside of the education system) of the majority of opportunities to participate in organised sport. Legacies of the emergence of this sector in the second half of the nineteenth century (Holt 1990) are the governing body structure, the plethora of small clubs identified with geographical locations (opposed to the large multi sport clubs in Germany or Holland) and a fierce sense of independence. This chapter starts by considering what the voluntary sector is and its relevance to leisure. It reviews evidence on the size of the voluntary sector, especially in sport. It considers ways in which local government and the Sports Council have attempted to use the voluntary sector as policy instruments, which leads into a general consideration of problems facing the voluntary sector. The discussion draws on recent research into volunteers in sport and in the Guide Association, which is the largest formal voluntary youth organisation in Britain. The chapter concludes by relating the discussion back to the nature of the voluntary sector and how this may be changing in response to pressures from the public and private sectors.

Related Chapters

Chapter 7: Access and Leisure Policy: The power of groups and how groups can influence policy decision-making is the main link between these two chapters.

Chapter 12: The Management of Change in the Leisure and Sport Management Sector: The voluntary leisure sector is experiencing significant change particularly with regard to the requirements of increased accountability and of professionalisation.

Learning Outcomes

- to appreciate the complexity of the voluntary sector as both a producer of leisure opportunities and as a leisure experience for those who volunteer
- to introduce the significance of the voluntary sector as an instrument of public policy
- to introduce the significance of the voluntary sector as a contribution to the quality of communities
- to understand the pressures on the voluntary sector

Introduction

There is not a simple distinction between the public, commercial and voluntary sectors. As Critcher *et al.* (1995) have pointed out, a voluntary sector football team may play on a publicly subsidised local authority pitch and have committee meetings in a commercial sector pub. Lyons *et al.* (1998) raise a more fundamental issue of definition and of understanding what the voluntary sector is. They conclude that there are two main approaches to understanding the voluntary sector: one has its roots in economics, and the other in sociology and political theory. These have implications for research into the voluntary sector, understanding the motivations of volunteers, and the role of public policy.

One way of defining the voluntary sector is by economic function; plugging the provision gap between the public and commercial sectors. This residual definition of non-profit organisations has been prevalent in the United States of America. For example, Weisbrod (1978) analyses the voluntary sector as meeting the demand for goods, such as sports clubs, that cannot be met effectively by the private or public sectors. Gratton and Taylor (1985, 1991) explain that Weisbrod's analysis is particularly relevant to collective goods where there is insufficient consensus on their value to justify public provision or to make such provision effectively. The infinite clusters of interests can only be met by small groups acting collectively in the voluntary sector. The policy importance of this sector is in its contribution to the economy. This means that it is justifiable to measure the 'work' of volunteers, as far as one is able to do so and compare it to the economic contribution of workers in other sectors of the economy. This approach was taken in the Sports Council research 'Valuing Volunteers' (Gratton *et al.* 1997). The implications of this approach for understanding the motivations of volunteers are not entirely clear. For example, in a review of American research into volunteers' motivations, while Smith (1994) notes that altruism is often given as a reason for participation, he cites his earlier work (1981) in which he argued that 'there was little pure altruism in participation, since people gain some pleasure for themselves even when acting altruistically'. The motivation of volunteers could be understood as a calculative rationality of self interest, in which participants give in relation to what they will get. More recent American work (Caan *et al.* 1996) has shown that people's understanding of volunteering includes an element of altruism.

However, an alternative approach to understanding volunteering, more common in the UK and Europe, is typified by Hoggett and Bishops' (1985) study of organising around enthusiasms. This approach is interested in mutual-aid, self-help organisations. As Lyons *et al.* (1998:52) state: 'they are the product of people's ability to work together to meet shared needs and address common problems.' This approach emphasises the role of the voluntary sector as an expression of active citizenship and enriching social capital. It stresses a social rather than an economic understanding of the relationship between volunteering and leisure.

The two approaches imply different understandings of the relationship between voluntary activity and leisure. Weisbrod's economic analysis is in terms of the output of the organisation; what it produces, in relation to the leisure opportunities produced by the public and private sector. This approach only regards leisure as a commodity to be exchanged – bought and sold – and ignores the possibility that the act of production of the output may itself be a leisure experience. In contrast, the mutual-aid approach would have a different understanding of the relationship between the voluntary sector and leisure. For example, an amateur dramatic society may spend many weeks preparing a production. The play they produce at the end is part of the output; people may pay to come and see it, so it is a commodity to be exchanged. However, for the members of the society the act of production, expressing a shared enthusiasm for drama, may be more important. It is this experience of organising around enthusiasms that Hoggett and Bishop (1985) felt was distinctive of the voluntary sector when they made their early study. Thus, in the voluntary sector, leisure may be produced and consumed by the same people and the act of production can also be a leisure experience. Within the organising around enthusiasms paradigm, a concern of public policy would be to provide encouragement for the voluntary sector as an expression of active citizenship, an expression of a plurality of interest groups, and an enrichment of social capital.

The organising around enthusiasms paradigm also gives a different perspective on the motivations of volunteers. On the one hand, one could regard volunteers as being involved to pursue their own particular interests. For example, volunteers in a sports club create an opportunity for their own participation in the sport. Alternatively, for some volunteers, enthusiasm for the activity may be beyond self interest in the way that Gorz describes personal and emotional relationships as not involving a question of equal exchange. In these relationships, which for Gorz would predominate in his ideal society, individuals give generously of themselves. 'At this level, economic goals and market values do not exist' (Gorz 1985:72). This might be typical of volunteers involved in coaching sport to young people, or those in voluntary sector youth organisations, both of which are discussed below.

Thus, in both paradigms, the view of the voluntary sector as meeting an economic need, or as a vehicle for shared enthusiasms; volunteers' motivations are understood as a balance between self interest and altruism. These motivations were identified by Cuskelly *et al.* (1998) in a study of changes in voluntary sports administrators' motivations over a year; relating commitment to perceptions of committee functioning. They found that over six months a more negative view of the committee led to reduced commitment, although this finding did not hold over a year. Of more interest to the general discussion of volunteers' motivations was the finding that altruism was rated as the most important benefit of volunteerism and that 'volunteer administrators who place a higher level of importance on altruism develop higher levels of organizational commitment' (Cuskelly *et al.* 1998:197).

Thus, we must take care when viewing the voluntary sector as part of the leisure and sport industry, as this has certain implications associated with the economic function approach. It implies a definition based predominantly on output that is exchanged in the market, rather than by the experience of those creating the leisure opportunity. It implies a perspective on public policy which might not always be sensitive to the nature of the voluntary sector, and the way volunteers see it. For example, in research investigating the reaction of volunteers in sport to the possibility of the Sports Council charging them for information, it was found that, 'a danger of charging is the alienation of those whose culture is opposed to it, but who may give the greatest personal effort to the promotion of sport' (Nichols and Taylor 1993:40). Volunteers in sport gave their own time and effort freely as a reflection of their commitment to the sport, and perhaps altruistically to help others enjoy it. Being asked to pay for information from the Sports Council, especially when they gave information freely to support sport, would have been insensitive to the nature of the voluntary sector.

The Scale of the Voluntary Sector

The voluntary sector in general

Despite its importance, knowledge of the voluntary sector in leisure provision is very limited. Little is known about its size, the roles of volunteers and their motivations. One of the few studies of volunteers in leisure was made by Hoggett and Bishop in 1985. The initial questionnaire-based phase of their study, which was conducted in two suburbs of Leicester and Bristol, revealed a very wide diversity of voluntary organisations and highlighted methodological problems that future studies will have to confront. For example, delimiting the range of organisations to study, making contact with the volunteers, defining what voluntary work is, and deciding how to measure it.

Any measurement of the voluntary sector has first to find a way of dealing with the issues of definition raised above. Measurement has to involve a definition that can produce quantifiable results. The three surveys described below did this. One difficulty in definition is that the voluntary sector, if defined as not the commercial public sector, may still include people in paid employment. For example, governing bodies of sport almost all include some paid officials. As we shall see these are usually excluded from measurement of volunteers. Thus in quantitative surveys, there is a difference between measuring the voluntary sector, and measuring the number of volunteers within it. There is also a difference between considering the problems of the voluntary sector and those of individual volunteers.

A different approach is taken by Stebbins (1997:117) for whom volunteer activity is one variety of serious leisure. The concept of serious leisure is defined as 'the systematic pursuit of an amateur, hobbyist, or volunteer activity that participants find so substantial and interesting that, in the typical case, they launch themselves on a career centred on acquiring and expressing its special skills, knowledge and experience'. As the word 'typical' indicates, serious leisure is an 'ideal type' in the Weberian sense (Freund 1972:59–70). For Stebbins, volunteer activity is only one type of serious leisure, distinguished from other types by 'its altruism, which invariably propels it', 'the unselfish regard for another or a set of others' (Stebbins 1996:219). Within volunteering, a narrower field of activity is defined as 'career volunteering'. This involves sustained voluntary activity, in contrast to a single act or single donation of money. A career in serious leisure will have 'turning points and stages of achievement and involvement' (Stebbins 1997:119). This type of volunteering is usually connected to an organisation.

Stebbins' definition focuses on the experience of the individual volunteer. It matches the type of activity studied by Hoggett and Bishop (1985). It would be more useful in qualitative research. This is the way that Stebbins used it, in lengthy unstructured interviews of amateur groups, including those involved in classical music, archaeology, entertainment magic and barbershop singers.

The General Household Surveys (GHS) of 1981, 1987 and 1992 asked questions about voluntary work (Goddard 1994). These surveys used a definition of voluntary work as 'unpaid work (except for expenses) done through a group or on behalf of an organisation of some kind, but not for a trade union or political party' (Goddard 1994:1). To check that respondents' activities met these criteria, a question was asked about the organisation that the respondent contributed voluntary work to. However, this was the only function of this question and separate responses were not recorded. This meant it was not subsequently possible to analyse volunteers by the type of organisation they worked for, in particular, sport and leisure clubs. The surveys did however give a general picture of volunteers.

The GHS showed that in 1992, 24 per cent of people aged 16 and over had done voluntary work in the last 12 months. Those that had done voluntary work in the previous four weeks had given just under four hours a week, which could be used to estimate a total amount of voluntary work per week by adults in Great Britain: 20 million hours. Voluntary workers were more likely to come from higher socio-economic groups and to have higher than average levels of educational attainment. Interestingly, volunteers were under-represented in groups that might be expected to have most time available, such as the unemployed, people without children and the recently retired. Women were more likely to volunteer than men and were more likely to have been involved in fund raising. The fact that volunteers are more likely to have dependant children and that the propensity to volunteer increases as the number of dependant children increases from one to three or more (Goddard 1994:6), suggests that a large proportion of voluntary work is set in the context of schools or youth organisations. The amount of time spent on voluntary work was not evenly distributed. The largest proportion of voluntary work was done by those involved in administration. Between 1987 and 1992 there was a small increase in the proportion of adults doing voluntary work, but little change in the total amount of time being given.

Further general information on volunteers is provided by surveys conducted by the volunteer society in 1981, 1991 (Hedley R and Davis Smith J 1992) and in 1997 (Davis Smith 1998). These surveys used a wider definition of volunteering than the GHS; defined as 'any activity which involves spending time, unpaid, doing something which aims to benefit someone (individuals or groups) other than or in addition to close relatives, or to benefit the environment' (Davis Smith 1998:13). This is a wider definition than that used in the GHS, although the survey distinguished between formal volunteering, defined as taking place through a group or organisation, and informal volunteering, which took place outside an organisational context. The surveys concluded that the number of respondents who had been involved in formal volunteering over the last year, in 1981, 1991 and 1997, were 44 per cent, 51 per cent and 48 per cent respectively. It is interesting to note the difference between the 51 per cent of respondents in this survey in 1991 and the 24 per cent in 1992 in the GHS. This must reflect methodological differences in the surveys and illustrates the difficulties of researching this activity.

The National Survey of Volunteering, conducted in 1997, was able to compare trends in volunteering by age between the surveys conducted in 1981, 1991 and 1997. Results from the 1991–97 period offered 'hints of a generation gap emerging in volunteering. Between 1991 and 1997 volunteering by 16–24 year olds and 25–34 year olds had dropped back to its 1981 level. Across a range of attitudinal measures on the role of volunteering and volunteers, young people were found to hold more negative views than older people. Young people were also far more likely to play down the altruistic motivations to volunteer and to highlight the self-interested or instrumental reasons' (Davis Smith 1998:158). The 1997 survey found that 26 per cent of respondents who had volunteered through a group or organisation (formal volunteering) in the previous 12 months, had done so in sport and exercise.

Volunteers in sport

Research in 1995, conducted by the Leisure Industries Research Centre (Gratton *et al.* 1997:i) for the Sports Council used a definition of a volunteer as: 'individual volunteers, helping others in sport, in formal organisations such as clubs or governing bodies, and receiving either no remuneration or only expenses.' The study concluded that 'there are nearly 1.5 million volunteers in UK sport, each contributing an average of 2.5 hours a week for 48 weeks of the year. Eighty per cent of these volunteers are involved in the running of voluntary sports clubs'. They also make a vital contribution to the running of national and international sporting events. Volunteers on club committees each give 4.6 hours a week to the sport.

Sports that are played in a formal club environment, such as bowls, football, cricket and rugby, are those most reliant on volunteers. Volunteers are also more likely to be important in clubs that own and manage their facilities, for example, club houses or specialist equipment. Volunteers play a crucial role in coaching programmes for young people and this role takes a considerable amount of time. Within sports clubs, coaches give considerably more hours of voluntary work than the average club committee member. As this suggests, voluntary work is not evenly distributed within clubs, 35 per cent of the volunteers in club committees contributing 50 per cent of the work. Key roles are those of chair, secretary, treasurer and fixture secretary. All of these officers contribute above average hours. Volunteers in sports club committees tend to be male, in employment and have a higher than average educational attainment. The characteristics of sports volunteers mirrored and accentuated the characteristics of volunteers in the GHS (see above), with the exception of the gender split. The GHS found that the average volunteer gave 3.9 hours a week. This is less than the 4.6 hours given by sports club committee members and the GHS figure included all voluntary work for any organisation in that period. Thus sports club committee members appear to give more time than the average volunteer.

This general picture of volunteers is within a very diverse range of sports clubs. These may range from semi-professional clubs competing internationally to Sunday morning pub teams. This diversity reflects both different interests in sport and different needs of the clubs and volunteers. The size of the voluntary sector in sport in the UK is equivalent to over 108,000 full-time workers. To make a comparison with the public sector, in 1990 the *Employment Gazette* reported that there were 81,000 full-time and 36,000 part-time local authority employees in Recreation, Parks and Baths departments in England and Wales.

The Policy Significance of the Voluntary Sector

The foundation of a pluralist society

The voluntary sector has been seen as both a reflection and a prerequisite of a pluralist society. For Roberts, 'in recreation and other spheres the public uses its leisure to nurture life styles that supply experiences which the individuals concerned seek and value' (Roberts 1978:86). People freely express themselves in leisure, and combine around shared interests (Veal 1989). An incredibly diverse voluntary sector is used as robust evidence of a pluralist society. Within such a society, public policy should facilitate the development of voluntary action that helps people develop their own leisure interests. This was the stance of Dower in the report, 'Leisure provision and people's needs' (1981), which understood leisure provision as a complex mesh of organisations and people, which was in flux. It was recognised by Hoggett and Bishop (1985:105), who recommended that public support for the voluntary sector would have to be offered in a way that was sensitive to the strong independent spirit of the local community and, 'that anybody wishing to relate to the worlds of communal leisure must understand and appreciate it in its own terms'. Public support for the voluntary sector can be seen as not only a recognition of, but a contribution to a pluralist society. However, such a society is dependant on the willingness and capacity of individuals to volunteer.

Public policy and sport

There have been concerns in Britain that young people have experienced a reduction in opportunities to develop sports literacy and commitment, especially in the traditional team sports. This has been attributed to education legislation and a loss of goodwill among teachers, who were formally more prepared to offer sports opportunities on a voluntary basis out of school hours (Sports Council 1993). Volunteers have been seen as a crucial resource in sports opportunities for young people. This is recognised in the English Sports Council's strategy (1997) and the Department of National Heritage's agenda for 'Raising the Game' (1995). Largely through the efforts of volunteers, the English Sports Council would like to see a 10 per cent increase in the number of boys and a 20 per cent increase in the number of girls who are members of sports clubs by 2001.

While one of the focal concerns of the English Sports Council is young people, the other is excellence. Excellent performers are more likely to emerge from a pyramid of participation with a broad base, thus volunteers at all levels of sports provision contribute indirectly to the development of excellence. The development of excellent performers depends on the coaching support given by the governing bodies, coaches and parents of participants (Taylor 1993). Taylor's research, conducted in 1988, estimated that it was not uncommon for sports people, or their parents, to incur annual expenses on training, equipment and travel of between £2,000 and £5,000.

Partnerships with local authorities

The reduced ability of local authorities to directly provide leisure opportunities, as a consequence of financial constraints, has led to a greater emphasis on partnerships with the voluntary sector. While partnerships between the public and voluntary sector can be seen as the local authority getting something done it could not afford to do itself, through voluntary labour, they can also be seen as enriching the community and enhancing the lives of the volunteers through enabling them to express their own leisure needs. Local authorities' role is changing from direct provider to enabler (Leach *et al.* 1994:37–44). Partnerships with the voluntary sector have been encouraged by Compulsory Competitive Tendering, either directly, as a means of avoiding having to tender the management of facilities competitively, or indirectly, by providing a model for a management contract. For example, significant partnerships with recreational trusts have been established in Peterborough, Milton Keynes, Welwyn-Hatfield, and Cambridge (Curson 1995).

Problems Faced by Volunteers

The National Survey of Volunteering (Davis Smith 1998:96) found, in response to a prompted question on the drawbacks of volunteering, that, of those who volunteered at least once a month, 24 per cent definitely felt that 'things could be much better organised', 7 per cent that 'you can't always cope with the things you get asked to do', and 6 per cent that 'your efforts aren't always appreciated'. A different set of prompted questions were asked in the survey of sports volunteers (Gratton *et al.* 1997) and a survey conducted by the author of volunteers in the Guide Association (Nichols and King 1997). In 1997 the Guide Association was the largest voluntary youth organisation in the UK with a total membership of almost 661,000 women and girls. Table 3.1 shows the responses in these surveys.

The National Survey of Volunteering (Davis Smith 1998:143) found that of 173 non-volunteers who would 'like to get involved', 58 per cent did not think they had enough time to spare, 53 per cent did not know many people who are interested in that sort of thing, and 52 per cent felt they had not got the right skills or experience to help. These survey results, combined with qualitative data from the studies of sports volunteers and Guide leaders, suggest several pressures on the voluntary sector (Nichols *et al.* 1998).

Table 3.1 The results of surveys to pinpoint difficulties faced by volunteers in sports clubs (A) and by leaders in the Guide Association (B)

Reported difficulties	*A%*	*B%*
There are not enough other people to volunteer	74	71
Increasingly the work is left to fewer people	55	59
Dissatisfaction with parents' contributions		41
There is little time left after your paid work	19	39
Rules and regulations of the Association		28
Conflict with family commitments	16	25
Increasingly my work as a volunteer needs specialist skills	23	20
Things could be better organised in the Association so you feel that your efforts are sometimes wasted	16	16
Poor support from other leaders	–	12
Attitude of the members of the unit you lead	–	10
There is little time left after your partner's work commitments	–	9
Poor support in training offered by the Association	–	8
Your children are no longer involved in the Association so you feel less motivated	–	5

Source: Survey of voluntary sports club committee members (Gratton *et al.* 1997): sample size 353; Guide Association survey (Nichols and King 1997): sample size 1494

Note: Sports volunteers (A) were asked a more limited range of questions.

Pressures on the voluntary sector

Time pressures on potential and existing volunteers

Nineteen per cent of sports club committee members and 39 per cent of Guiders reported that a major problem was little time left after paid work. It is debatable whether there has been a recent increase in working hours in the UK (Holliday 1996; Martin and Mason 1998), whether time pressures are just greater for the increasing proportion of two income families, or if a perceived time squeeze is merely the consequence of an increased and competing range of leisure opportunities (Robinson 1990). The UK Labour Force Survey indicates that hours worked have increased for full-time males since the mid eighties. The General Household Surveys show the same broad pattern, with the greatest increases for the A/B socio-economic groups (Holliday 1996); those the GHS (Goddard 1994) has shown have the greatest propensity to volunteer. The pressures on Guide leaders will be particularly related to the increase in the proportion of females in the labour force. This was also apparent in the study of sports volunteers in women's national governing bodies of sport, for example, women's hockey or golf organisations. Reduced numbers of volunteers may result in more demands on the time of those that do volunteer, as is suggested by the 55 per cent of sports club committee members and 59 per cent of Guiders who reported that 'increasingly the work is left to fewer people' (Nichols and King 1998:23).

A demand for professionalism

In both sports clubs and the Guide Association volunteers felt they had to increasingly deliver a service in ways that were common to, and comparable with, the private or public sectors. For example, a sports club secretary:

> *Organisation five years ago was more of a back of a cigarette packet job, now it is all computers, with things going out on the Internet, which is much more professional. And if you put something forward it has to look good, it can't just be hand written and passed around the boys, it has to go to one committee and on to the next.* (Nichols, Shibli and Taylor 1998:42)

Professionalism can be linked to the demands made by external organisations, such as the Sports Council, or local authorities. As national and local government increasingly recognises the potential for the voluntary sector in sport as a policy instrument, grants will be attached to conditions that meet the objectives of the grant-giving body. Houlihan (1991:115–149) has argued that while the finances of governing bodies have become increasingly reliant on grants from the Sports Council, since the late 1980s these grants, consistent with the Council's desire to strengthen financial control and accountability, have become increasingly tied to development plans that incorporate the Sports Council's policy objectives. In the same way, Houlihan reports that since the late 1970s elements of the Sports Council's grant from central government have been allocated by central government for specific purposes (Houlihan 1991:102).

The fierce independence of the voluntary sector in British sport has meant that clubs, and national governing bodies, have always been wary of support with strings attached. A fell running club in the research into volunteers in sport (Gratton *et al.* 1997), when asked if they had a message to give to the Sports Council on the best thing it could do for their club, replied:

> *leave us and it alone. Leave it as the low key, underground, friendly, social sport that it has always been.* (Nichols, Shibli and Taylor 1998:43)

This again illustrates the point made above, that the public sector has to be sensitive to the nature of the voluntary sector when giving support.

Increased complexity of voluntary skills

The surveys of the Guiders (Nichols and King 1997), sports volunteers (Gratton *et al.* 1997), and non-volunteers in the 1997 National Survey of Volunteering (Davis Smith 1998), showed that volunteers were concerned by the greater demands on their skills. These might include making National Lottery applications, dealing with legislation, learning specialist coaching or leadership skills, or word processing skills. Skills might also include handling relations with partner organisations.

Increased choice and competition

The demands of professionalism (acting as if one was being paid to do the job) and increasing skill requirements are related to the increasing competition the voluntary sector faces from the private and public sector. New members of a sports club may become more able to choose alternative provision from the private or public sectors. For example, where once the only way to play badminton was in the church hall on Wednesday evenings, now one may be able to book a local authority court at a time of one's convenience. Similarly, the Guide leaders interviewed in the research for the Guide Association claimed that young people had an increasingly wide range of activities to choose from and Guiding had to compete more strongly for their interest, even if it was against a soap opera.

A changed attitude to volunteering

The overall impression from both the research projects drawn on here was that there had been a reduction in the number of volunteers. In the sports volunteers and the Guiders high proportions reported that 'there were not enough other people willing to volunteer in the club' and that the work was left to fewer people. For example, a respondent involved in football administration for the sport's governing body reported that:

> *I have a council of 30 people. At 60 I am the third youngest. What used to happen is that you played to a certain age and then took up refereeing or administrative work. What happens now is that people play up to the age of 30 and then go and do other things.* (Nichols, Shibli and Taylor 1998:39)

However, is there really a changed attitude to volunteering if the National Survey of Voluntary Action and the GHS show little decline in overall numbers of volunteers? Could it just be that existing volunteers are pessimistic? The National Survey does show a decline in younger volunteers (Davis Smith 1998:158) and suggests that different attitudes are one possible reason for this.

A hegemonic redefinition of the voluntary sector

The pressures above could be understood as part of a hegemonic redefinition of the voluntary sector such that it is increasingly equated to the understanding of leisure as consumption, a commodity to be bought and sold (Clarke and Critcher 1985:225–229).

A challenge to the traditional approach to volunteering from Thatcherite hegemony has also been implied by Henry's analysis of the changing environment of the leisure professional and leisure policy (1993:175–190). Comparable with what Henry terms a 'post-Fordist' regime are new socio-political arrangements. These include an increasing division in society between those in full-time employment and those on the periphery or out of the workforce. Differences in income between these groups are accentuated by the reduction in public welfare services. Rights of citizenship are replaced by rights of the consumer and such a change is legitimised by an ideology of self-help and individualism. The economic differences between groups in society are accentuated as the rights of the consumer are dependant on income levels. Thus only those in steady employment are able to supplement the increasingly inadequate public services. While the focus of Henry's analysis is on the impact of these socio-economic changes on public leisure policy the impact on the individual is likely to be an increased concern with their own welfare, maintaining their position of relative prosperity or trying to improve their position of relative disadvantage, and thus contributing to a reduced propensity to volunteer. These factors were reflected in the analysis offered by an experienced national level administrator in orienteering.

> *I think the increase in the responsibilities of volunteers is to do with the socio-economic changes in the country. I think people who are in work, are having to work much longer hours, which means less time for voluntary activity. If there is time they want to be paid for it. At the same time there are others who are in work, but under a lot of stress because they are thinking they may lose their job, or they are in and out of work a lot. They are obviously under pressure which takes their minds off voluntary activities like sport. Then you have the unemployed who are desperately looking for jobs. We find it is much more difficult now to get people who are willing to go and work with juniors, travel overseas etc., than it was five or six years ago. Orienteering is extremely heavy on volunteer help because we make all our own maps, and organise all our own competitions. I think it is a great tragedy the way the market philosophy has hit sport, it has certainly hit the opportunity of thousands of youngsters.* (Nichols, Shibli and Taylor 1998:41)

For both Henry (1993) and Hedley and Davis Smith (1992), the rights and responsibilities of citizens are being replaced by the rights and responsibilities of consumers. This erodes the sense of obligation to volunteer, to contribute to society, and supports the hegemonic view that relations must be mediated by the cash nexus. Relationships are increasingly defined in terms of economic costs and benefits. This explains the comments by sports volunteers that parents use their junior sessions as cheap childminding facilities for their children and are not prepared to contribute effort themselves, for example, something as simple as putting away the equipment. It helps to explain similar comments from Guiders, 41 per cent of whom were dissatisfied with parents' contributions (Nichols and King 1998:23).

Economic approaches to analysing the voluntary sector (Weisbrod 1978) can also be understood as reflecting a hegemonic definition of leisure as a product to be bought and sold, if they fail to acknowledge the distinctive nature of the voluntary sector and the motivations of volunteers, including altruism. Thus, the combination of pressures on voluntary sports clubs towards change can be understood as reflecting 'a whole body of practices and expectations, over the whole of living: our shaped perceptions of ourselves and our world' (Williams 1977:110).

Sources of Support for the Voluntary Sector

This section provides examples of support to organisations in the voluntary sector and to individual volunteers. Support may come in the form of grants, subsidies, lottery awards, training courses for specific skills, training in volunteer management and changing the structure of organisations. The major sources of support are local authorities, the English Sports Council, and national levels of the voluntary organisations. Interestingly the research into voluntary sports clubs (Gratton *et al.* 1997) found very few examples of support from the commercial sector. Support was usually at a minor level; for example a hockey team, who competed at European level, were sponsored in kind. One company provided the match balls and another provided a crate of bananas for each training session.

From local authorities

The voluntary sector may be helped by local authorities through support in making Lottery applications (Nichols and Sparrowhawk 1999), provision and co-ordination of training courses for coaches and officials, networking of volunteers, the production of local directories of sports clubs, and training volunteers in management skills. Support is often channelled through sports development officers. An example of local authority support is that given by Birmingham City Council. A project called Coach Train has involved the setting up of a database of voluntary coaches. This can be used as a marketing tool to identify the training courses that would be most effective in meeting the needs of coaches and to target their promotion. It can also be used to support voluntary clubs who needed to contact a particular type of coach or official. Birmingham City Council have run a series of sports forums that are sport specific. These have been used as a medium for disseminating information on authority support and initiatives for voluntary clubs, as well as enabling clubs to learn from each other. In a city the size of Birmingham it is practical to do this by individual sports but in smaller places it is necessary to involve all sports in one forum. A forum may fulfil the role of allowing information to be shared but the role of this body can be extended to include sports development. In Birmingham the authority supports a Sports Advisory Council, comprised of representative volunteers from sports. This body plays an important role in administering the authority's Community Sports Club project. Within this project sports clubs are matched to one of five levels of development, which accord to criteria that reflect the authority's objectives. Each level is eligible for different levels of support. This project again illustrates the balance between giving support and meeting the authority's objectives but it also illustrates the importance given to working through volunteers in the Sports Advisory Council so they feel ownership of the project and support it. This attempts to maintain the motivation and support of volunteers, and use their skills in partnership while achieving the authority's objectives. Birmingham appears to fit well the model of a 'community oriented enabler' but within this it seeks to meet its own objectives as well as those of the sports clubs.

From the English Sports Council

The English Sports Council have recently reviewed their work with the voluntary sector. They realised that they needed to be more sensitive to the needs of voluntary sector clubs and to appreciate the impact on clubs of asking them to meet Sports Council policy objectives. As a consequence the English Sports Council set up the volunteer investment programme (VIP).

The VIP has four main elements:

- *More information is being provided for volunteers*: A free information pack for volunteers includes details of the VIP awards scheme, examples of 19 award winners including practical examples of methods of recruiting, managing and retaining volunteers, and the booklet 'Getting Things Done' which is one of a series associated with the Running Sport training programme. Some practical examples of volunteer management, taken from the 19 award winners described in the pack, include good communication with existing volunteers, clear understanding by volunteers of their roles, matching volunteers' skills to the tasks they are asked to undertake, making sure the organisation's constitution allows a clear policy of succession between roles, delegating responsibility to a smaller number of volunteers to share the workload, providing support for new volunteers through a 'buddy' system, and showing appreciation of volunteers' efforts.

- *Training for volunteers*: The English Sports Council has extended its 'Running Sport' programme. This involves a series of booklets and regional workshops. The booklets and workshops cover 17 topics, including one specifically on 'valuing volunteers'. Over 70 per cent of those attending workshops are volunteers in sports clubs. The total number of workshops has been increased from 74 in 1996 to 222 in 1997. It was an aim to run 500 workshops in 1998.
- *Recognition of volunteers' work*: As part of the VIP programme, clubs, or governing bodies of sport, can apply for an award of up to £3,000 if they can provide an example of good practice in volunteer management. In the first year of operation, July 1996–97, over 250 applications were received and this is likely to have doubled in 1997–98. Awards have been made, totalling £39,000. This has been a good attempt to overcome the criticism that awards tended to be made to larger organisations.
- *Other support*: Thirteen national governing bodies of sport are now developing their own volunteer support strategies incorporating VIP. The Lawn Tennis Association (LTA) is an example of support given by a national governing body. The LTA has trained 80 of the English Sports Council's Running Sport tutors to deliver courses especially adapted for the needs of volunteers in tennis. These courses are then marketed through county newsletters. In 1997, 57 courses were run for 700 volunteers. The target for 1998 is to get 1,500 volunteers on courses. At county level the LTA has appointed full-time development officers. These officers support volunteers through organising courses, for example for club secretaries or officials, and also by providing a source of information and advice. County publications can provide examples of good practice. At county level one of the posts on the county committee is a volunteer co-ordinator. In this way a network of professional staff at county level provide a structure and support for volunteers. Recognising the problems of time constraints on volunteers the LTA is experimenting with various ways to reduce the burden on individual volunteers. Role profiles are being tried as a way of defining voluntary posts and what is expected of them. Fixed term appointments are being tried as a way of encouraging new volunteers to come forward who might otherwise have been deterred by a post having been held by an existing volunteer for many years. Workshops run by the English Sports Council give national governing bodies, such as the LTA, an opportunity to share their experiences.

In addition to these initiatives, up to December 1997, the English Sports Council have made 1,675 awards to voluntary sports organisations from the Lottery Sport Fund, totalling £180m. By May 1998 it was estimated that 2 per cent of sports clubs in England had received an award. The voluntary sector in sport has received 68 per cent of the Sports Lottery awards; which equates to 28 per cent of the value of awards distributed so far. This understates support to the voluntary sector through the Lottery as the large majority of all awards will provide future opportunities for voluntary sports through improved facilities.

From national organisations – examples of the Guide Association and national governing bodies of sport

The Guide Association

To meet the problem that volunteers do not feel they have sufficent skills to deliver a more exciting programme the Guide Association is developing local networks of specialist volunteers to deliver particular skills. These will be connected to local authorities' networks of specialist instructors. Another way of increasing the skills base is through internal training courses, although these just give more skills to existing volunteers rather than widen the volunteer pool.

Recruitment of volunteers in the Guide Association is heavily influenced by the association's strong and distinctive ethos. Membership is only open to females and it is recognised that to change the organisational culture of the Guide Association such that men, beyond the close family of Guiders, are seen as suitable recruits to volunteer, is a very big step. Politically this would be unacceptable because it would be a direct challenge to the Scout Association, competing for their leaders, and because it would be too directly in opposition to the nature of the Association as a single sex organisation. In this respect the ethos of the organisation limits the groups it can recruit from.

Another initiative to encourage volunteers has been to link leadership training to nationally recognised awards. For example, Guider training qualifications have been linked to National Vocational Qualification (NVQ) level 3. It is unclear the extent to which linking Guiding leadership training to NVQs will have a positive effect of recruitment. It may be significant in enhancing the employment portfolio of young Guiders who are seeking to establish their career. It may be less significant for a Guide leader who becomes involved through her children. Perhaps it can be regarded as an additional incentive that may be relevant to some volunteers.

National governing bodies of sport

Examples have been given above of support offered by the Lawn Tennis Association. In general NGBs may give support through training courses, national and regional forums to share ideas, advice with making Lottery bids, handbooks (which often contain a wealth of practical information – the Lawn Tennis Association handbook has advice on alternative club constitutions, club management, budgeting, accounting, taxes, rating assessments, etc.) and a range of other specific and general advice. Some governing bodies are able to give this advice through regional officers. As in the Guide Association, some NGBs have attempted to link their training awards to NVQs.

General conclusions on support

As Hoggert and Bishop (1985:105) noted, 'anybody wishing to relate to the worlds of communal leisure must understand and appreciate it in its own terms', and 'each group sees itself as almost assertively independant'. Support for volunteers needs to be sensitive to their needs. Local authorities may be more sensitive to the needs of sports volunteers because of their close contact with them and ability to give support in relation to local conditions; frequently through sports development officers. However, the English Sports Council has become more sensitive to this problem. Many organisations offer support in the form of training courses, but a problem with this is that volunteers need to find the time to attend them. There is great potential for organisations working in partnerships to support volunteers, for example NGBs working with the English Sports Council, or the Guide Association working with local authorities. There will always be a tension, discussed below, between support with conditions attached, and meeting the needs of volunteers. For example, the Lawn Tennis Association is willing to give clubs financial assistance to make Lottery bids to develop new facilities, but on condition that small clubs merge to gain economies of scale, allowing them to provide facilities of a high quality, comparable to the private sector. Traditional clubs may not wish to do this. Another example of this tension might be the support given by Birmingham City Council, described above.

Summary and Conclusions

There are two main ways of understanding the voluntary sector and volunteers. One is as fulfilling an economic function, producing leisure opportunities, or other services, which are not provided by the private or public sectors. The second is as the free expression of shared enthusiasms, in which the act of volunteering may be as important as the output from the activity. The two different perspectives have implications for understanding the motivations of volunteers as a balance between self interest and altruism. However, the public perception of volunteering is that altruism should be an important motivation.

The different understandings of the voluntary sector also have implications for public policy. Policy may be directed towards supporting the voluntary sector because of the benefits from the services it creates. For example, the English Sports Council wants to ensure that opportunities are created for young people to take part in sport, partly through the efforts of volunteers. Alternatively, support for the voluntary sector could be to engender active citizenship and the expression of interest groups in a pluralist society.

In practice, while there is a balance between the two approaches, local authority support for voluntary sports clubs has become increasingly conditional. In a climate of financial constraint, and where local authority, or Sports Council, expenditure is expected to be justified with reference to its contribution to strategic plans and measurable performance indicators, support for the voluntary sector is unlikely to merely have the objective of nurturing a pluralist society; allowing interest groups to freely express themselves in their leisure. Support is much more likely to 'have strings attached', to be conditional on the voluntary organisation acting in a way that will help achieve the grant-giver's policies. For example, there are a range of conditions attached to the award of Sports Lottery grants. However, as the English Sports Council have found, Hoggert and Bishops' conclusion that public sector support should be sensitive to the nature of the voluntary sector is valid. If conditions of support are too onerous it will not be accepted, or there may be unacceptable pressures put on volunteers. This is one source of general pressures on the voluntary sector.

The examples of support above show that there may be a lot to be gained by voluntary organisations just sharing good practice, and helping them to do this. The Sports Council VIP programme is set up to do this. There are training courses available to volunteers, but this form of support is limited by the time volunteers have to attend such courses. Lack of time was the main reason why non volunteers in the National Survey of Volunteering (Davis Smith 1998) did not volunteer, and why sports secretaries did not attend Running Sport courses.

The distinctive character of the voluntary sector in Britain is a consequence of its historical development. However, it can be argued that changes in the time people feel they are able to give to volunteering, changes in attitudes, competition from other leisure opportunities, and an increasing tendency to view leisure as a commodity subject to market exchange, may all contribute to the sector's decline. It is very difficult to prove conclusively that this is happening because of the lack of longitudinal evidence, but if it is, it would constitute a reduction of the opportunities for free expression through leisure.

Suggested Tasks for Further Study

1. Interview a volunteer, or a group of volunteers in a formal organisation. To what extent are the difficulties they face similar to those of the volunteers discussed above?
2. Examine a partnership between the public and the voluntary sector. What are the objectives of each partner? How do they have to compromise them in making the partnership work? Does a partnership imply equal power between partners?
3. How has a voluntary sector organisation attempted to recruit more volunteers or share work around the existing ones?
4. What support is offered to volunteers by a local authority, national governing bodies of sport, a national organisation such as the Guide Association, or the English Sports Council? Are conditions attached to this support and if so, how do they affect the voluntary organisation?
5. How does a sports development officer both support voluntary sector sports clubs and use them to achieve particular objectives?
6. Analyse the handbooks provided for clubs by national governing bodies of sport. What range of advice do they give and how useful is it? You may like to gain the opinion of a club official.

References

- Caan R, Handy F and Wadsworth M 1996 'Defining who is a volunteer' *Social Policy and Administration* 30(3) pp.206–226
- Clarke A and Critcher C 1985 *The devil makes work; leisure in capitalist Britain* Macmillan, Basingstoke
- Critcher C, Bramham P and Tomlinson A 1995 *Sociology of Leisure* E and F N Spon, London
- Curson T 1995 'Can you place your trust in them? The role of charitable trusts in leisure management' in Leslie D (Ed) *Tourism and leisure perspectives on provision* (LSA publication No.52) Leisure Studies Association, Eastbourne
- Cuskelly G, McIntyre N and Boag A 1998 'A longitudinal study of the development of organizational commitment amongst volunteer sport administrators' *Journal of Sport Management* 12(3) pp.181–202
- Davis Smith J 1998 *The 1997 National Survey of Volunteering* National Centre for Volunteering, London
- Department of National Heritage 1995 *Sport, Raising the Game* DNH, London
- Dower M *et al.* 1981 *Leisure provision and peoples' needs* HMSO, London
- English Sports Council 1997 *England, the sporting nation; a strategy* English Sports Council, London
- Freund J 1972 *The sociology of Max Weber* Penguin, London
- Goddard E 1994 *Voluntary work* HMSO, London
- Gorz A 1985 *Paths to paradise* Pluto Press, London
- Gratton C and Taylor P 1985 *Sport and recreation* E and F Spon, London
- Gratton C and Taylor P 1991 *Government and the economics of sport* E and F Spon, London
- Gratton C *et al.* 1997 *Valuing volunteers in UK sport* Sports Council, London
- Hedley R and Davis Smith J 1992 *Volunteering and society* Bedford Square Press, London
- Henry I 1993 *The politics of leisure policy* Macmillan, Basingstoke

- Hoggett P and Bishop J 1985 *The social organisation of leisure* Sports Council, London
- Holliday S 1996 'Trends in British working time: has the British worker's increasing workload become a barrier to leisure participation?' in Gratton C (Ed) *Work, leisure and the quality of life: a global perspective* Leisure Industries Research Centre, Sheffield
- Holt R 1990 *Sport and the British* Oxford University Press, Oxford
- Houlihan B 1991 *The government and politics of sport* Routledge, London
- Leach S, Stewart J and Walsh K 1994 *The changing organisation and management of local government* Macmillan, Basingstoke
- Lyons M, Wijkstrom P and Clary G 1998 Comparative studies of volunteering: what is being studied? *Voluntary Action* 1(1) pp.45–54
- Martin W H and Mason S 1998 *Transforming the future quality of life; rethinking free time and work* Leisure Consultants, Sudbury
- Nichols G and Taylor P 1993 *UK sports information services, an investigation of demand by people with a professional interest in sport* Sports Council, London
- Nichols G and King L 1997 *Research for the Guide Association* London: Guide Association, unpublished
- Nichols G and Sparrowhawk J 1999 'Local authorities' role in distributing the lottery to sport' *Local Government Studies* 25(3) pp.1–15
- Roberts K 1978 *Contemporary society and the growth of leisure* Longman, London
- Robinson J 1990 'The time squeeze' *American Demographics* February 1990 pp.30–33.
- Smith D H 1981 'Altruism, volunteers, and volunteerism' *Journal of Voluntary Action Research* 10 pp.21–36
- Smith D H 1994 'Determinants of voluntary participation and volunteering: a literature review' *Nonprofit and Voluntary Sector Quarterly* 23(3) pp.243–263
- Sports Council 1993 *Young people and sport, policy and frameworks for action* Sports Council, London
- Stebbins R 1996 'Volunteering: a serious leisure perspective' *Non-profit and Voluntary Sector Quarterly* 25(2) pp.211–224
- Stebbins R 1997 'Serious leisure and well-being' in Haworth J (Ed) *Work, leisure and well-being* Routledge, London
- Taylor P D 1993 *Financing of excellence in sport* Sports Council, London
- Veal A J 1989 'Leisure, lifestyle and status: a pluralist framework for analysis' *Leisure Studies* 8 pp.141–153
- Weisbrod B A 1978 'The voluntary non-profit sector' in Gratton and Taylor, *op. cit.* Lexington Books, Lexington, Massachusetts
- Williams R 1977 'Marxism and literature' OUP p.110 in Clarke and Critcher, 1985 pp.228, *op. cit.*

Material in this chapter has appeared previously in:

- Gratton C, Nichols G, Shibli S and Taylor P 1998 'Local authority support to volunteers in sports clubs' *Managing Leisure: an International Journal* 3(3), pp.119–127, July 1998
- Gratton C, Nichols G, Shibli S and Taylor P 1998 'Can the Sports Council rely on volunteers?' *Recreation* June 1998 pp.14–16
- Nichols G and King L 1998 'Volunteers in the Guide Association; problems and solutions' *The Journal for Volunteering Research* 1(1) pp.21–32
- Nichols G, Shibli S and Taylor P 1998 'Pressures that contribute to a change in the nature of the voluntary sector in British sport' *Vrijetijdstudies* 16(2) pp.34–46
- Nichols G and Taylor P 1998 'Volunteers: the Sports Council strikes back' *Recreation* December 1998 pp.16–19

Chapter 4

The UK and International Sports Organisations

Mel Welch
Leeds Metropolitan University

Chapter Content

- Introduction
- The Perspective of the Various Sectors
- The Range of Organisations
- The Impact of the Market Place
- Summary and Conclusions
- Suggested Tasks for Further Study

Abstract

This chapter provides a coherent reference point for all studies of the organisation and government of sport; it is essential to be aware of the existence and the motivation of the various parties before predicting how they are likely to react and contribute to any new initiative or development.

The structure of the government of sport is a complex jigsaw, in which international, UK, home country, regional and local associations and their member clubs, interlock in a manner which is not always harmonious. The wide range of organisations, their motivation and their frustrations provides a dynamic framework in which the various players compete for their interpretation of success.

The organisation and government of sport has traditionally followed the Victorian model of voluntary management and self-regulation, and most sports organisations in Britain evolved along these lines. More recently, however, the influences of the market place (most in evidence in USA, but now universal) and state control (as demonstrated by the Eastern European model) has led the public and commercial sectors into the framework of sports organisation and management, sometimes in partnership and sometimes in conflict with the voluntary sector.

Related Chapters

Chapter 12: The Management of Change in the Leisure and Sport Management Sector: This chapter is a very good practical example of how change has developed within the international sports arena. The theory and practice of change management, particularly, issues of power and politics are relevant to these changes.

Learning Outcomes

- to provide an insight into the existence and functions of the various bodies involved in the organisation and government of sport
- to enable comparisons to be made between the role and aspirations of the different sectors (public, private, voluntary) involved in the organisation and government of sport
- to relate the impact of market forces to the various bodies involved in the organisation and government of sport
- to enable predictions to be made of the likely impact of possible future developments on the structure and nature of sport

Introduction

The organisation and government of sport was first developed during the Victorian era in England, and the model of voluntary management and self-regulation devised at that time has been adopted throughout the world and prevails to this day.

Most organised sport in Britain was first developed in the educational sector, notably the universities and public schools. Similar educational development took place in the USA. Naturally, it was only a matter of time before the wealthy graduates decided that they wished to continue playing their sport after they had finished their education. Sport had become a desirable leisure activity and the rapid development of the railway meant that for the first time, it was possible to have regular competition with those from other parts of the country. This meant there was a need to codify rules and regulations, to ensure consistency, and this led to the co-ordination of competitions and the formation of national sports associations.

These associations are known in Britain as national governing bodies of sport and they do indeed seek to govern and control the sport that they represent, acting as quasi governmental organisations setting and establishing rules and then providing a legal framework to implement those rules and to take sanctions against those who break them.

Sports clubs developed to provide for those who had completed their education initially mostly based on school old boys, military establishments or similar organisations. The development of the sports club, in its own right, was initially slow and sport in England, especially the south of England, was still very much something for the leisured classes.

Golf had developed in Scotland from the Middle Ages and the game of lawn tennis, invented as sphairistike in 1873, quickly developed appeal. Cricket clubs were by then well established and the sports of association football and rugby football were gaining favour. Spectator following of these team sports soon led to the introduction of formal competitions such as:

- the Football Association Challenge Cup (started in 1871)
- the All England Lawn Tennis Championships (started in 1877)
- the Open Golf Championship (started by a canny group of Scottish professional golfers in 1860) and
- the County Cricket Championships (which began in 1890).

Ambitious football clubs, especially those in the north west of England and the midlands, realised that the recruitment of players could be greatly improved if the working classes could be a source of talent for them, and they quickly began to overhaul the military and gentlemen's clubs such as the Royal Engineers, Old Etonians, and the Wanderers who had dominated the early years of the FA Cup. In 1888, the Football League was established by 12 professional clubs, and they immediately dominated the Football Association's Cup. No team from the south of England reached the cup final between 1883 and 1900.

Many of the rugby clubs in the north of England wished to follow suit. These clubs were recruiting from working class people, who normally worked on Saturdays and had to give up work in order to play matches and to travel the increasing distances required to get a higher standard of competition. However, the Rugby Football Union, not wishing to see their sport go the same way as association football, opposed this move and this led to the great schism of 1895. The Northern Rugby Football Union, (subsequently to become known as the Rugby Football League) was formed when 21 rugby clubs from Yorkshire and Lancashire met together at the George Hotel in Huddersfield and decided that, if they were not to be allowed to pay broken time payments to their players by the Rugby Football Union, then they would form their own Union and be their own governing body.

Following the English model, other sports associations were formed, initially in Scotland and Ireland, and then in the USA, and the British Empire; then in Europe and the rest of the world. In the main they all followed the same model whereby a voluntary organisation, essentially a collection of voluntary sports clubs, set themselves up as the national governing body for their sport in that country. Naturally, the introduction of international competition between these countries soon followed. The first international football match was played between England and Scotland in 1872, the first rugby international took place between the same two countries in 1871, and the first Cricket Test match, between England and Australia, was held in 1877. The Davis Cup in tennis between Britain and the USA began in 1900.

In USA, from the earliest times, the organisation of competitive sport had taken a different route. Inter-Collegiate events took centre stage – the Inter-Collegiate (American) Football Association was founded in 1876 – and the top level of non-academic competition formed through independent leagues, comprising a small group of clubs who governed their own affairs and had little or no interaction with the rest of the sport. Major League Baseball (MLB) started in 1876 with the formation of the National League. The American League started in 1901, and the World Series, between the two league champion clubs, in 1903.

The French aristocrat, Baron Pierre de Coubertin, visited the traditional sports fair at Much Wenlock in Shropshire, England in the 1880s and was so impressed by what he saw that he decided to copy their celebrations to found the modern Olympic Games, which started in Athens in 1896. The epitaph to de Coubertin on his grave in Olympia, Greece has become the Olympic ideal: '*Ce n'est pas la victoire, mais la lutte qui est importante. L'essentiel n'est pas d'avoir gagné mais de s'être bien battu.*' ('The important thing is not winning but taking part. The essential is not to have won but to have fought well').

The Games of 1896 led to the formation of National Olympic Committees, the first being in the USA in 1896 followed by Greece, France, Great Britain and Ireland. Today there are over 200 National Olympic Committees recognised by the IOC.

International sports federations were founded by the national associations coming together. The Federation of International Football Associations was formed in 1904; the International Amateur Athletic Federation was formed in 1912; the International Swimming Federation in 1908; and the International Basketball Federation in 1932. These organisations continue to this day in the same democratic format, whereby each member national association has an equal voice, irrespective of the size of the country or the number of players in that country. The associations are voluntary bodies run without profit motive and the revenue raised is put back into the sport they represent.

Nevertheless many of these sports bodies have now become extremely commercially oriented, and in recent years, some of the clubs have themselves moved firmly into the public sector with profit as their main motive. This was the case from the earliest times in the major sports leagues in North America (NBA, NHL, NFL and Major League Baseball), but now is increasingly the case in Europe. Many of the Premiership football teams in England and Scotland have turned themselves into public limited companies, and shareholding has generated huge profits for some individuals.

The increasing commercialism has enabled individual sports performers to become extremely wealthy, either through prize money, appearance fees, or endorsements whereby the individual is seen to be using a particular brand of sports equipment or extolling the virtue of a product. Michael Jordan, the American basketball star, was reputed to be earning $100 million a year when he retired in 1999; $30 million came from his salary with the Chicago Bulls and the balance came from product endorsements and other personal fees. Golfers, tennis players and track athletes are among performers who can look forward to rich returns for their sporting performance.

The concept whereby the Olympic Games was reserved for amateur performers was abandoned when it became clear that without the world's superstars the Games might lose their appeal and the marketability; performers who had earned huge sums of money through their performance on the tennis court, or the basketball court (notably the 'Dream Team'), made their appearance in the Games of Barcelona in 1992, thereby finally laying the myth of Olympic amateurism to rest. Since that time Olympic stars have been able to earn large sums of money throughout the world based on the prestige to be gained by winning an Olympic medal.

The Perspective of the Various Sectors

The commercial sector

The influences of the market place, particularly in the sports which are well developed in North America and in the sport of association football, and now well in evidence throughout the world, has led the commercial sector to become involved in the organisation and management of sporting affairs sometimes in partnership with and sometimes in conflict with the voluntary sector and the governing bodies of sport.

In the UK in the 1990s, it was estimated that the commercial sector employed over 130,000 people in the sport and leisure industry, including the periphery industries of sports equipment and clothing and sports event management.

The private or commercial sector has recognised the desire for people to belong to clubs and therefore encourages a sense of belonging and ownership by introducing membership for a variety of clubs. In this way the 'member' feels that they in some way have a say in the way in which their club is run, while in reality they are simply customers paying for a season ticket to enable them to have use of facilities. Certainly, they have no say in the government or profit of the club in question.

The public sector

When we have match'd our rackets to these balls,
We will, in France, by God's grace, play a set
Shall strike his father's crown into the hazard.
Tell him he hath made a match with such a wrangler
That all the courts of France will be disturb'd
With chases (William Shakespeare, *Henry V* (1497) ACT I, SCENE II)

Governments throughout the world have recognised the value of sport to them in achieving their aims. Their involvement in sport is two-fold: firstly there are public relations advantages to be won or lost by implementing positive attitudes and policies towards sport and exercise: a successful national sports team or individual can raise national morale and help the government of the day to improve its popularity. On the world scene, many governments, especially those of a totalitarian nature, have tried to use sporting success to extol the virtues of their own particular political system. This could be seen as long ago as the original Olympic Games of Ancient Greece and was echoed by Hitler's overt propaganda use of the 1936 Olympics. The Soviet Union and its satellites were notable for their sporting achievements and many of the methods used to achieve that success are now being questioned as to their ethical values.

Then there is the role that government, especially local government, can play in the provision of opportunities for its local population to actively engage in sporting activity, which can lead to a sense of public well-being and improve their quality of life.

In a consultation paper published by the Department for Culture, Media and Sport, it states:

Sport offers direct economic benefits. It contributes to the re-generation of towns and cities improving health, productivity and quality of life. It contributes to savings in the cost of health care and leads to a reduction in crime and vandalism. It offers local environmental benefits that can change the image of a city or community and lead to increased inward investment.

(*The Comprehensive Spending Review – a New Approach to Investment in Culture* Department of Culture, Media and Sport 1998)

The voluntary sector

Today it is estimated that there are:

nearly 1,500,000 volunteers working in UK sport, each putting in an average of 125 voluntary hours a year, or just over 2.5 hours a week for 48 weeks a year . . . Assuming a standard working week and year, the hours worked by the estimated volunteer workforce in UK sport are equivalent to over 108,000 full-time equivalent workers added to the sports labour market . . . The total annual value of the UK sports volunteer market is thus estimated to be over £1.5 billion.

(*Valuing Volunteers in UK Sport* Sports Council 1995)

The establishment of voluntary sports clubs began in Britain in the eighteenth century, when clubs such as the Marylebone Cricket Club (founded 1787) and the Royal and Ancient Golf Club of St Andrews (founded 1754) came on the scene.

Horse racing also began to be established at about that time – the first Classic race, the St Leger, started in 1776, followed by the Derby in 1780. The French equivalent, the Prix du Jockey Club began in 1836, whilst the great Australian race, the Melbourne Cup, was first run in 1861. The first of the American Triple Crown races was the Belmont Stakes in 1867.

Blackheath Football Club is the oldest surviving rugby club, having been formed in 1857 when the separation of the two codes of football into *association* and *rugby* was still a few years off. An independent voluntary club, divorced from the connections with education or the military, was such a rare event in those days that Blackheath were known simply as 'The Club', a name that survives to this day. Sheffield FC has the same claim in association football – being the first club to have been formed, back in 1855.

Such was the uncertainty as to the best code that Manningham started life playing rugby union; switched to rugby league as a founder member of the Northern Union in 1895; became the first Northern Union league champions in 1896, and then in 1905 withdrew from rugby league to become Bradford City association football club.

> *The voluntary sector is vital to the delivery of sport in the UK*
> (UK Sports Council survey on 'Valuing Volunteers' 1996)

Most organised (as opposed to casual) sport in Britain takes place within the voluntary sector. This sector contains the vast majority of sports clubs and nearly all the national associations – known as national governing bodies (NGBs) – that co-ordinate their activities.

> *When many governing bodies of sport were formed in the last quarter of the 19th century, their main priority was the enforcement of amateur rules and the fair conduct of competition* (McNab *et al. Coaching Matters* Sports Council 1989)

The Range of Organisations

International

International sport is headed by the International Olympic Committee (IOC), a self-appointed group who are the custodians of the Olympic Games, one of the most powerful marketing images in the world today.

The IOC recognises a range of international sports federations who take control of various sports events that take place in the Olympic programme, but the IOC is not answerable to any of these federations, and the federations themselves have no direct voice in the IOC, other than through members of the IOC Council who may be associated with those particular sporting organisations.

The international sports federations themselves have a joint federation: GAISF (General Assembly of International Sports Federations); and the National Olympic Committees have together formed their own association: ANOC (Association of National Olympic Committees).

The major international sports federations (FIFA, IAAF, FINA, FIBA, etc.) now have 200 or more national associations affiliated to them, and control sports with huge commercial and social impact.

In contrast, the most successful sports leagues in the world, those in the four major team sports in North America, are owned and controlled simply by their member clubs. The National Football League (NFL) has 31 franchises that are commercially owned, marketed, and traded for profit. The League is owned by the clubs and profit from the marketing activities of the League, which can be enormous, are shared by the clubs. The players provide the raw material from which the League profit is generated, and inevitably there have been a number of labour disputes, leading to strikes or walk-outs, when the club owners and the players fail to reach agreement regarding the level of remuneration that the players should be receiving. Like most strikes, these disputes lead to difficulties for all parties concerned and the sport can receive a serious setback. The public sympathy and the moral high ground are the eventual weapons that all parties seek to win.

The most commercially developed team sport outside North America, association football, has so far resisted a complete take-over by the leading clubs, but this is a constant battle, which is fought at national and continental level. To date, the attraction and the earning power of international matches between national representative teams, and in particular the World Cup, has been sufficient to ensure that the clubs and players remain within the jurisdiction of the national football associations. Inevitably, however, each year the power of the clubs increases and they are able to secure more and more concessions leading to a larger share of the revenue being apportioned to a reducing number of elite clubs.

United Kingdom

The structure of sport in the United Kingdom is made particularly complex by virtue of the fact that most sports organisations were developed firstly in England and then copied in Scotland and the first international matches were between those two countries. Other sports were bound to imitate the model provided by football, rugby and hockey, and thus the structure of British sport is largely defined on a four-nation basis. However, the participation in the Olympic Games and membership of some international sports federations, has been in the name of Great Britain and therefore it has been necessary to bring together, for the purpose of providing British teams, representatives of the various component parts of the United Kingdom. The sports associations in Ireland were mostly formed before the separation of Northern Ireland from the Republic and many have continued with the unique cross border arrangements and are in membership of the international sports federation on behalf of both north and south of the country.

At governmental level, the United Kingdom Sports Council (now operating under the brand name UK Sport) was formed in 1997 to try to provide a representative voice for the United Kingdom and to harmonise the views being expressed by respective National Sports Councils from England, Scotland, Wales and Northern Ireland. Previously the Sports Council in London represented both English and British affairs, which inevitably led to some conflict with its counterparts in Scotland, Wales and Northern Ireland, who argued that their views should also be taken into account when Britain is being represented.

However, the early days of the UK Sports Council were frustrated by limited opportunity for successful development, since its powers did not extend to instructing or mandating the four national Councils. Governing bodies of sport were left with the dilemma of dealing with the UK Sports Council and, in some cases, the four National Sports Councils if they were operating both at British and separate national levels.

National

The range of national sports organisations in Britain is enormous. The situation in England is especially complex although Scotland, Wales and Northern Ireland have similar structures, made somewhat simpler by the fact that there is a clear separation between their own national organisation and any body serving Great Britain or the United Kingdom.

In England, the English Sports Council (now operating under the brand name Sport England) serves the developmental and excellence programmes of sport, paying particular attention to youth sport and a whole range of equity programmes. The Council is an approved distributor of the National Lottery Sports Fund, and since this is allocated on the basis of relative population, the English Sports Council enjoys 83 per cent of the total Lottery cake that is available to give out each year. In 1999 this amounted to over £200 million.

The English Sports Council is funded largely from the Exchequer through the Department for Culture, Media and Sport. Although it enjoys independent status with a Royal Charter, it is required 'in the exercise of its functions to have regard to any general statements in the policy of our Government that may from time to time be issued to it by our Secretary of State' (Sports Council Royal Charter 1972). Besides, the Sports Council could not ignore the wishes of central government who decide its revenue budgets and the membership of the Council's own governing board.

The main partners of the Council at national level are the national governing bodies of sport, each of which comprise the clubs and various county and regional associations. The national governing bodies are themselves combined with other organisations, and the regional federations of sport, in the Central Council of Physical Recreation (CCPR). The CCPR was founded in 1935 as the Central Council of Recreative and Physical Training and has always maintained its complete independence from government and has successfully lobbied government on behalf of sport on a variety of issues including limiting the sale of school playing fields and VAT exemptions for sports organisations.

The main objectives of the CCPR are to encourage as many people as possible to participate in all forms of sport and physical recreation, and to provide the separate governing bodies of the individual sports the central organisation that would represent and promote the individual and collective interests. The CCPR has in membership both British and English sports bodies and in 1997 its membership reached 285 organisations.

The national governing bodies of sport have responsibility for their own particular sport, often working through regions or county associations, schools sports organisations and various disability sports bodies. In addition, at national level there are various other national associations and charities including Sports Aid (which is responsible for fund raising and giving grants to promising young sports performers); the Youth Sport Trust; and the National Coaching Foundation (a subsidiary body to the Sports Council).

The other major player on the national sports scene is the British Olympic Association, founded in 1905 and comprising representatives of the British governing bodies of the sports in the Olympic programme. The BOA, through its involvement with the International Olympic Committee and through public appeals, is able to operate without relying on financial support from the Sports Council or central government. This has enabled the BOA to maintain its independence, which was perfectly illustrated during the time leading up to the 1980 Olympic Games in Moscow when the then Prime Minister, Margaret Thatcher, wished the BOA to support the US boycott of the Games. BOA did not share this viewpoint and went ahead with sending a British team despite the Government's displeasure.

Regional and local

In England most national governing bodies of sport are sub-divided into regional or local units. Confusingly, each sport has its own system for determining these divisions, which may be based on a wide variety of concepts, including county (or groups of counties), regions (governmental or otherwise), leagues (which are peculiar to that particular sport) and miscellaneous other geographical or sporting concepts. Particularly in the case of county boundaries, this is further complicated by the use by some sports of boundaries that existed prior to a number of local government reform acts, which has perpetuated such counties as Middlesex and Huntingdonshire; not recognised the separation of Yorkshire or Lancashire into several separate counties; and still splits London into four parts.

There is a move to a degree of conformity at regional level for sport in general with the formation of nine Regional Sports Boards (in each case conforming to the boundaries of the government regions), which are mirrored by offices of the English Sports Council and the Sports Aid Foundation and on which the governing bodies are represented by a Regional Sports Federation.

The Impact of the Market Place

Professionalism

Professionalism followed gradually in many other sports – sometimes with traumatic impact, such as:

- the great schism of 1895, which led to two codes of rugby
- the long-running separation of amateurs and professionals in tennis, only finally resolved when Wimbledon unilaterally declared itself to be open in 1968
- the continuing separation of boxing into the amateur code, properly regarded as the only true embodiment of the sport by the International Olympic Committee (IOC) and the multiplicity of bodies purporting to govern world professional boxing
- a continuing artificial divide maintained to this day in a few sports (including golf) where amateur status still has a meaning, and competition is largely segregated
- the abandonment by the IOC of the definition of amateurism and the requirement that only 'amateurs' can take part in the Olympic Games.

Professionalism plays an increasingly important role in sport. There has been an increase in the number of professional sporting events, and the financial returns for players in many sports have risen considerably in recent years. This has led to a number of difficulties for NGBs and clubs who seek to employ or promote events involving professional players. The intrinsic love of the game may, in some cases, be replaced by the profit-motive.

Sports administration, coaching and officiating has also taken a turn towards the increasing use of paid personnel, either as full-time members of staff or (effectively) as self-employed fee earners (e.g. a referee who is paid a match fee).

The match official is subjected to very visible and well-known pressures and faces possible condemnation from players, coaches, team owners, fans, the media and even fellow officials. The pressure on the professional coach is similarly well-known. Failure to produce a winning performer or team is likely to lead to their being relieved of their duties. Even those coaching at beginner or participation level are likely to be judged by their pupils, who will make a personal judgement as to the effectiveness of the coach to deliver the increased level of skill that the player considers him or herself to be inherently capable.

Legal impacts

Any move towards increased financial outlay and reward inevitably leads to an increase in the involvement of lawyers in the management of sport. Every contract needs careful scrutiny and every decision taken by sporting bodies can be expected to be the subject of legal challenge if anybody feels that they may stand to lose by the decision. The old adage 'the referee's decision is final' may no longer be the case.

The European Commission, notably through the Bosman ruling of the European Court of Justice (Case C-415/93, *URBSFA* v. *Bosman*, (1995) ECR 4921, 15 December 1995), has had a major impact on the eligibility and transfer regulations for sporting competitions. The anti-doping regulations introduced by all major international sports federations have generated several major legal battles which have been known to bankrupt the sports bodies defending their actions; and the leading clubs or teams in sports such as football, basketball and motor racing are multi-million pound businesses.

Media involvement

Traditionally, the media has reported sport as it has found it, by faithfully recording the progress of the event. Today, many sports have exclusive broadcasting contracts which provide the governing body, the clubs and the individual players with the majority of the income. From being a passive observer of sport, the media has become a key player in the game.

Summary and Conclusions

The organisation and government of sport has traditionally followed the Victorian model of voluntary management and self-regulation. Today, however, the influences of the market place and state control has led the public and commercial sectors into the framework of sports organisation and management, sometimes in partnership and sometimes in conflict with the voluntary sector.

The future of sport in the United Kingdom and Europe is likely to follow the media-led model, until there are essentially two distinct forms of sport – sport you play and sport you watch. The two forms will move apart as sport as an entertainment industry becomes more and more geared to interesting and pleasing the viewing public. Influence and control by the mass media will increase and the key to success will be the viewing figures and the company profits, not the results of the matches. Alongside this, the leisure and recreation industry will also expand, but it is likely that conflict for the control of the two forms will increase, as the clubs, the players, their agents and lawyers demand an ever increasing say in the government of their sport.

Many sporting expressions have passed into everyday language: 'It's not cricket'; 'Play to the whistle'; 'A level playing field'; 'Be a good sport'. It is likely that, in the future, sport itself will have to fight hard to continue to hold on to many of these expressions.

Suggested Tasks for Further Study

1. As a result of the Bosman ruling and its impact on eligibility regulations, Chelsea FC (England) and Glasgow Rangers FC (Scotland) regularly fielded teams in the 1999–2000 football season which did not contain a single player eligible to play for their respective countries. Consider the advantages and disadvantages of this for the sport.

2. Explore the website of the English Sports Council, www.english.sports.gov.uk. By following appropriate links or otherwise, identify:

- the location of the nearest outdoor basketball goal to your home (English residents only)
- the date of the next FA Cup Final
- the opening line of the Olympic Charter.

3. 'Sport matters. It is vitally important to the physical health of the nation, and is a multi-billion pound industry. At its best sport is exciting, passionate, and hugely enjoyable. In short, it can help to improve our quality of life. It offers a sense of personal accomplishment and health related benefits; it teaches people how to win and lose with equanimity and can improve cognitive skills such as literacy and numeracy. For society as a whole, sport can help to reduce the level of crime; it can help channel aggression; and it can play an important role in dismantling social and ethnic barriers.'

(*A Future for Sport*, Conservative Party Blue Paper, published January 2000)

- identify the various elements of the above statement
- discuss each in turn
- what evidence exists to support the above assertions?
- what evidence exists to refute the above assertions?

4. George Orwell once made a statement about sport and fairplay. However, there is no consensus of the exact words he spoke. Consider, compare and contrast the two alternative versions of his quote:

- 'Sport is nothing to do with fairplay; it's just war without the shooting'
- 'Sport is nothing without fairplay; for then it's just war without the shooting'.

The Leisure and Sport Markets

This section draws upon existing literature and research in order to rationalise the complexities and competitive pressures within today's leisure markets. These pressures and external realities will shape the leisure choices of the future. The section begins by discussing individual consumer behaviour and moves on to discuss the wider global issues that leisure providers need to be aware of.

Chapter 5 focuses on individual leisure consumer behaviour. The literature involving consumer choice is explored, as are the issues of disposal income and time constraints as they apply to consumer behaviour. The authors, *Chris Wolsey* and *Helen Whitrod Brown*, set the chapter within the context of applied social psychology and consumer behaviour literature.

Chapter 6 is entitled *Strategy, Competition and the Commercial Leisure Markets* and provides an overview of the relevant literature as it applies to the leisure and sport context. This review is a critique of the existing literature both from a pragmatic and an academic point of view. The author, *Chris Wolsey*, also sets the chapter within the wider context of macroeconomics. A range of leisure and sport management examples are used throughout the chapter to reinforce the points made and to provide a clear focus for the reader. Issues to do with competitive strategy from an organisational and human resource perspective are also considered.

Chapter 7 explores the ideological ethos underpinning postwar policy-making within Britain. This is done with a focus on access to the countryside as an illustration of how policy issues have developed over time. A range of theoretical perspectives are discussed from social reformist views through to neo-liberal New Right perspectives. The authors, *John Spink* and *Peter Bramham*, set this discussion within the access to the countryside debate. The chapter also explores the managerial implications of leisure policy as well as the role of public policy in a changing consumer market. The role of pressure groups and how power is exerted within a public policy context is also explored.

Chapter 8, on globalisation, provides a sound basis to understand much of what has been discussed in the previous two sections. The chapter's authors, *Peter Bramham* and *John Spink*, provide an overview of the processes, meaning and impact of globalisation on leisure markets. This is achieved through the use of a model of globalisation, which includes the following: ecological, technological, cultural, social, political and economic change. These broad areas are set in the context of three levels of analysis – transnational, the national and the local. A case study of the UK Premiership football league is used to reinforce the model presented.

Chapter 5

Consumerism and the Leisure Markets

Chris Wolsey and Helen Whitrod Brown
Leeds Metropolitan University

Chapter Content

- Introduction
- Leisure Time
- The Economics of Consumption
- Consumer Behaviour in a Turbulent World
- The History of Consumption Research
- Contemporary Theories of Consumption
- Consumer Behaviour and Leisure Choices
- The Leisure Experience
- Leisure Lifestyles in the New Millennium
- A Question of Balance
- Back to Basics, Back to the Future
- Summary and Conclusions
- Suggested Tasks for Further Study
- References

Abstract

This chapter seeks to establish the context in which individual leisure production and consumption decisions are made. It will locate this within the disciplinary areas of economics, psychology, sociology and social psychology as applied to the study of consumer and market behaviour. The chapter reviews the antecedents of individual leisure choices and the implications for the marketing undertaken by leisure organisations. It concludes that consumer behaviour is likely to become more difficult to predict in the future. This has consequences for leisure organisations, who must work hard to ensure that consumers have an appropriate mix of choices. Leisure organisations should respond to heterogeneous markets by adopting a clear strategy to deliver a coherent and well targeted market proposition to an increasingly discerning leisure consumer.

Related Chapter

Chapter 2: This provides a wider *international* perspective of the factors affecting leisure demands. This is particularly true of discussions relating to the cultural context and the section dealing specifically with technology.

Learning Outcomes

- to develop an understanding of the context in which leisure production and consumption decisions are made
- to develop an understanding of related literature in the area of consumer behaviour
- to be able to apply relevant theory to a variety of leisure contexts
- to develop an understanding of the factors affecting future leisure choices

Introduction

The nineteenth-century philosophers J S Mill and Jeremy Bentham both agreed that the greatest moral good was to maximise the happiness of the greatest number of people. This utilitarian treatise provides an interesting comparator with which to measure the success of contemporary society. However, as we enter the twenty-first century, we are forced to contend with an accelerating rate of industrial, technological, economic and cultural change. This, in turn, impacts the very social fabric of nation states and the day-to-day lives of individual citizens. The leisure industry is not insulated from such trends and is reflective of similar patterns in the wider national and global economies. Such structural changes have fundamental consequences for both existing and future leisure choices.

In 1965 Michael Dower was optimistic in his appraisal of the situation. He predicted a 'Fourth Wave' of a leisure oriented society. Other writers have been equally sanguine about 'The Collapse of Work' (Jenkins and Sherman 1979) and the emergence of a utopian society based on wealth redistribution and leisure as the central construct in people's lives, (Neulinger 1980). Unfortunately, in a capitalist system where inequalities are often perpetuated rather than equalised, such visions remain illusory (Handy 1997).

Measures of both material wealth and poverty are moving targets in western societies driven by economic performance and material growth. For Sahlins (1974 in Miller 1995c), societal inequalities are fundamental to individual perceptions of happiness. Moreover, Belk (1995) argues that quantitative studies of materialism indicate a moderate negative relationship between wealth and individual notions of well being. Neulinger (1980:16) provides a useful synopsis of the issues:

> *Since about the 1960s, the dissatisfaction with the GNP as an adequate measure of our national well-being has steadily grown. We have come to realize that as our nation is getting richer and richer, many and much of our individual lives is*

getting poorer and poorer. Money does not guarantee happiness to all, and particularly not if it is extremely unevenly distributed.

It is, therefore, spurious to equate individual happiness with aggregated measures of economic performance in isolation. Indeed, despite the inexorable rise in consumer power, there is little evidence to suggest that improved living standards are mirrored by individual perceptions of life quality (Earl 1986; Bosserman 1989; Csikszentmihalyi 1992; Belk 1995).

Leisure Time

As UK unemployment hovers around one million, from 1987 levels in excess of three million, it would appear that Lindler's (1970) notion of 'the harried leisure class' has finally come home to roost. The United Kingdom currently has the longest working hours in Europe and before the 1998 European Union Directive on Working Practices there were no statutory rights to annual holidays. Given a continuing context of employment insecurity, there is a tendency for workers to work harder and longer in order to safeguard the holy grail of improving living standards. For some, the rat race is one that cannot be won. The threat of 'downsizing' is exchanged for 'downshifting' in the pursuit of more acceptable notions of individual utopia (Schor 1993, 1999; Bull 1997; Frank 1999). For those who remain on the treadmill, there is increasing evidence to suggest the emergence of a 'money rich, time poor' consumer (Crace 1999). This has important consequences for both leisure consumers and producers. As Vogel (1990:5) argues:

investigations into the economics of time, including those of Becker (1965) and DeSerpa (1971), have suggested that the demand for leisure is affected in a complicated way by the cost of time to both produce and consume . . . From this it can be seen that the cost of time and the consumption-time intensity of goods and services are significant factors when selecting from among entertainment alternatives.

For many, work is still regarded as the single most tangible indicator of self identity and societal worth. The economic rewards derived from work are seen to be compensatory; both in the short-term and as an investment against future uncertainty. The now ubiquitous notion of 'quality time' signifies the rising opportunity cost of leisure when measured against more profitable work-oriented activities. Economists refer to such work/leisure trade-offs as substitution and income effects. Substitution effects signify the choice to substitute more expensive activities, such as the cost of leisure time in times of wage inflation, with those that are less expensive, i.e. work. Conversely, income effects are defined by choices where the opposite is true. Under this scenario, increasing levels of income are used to effectively 'buy' more leisure time.

However, despite rising affluence, the notion of free choice between work and leisure is a misnomer, constrained by the legal and psychological contracts imposed by societal, work and other personal commitments. Not surprisingly, there is little evidence to suggest that working hours are decreasing (income effect dominates). Indeed, for some, the pressures and demands of life dictate that longer hours are deemed necessary (substitution effect dominates), in an effort to negate future uncertainty and/or maintain current lifestyle aspirations. Against this context, leisure is increasingly seen as a commodity to be both produced and consumed. Nowhere is this more apparent than in the booming health and fitness industry where individuals are prepared to spend between £300 and £1,000 annually as both an investment against, and compensation for, their increasingly stressful and sedentary lifestyles (Govaerts 1989).

The Economics of Consumption

Until relatively recently economics has dominated industrial theory and praxis in this area. The economic theory of revealed preference, posits that existing demand information provides a useful indicator of the value ascribed to a commodity by any given society. This information can be triangulated from a number of disparate government and commercial sources, such as the General Household Survey, the Family Expenditure Survey, *Business Monitor* and Mintel's *Leisure Intelligence* series. However, the mere extrapolation of expressed demand does not take account of the consumers' underlying motives for purchase. Moreover, there is a tacit assumption that consumers are making rational choices, based on perfect information of alternatives.

Whilst advertising may inform the consumer of alternative choices, it also serves to persuade and influence attitudes and thus behaviour. As a consequence, it has the power to subvert rational choice. The notion of perfect information is a myth and militates against the optimisation of purchase decisions. Often, consumers are 'saticficing' based on heuristic assumptions (i.e. compromising based on general rules of thumb). Rational decisions are therefore constrained by a number of factors including a lack of time, income, information, peer pressure, expertise and consumption skills (c.f. Simon's 1955/1957 discussion of bounded rationality). Traditional economic models perpetuate the stereotypes of mass markets. The aggregation of demand is a convenient oversimplification which does little to address the more fundamental/innate drivers of purchase decisions (Scitovsky 1992; Belk 1995).

As individual freedom increases, there is a growing realisation, amongst suppliers, that homogenous markets represent a multiplicity of transient demands. Product differentiation provides increased consumer choice and allows producers the opportunity to increase revenues and/or profit margins by tapping into this latent demand. It is also clear that an understanding of individual consumer choices is required to inform future investment decisions. Existing measures of expressed demand may provide a useful indicator of the current economic importance of different commodities/markets. However, this communicates only a partial picture.

Consumer Behaviour in a Turbulent World

> *An understanding of such fundamental theories (of consumer behaviour) may be more important to the practising marketer than a knowledge of the tools and techniques which worked effectively in the past.*
>
> (McGregor 1995, quoted in Marsden and Littler 1998:40)

As we move into a world where previous rules and boundaries are being questioned and rewritten, it is not surprising that the study of consumer behaviour now represents an eclectic mix of academic disciplines. This is symptomatic of the changing hegemony between the producer and the consumer (Miller 1995b). For producers, it is myopic to adopt a product oriented vision of the future where it is assumed the public will continue to purchase previously successful products/services. Instead, there is a need to adopt a marketing-led approach, where the mission of producers is to understand underlying consumer needs and develop market offers designed to meet such purchase drivers.

Whilst attitudes are relatively stable, the tastes of consumers vary through time. Similarly, whilst underlying needs often dictate future decisions, wants/tastes are transient and subject to individual differences. Traditional economic models are guilty of viewing the consumer through the lens of the producer. While it makes sense for industry to simplify models of consumer demand when choices are limited, it is unwise to adopt this approach in highly competitive environments. The increasing fragmentation of society has led to a growing interest in alternate disciplinary approaches to help explain the complexity of individual cognition and subsequent action.

The History of Consumption Research

> *The analysis of consumer behaviour often takes place at a very high level of abstraction. Of course, the theoretical and conceptual analysis of consumption is central to understanding not only marketing management but also our place as consumers in a complex economic system.* (Foxall p.vii in Evans *et al.* 1996)

Whilst economists assume that needs are instinctive and are best monitored through purchase decisions, psychologists seek to develop a more informed understanding of individual behaviour. In the 1950s, motivation and behavioural research attempted to investigate the meaning and environmental antecedents of individual action. Freudian interpretations posited behaviours as surrogates for more fundamental needs/drivers. Freud argues that the human psyche is dominated by three basic drivers; the id, the ego and the superego. The id is best explained as a primitive survival instinct and incorporates the characteristics of both life (Eros:sex) and death (aggression). It operates at a subconscious level and is held in check by the superego which seeks to control behaviour in order to conform to social norms. The ego is the conscious manifestation of the subliminal battles between the id and superego. It is the ego that governs attitudes and ultimately action.

Freudian psychoanalysis represents a useful way to conceptualise some of the contemporary drivers of the leisure market and helps explain the popularity of leisure pursuits designed to escape the superego, in favour of more pleasurable and primaeval instincts of the id. Under this scenario, the responsibilities and stresses of modern society are temporarily banished in favour of more hedonistic tendencies. There are many potential examples of such leisure activities. From opera to alcohol; the club scene to the cinema; Disneyland to computer games; the aim is to produce a virtual reality in which the superego is subjugated by the id. In opera and high arts, for example, the ego works to transform the energies of the id into activities that are acceptable to the superego. In this way, the fundamental drivers of the id are *displaced* (i.e. transformed not repressed) into surrogate activities that are more acceptable to civilised society.

Latterly, research in this area has tended to concentrate on the influence of the environment in behaviour modification. This has many applications and helps explain the controversial policy adopted by some local authorities of sending adolescent offenders on expensive overseas holidays. The aim is to remove offenders from environments that are not conducive to rehabilitation and, instead, to reinforce more positive behaviours. In a similar way this helps explain the importance of external context in areas such as drug abuse and football hooliganism. However, responses to environmental antecedents are subject to individual differences and thus behaviour; the footballers Pelé and Maradona being a case in point. Both were regarded as the greatest footballers of their generation and, as such, subject to similar pressures and temptations. Pelé is now the Minister for Sport in Brazil, whilst Maradona fights an on-going battle with drug addiction.

Of course, a preoccupation with external and observable phenomenon tells us little about the internal processes/attitudes that guide individual choices. During the 1960s, there was a growing interest in the process of decision-making. This gave rise to cognitive models of information processing where choices are filtered through the brain either centrally or peripherally, dependant upon the relative importance of the message. Neulinger (1980:15) argues that:

> *Attitudes are considered by some not to be worth studying because they often do not relate to observed behavior. Such an argument relates to rather naive thinking. Of course attitudes do not relate to real-life behavior! Do we live in a society where we can do what we would like to do? The importance of attitudes lies in the very fact that they frequently do not correlate with behavior. It is only when we become aware of that fact (by measuring attitudes and behavior independently), that we can start to do something about it.*

This has relevance to previous Freudian interpretations of behaviour in a societal context that engenders an increasingly liberalised attitude towards acceptable behavioural standards. This also means that the link between attitude and behaviour becomes more important and thus predictive of individual action. Petty, Faith and Baker (1991) advance the Elaboration Likelihood Model to explain the fluid relationship between central and peripheral processing. They argue that High Elaboration (information processing) is likely if emotions are important to the decision, whilst Low Elaboration is more likely if emotion is seen to be peripheral. The potential of this approach lies in its ability to modify attitudes. These can be formed, influenced or changed through both information processing channels. However, they tend to be more stable and predictive of behaviour if information is systematically processed through the central channel.

According to McQuire (1969 in Petty *et al.* 1991), humans are 'lazy organisms', whilst Taylor (1981 in Petty *et al.* 1991) prefers the phrase 'cognitive misers' to signify the proposition that decisions are rarely taken based on a detailed analysis of the situation. This has important consequences for marketers who should work hard to package information in a way that leads to cognition and ultimately promotes the likelihood of purchase. To do this, marketers must understand the needs of consumers and search for communication channels and emotive messages that have a positive resonance with potential customers. The aim should be to promote a frequency of exposure to messages that engender positive mental rehearsal. Such messages should seek to reinforce the stated communication/ marketing objective, whilst minimising the cost per exposure within the identified market segment. In India, for example, in an effort to maintain the awareness and thus market dominance of Coca-Cola, the ubiquitous trademark can be seen beneath virtually every road sign!

Unfortunately, this is much easier said that done and relies on the targeting of a previously identified market segment. However, according to Kotler (1997:201) '. . . segment descriptions represent a compromise between viewing all buyers as similar versus all buyers as individually different'. Similarly, cognitive models have been criticised for their inability to deal adequately with individual differences. Moreover, individual choices are often influenced by environmental factors. These have been largely ignored by this line of research.

Trait theories attempt to identify more holistic models of individual cognition and action through the study of personality. Psychologists have identified over 18,000 words, in the English language, that can be used to describe personality characteristics. Broadly, personality consists of a series of traits or descriptors which are thought to be predictive of individual behaviours. In an effort to explain increasingly dynamic consumer demand, trait theories were used to develop psychographic profiles of consumers which, in turn, led to marketing initiatives such as lifestyle segmentation during the 1980s. For example, the Values, Attitudes and Lifestyles programme (VALS2) uses factor analysis to differentiate between eight consumer lifestyle segments using 65 identified traits (Gates 1989). However, despite the intuitive appeal of trait theory, there are also several weaknesses. Not withstanding the obvious marketing applications, lifestyle segmentation is argued by Campbell (1995) to lack any real sociological significance and relies on the accuracy of personality inventories to discriminate between individual perception and behaviour. Moreover, even pre-supposing the accuracy of the test, the results may not be reliable if compared against inappropriate reference groups. For example, it would be misleading to compare attitudes to risk from an American commercial leisure manager against a reference group drawn predominantly from the British public/voluntary sector.

Traditional psychological models of consumer behaviour are now viewed as overly deterministic in their orientation. They are predicated on the notion that patterns of decision-making remain relatively fixed and therefore predictable with consumers being viewed as little more than passive recipients of marketing information. Furthermore, empirical investigations are guilty of oversimplification, often based upon 'experimental' laboratory conditions that attempt to ameliorate the affects of other contributory variables. It is for this reason that research in this area has a tendency to deal with relatively simple choices in an attempt to control for such sources of variation. Moreover, Mannell (1980) argues that it is difficult to produce 'experimental' research methodologies designed to investigate 'leisure' as either the dependent or independent variable. This difficulty is further exacerbated when one considers the plurality of influences affecting leisure choices in the real world and at different moments in time. To investigate leisure experiences as a series of mutually exclusive constituent parts is to belie the complexities and interdependencies of the construct under investigation (Elementalism vs Holism). For behavioural and cognitive theories the influence of personality and social context is largely marginalised and does little to account for individual differences. Indeed, according to Marsden and Littler (1998:13) '. . . . in order to understand consumer behaviour in dynamic competitive environments (McGregor 1995) it may no longer be sufficient to ask "what marketing stimuli do to consumers?" but rather "what consumers do to marketing stimuli?" (Lannon 1996; Stewart 1991)'. As a consequence, the epistemology of consumer behaviour has evolved through traditional cognitive, behavioural and trait theories, to more contemporary interpretive and post-modern discourse.

Contemporary Theories of Consumption

> *Consumer goods may serve to fulfil a wide range of personal and social functions. Fairly obviously, they commonly serve to satisfy needs or indulge wants or desires. In addition they may serve to compensate the individual for feelings of inferiority, insecurity or loss, or to symbolise achievement, success or power. They also commonly serve to communicate social distinctions or reinforce relationships of superiority and inferiority between individuals and groups. They can also, on some occasions, express attitudes or states of mind, or communicate specific messages from one person to another. Finally, they may be instrumental in creating or confirming an individual's sense of self or personal identity.* (Campbell 1995:111)

Whilst traditional models of consumer behaviour reflect an approach largely underpinned by psychology, more contemporary perspectives have a tendency to reflect the interdisciplinary field of social psychology. This has been defined by Allport (1968:3) as 'an attempt to understand and explain how the thought, feeling, and behavior of individuals are influenced by the actual, imagined, or implied presence of others'. This represents a clear and positive development in the field of consumer behaviour. It moves research forward by attempting to understand not just the individual (psychology), but the individual within a social context (social psychology). This is not to disregard previous work, but to integrate this within a more holistic and thus realistic model of individual cognition and behaviour.

Interpretive models of consumer behaviour emerged during the 1980s and characterise the consumer as autonomous and free thinking. However, unlike the more traditional models, responses to external stimuli may not be stable and are likely to be conditioned by a number of variables that are subject to individual interpretation. These tend to be experiential in nature, helping the consumer to build 'subjective maps' of the world. These are assumed to be shared within society as a whole allowing marketers to target different groupings. Unlike more traditional theories, this leads to decisions that are semi-fixed through time, influenced by prior experience, societal norms and the likely reactions of referent others. More recently, post-modern perspectives of consumer behaviour assume that no conceptual maps dominate for either the individual or groupings of individuals within society. Anything goes, for any one or group, at any time! Hence, decisions are fluid, mitigated by individual perceptions of identity and context. Saren and Tzokas (1998) argue that *marketing* has little to say about the symbolic characteristics of consumer decisions. However, this has dominated sociological discourse in this area over recent years.

Influenced by the work of Robert Mayers and Peter Saunders (in Campbell 1995), there has been a reconfiguration of traditional production and class-dominated paradigms of sociological analysis. There is now an increasing body of literature that refocuses the academic lens to concentrate upon the changing relationship between consumer and producer. The literature traces this dynamic from a capitalist mind set which is exploitative of mass cultures to an increasing recognition of consumer power within micro cultures. Prior to this, 'consumer culture' was identified with a hegemonic system that encourages materialistic values in order to induce purchase and thus profit. Veblen (1925) labelled this 'conspicuous consumption'. However, contemporary literature has moved the thinking on from Marx's concept of commodity, *per se*, to the symbolic meaning of the labels associated with consumption. Bourdieu (1984 in Campbell 1995), for example, provides a social critique of the judgement of taste by arguing that consumption is used to establish a social hierarchy. However, unlike Veblen, Bourdieu concentrates on the accumulation of the caché that surrounds the purchases. Hence, National Lottery winners may be able to afford the trappings of success but may find it more difficult to acquire the cultural capital which acts as a surrogate for social status. You may be able to afford the horse, but would you really enjoy yourself at a polo match or in the Royal Enclosure at Ascot? An interpretive viewpoint would argue that such qualitative lifestyle changes take place over a period of time and adjustment. This allows for the development of more appropriate 'subjective maps' that govern expectations, aspirations, attitudes and thus behaviour. Post-modernists, would question the importance of such symbolism. They would see it as being predicated upon bourgeoisie demarcation lines that no longer hold value in a society where lifestyle and leisure choices are merely a function of individual preference. Yachting is stereotypically viewed as an elitist leisure pursuit. However, recent evidence suggests that things are changing.

> *We have found that there is no one person of a certain status or age that is buying – they range from bricklayers to directors of big companies . . . It is much more about how they feel about themselves when they buy boats. They aren't interested so much in the social status.*
>
> (Exhibitor at The London Boat Show, Earl's Court, January 2000, quoted in Smith and Barot 2000)

Of course, as technology advances and living standards improve, you do not have to be a National Lottery winner to experience a change of lifestyle expectations. This is equally true of individual leisure choices and the meanings that underpin such decisions.

Consumer Behaviour and Leisure Choices

Scitovsky (1992) provides an eclectic view of the early literature in this area. Drawing upon trait theories, he argues that arousal levels affect personality, which, in turn, influence tastes and ultimately purchase decisions. The biological basis of this hypothesis is well established. From this, it is possible to infer that individuals are 'hard wired' along such personality dimensions as extroversion/introversion. For extroverts, the emphasis is on raising arousal levels to mitigate boredom. For introverts the opposite is true. As a consequence, extroverts have a tendency to engage in more adventurous activities (e.g. whitewater rafting) while introverts seek out experiences designed to reduce levels of excitement in an effort to reduce stress/anxiety (e.g. reading a good book). As technology increases the convenience of modern living, it is also possible to argue that there will be a move towards more stimulating leisure activities. The increasing popularity of so-called 'extreme sports' provides a useful exemplar of this trend. An understanding of how the physiological affects the psychological is an interesting and important area of future research into personality and, consequently, consumer behaviour.

While Scitovsky provides a useful but limited exploration of personality dimensions, his work does attempt to draw interrelationships between the disciplines of economics and psychology. This has particular value when attempting to understand the feeling of pleasure experienced through the (in)direct participation in a variety of leisure activities. For Scitovsky, pleasure is a psychological construct that is maximised when the information processing capacities of the individual are stretched to the limit. This hypothesis is also mirrored by Maslow's (1968) discussion of 'peak experiences', Mannell's (1980) concept of 'leisure experience' and Csikszentmihalyi's (1992) notion of 'flow'. Csikszentmihalyi (1992) draws distinctions between enjoyment, which involves personal growth, and pleasure which merely requires cortical stimulation and does not include self actualisation as a key driver. This helps explain why enjoyment is enhanced when competition is equalised. This is an inherent characteristic of sporting activities, which are always more enjoyable when the main protagonists are equally matched for skill and ability. Interestingly, the concept of flow has close similarities with earlier academic definitions of 'recreation'. Gray (quoted in Neulinger 1980:8) argues that:

> *Recreation is an emotional condition within an individual human being that flows from a feeling of well being and satisfaction. It is characterized by feelings of mastery, achievement, exhilaration, acceptance, success, personal worth and pleasure. It reinforces a positive self image. Recreation is a response to esthetic experience, achievement of personal goals or positive feedback from others. It is independent of activity, leisure or social acceptance.*

Despite the inherent limitations of phenomenological research, the literature in this area is both enduring and intuitively appealing. The relative success of squash ladders provides a useful application of this idea; allowing for competition, improvement and thus personal accomplishment. The same principal is transferable to a variety of leisure and sport contexts. In golf and horse racing, for example, the handicap system seeks to equalise abilities in order to facilitate increased competition. The same is true of computer games that contain different levels and difficulty settings. This allows all 'players' to participate at a level that is consistent with their ability and thus maximises enjoyment levels. Moreover:

> *Enjoyment often occurs in games, sports, and other leisure activities that are distinct from everyday life, where any number of bad things can happen. If a person loses a chess game or botches his hobby he need not worry . . . Thus the flow experience*

> *is typically described as involving a sense of control – or, more precisely, as lacking the sense of worry about losing control that is typical in many situations in normal life.* (Csikszentmihalyi 1992:59)

This lack of self-consciousness is reminiscent of early Freudian interpretations and helps explain the popularity of experiences that reduce perceived barriers to participation by threatening self image/identity. Female-only sessions within health and fitness clubs provide a useful example of how leisure operators can mitigate inhibitions that negatively affect participation. Another interesting characteristic of flow activities is a complete engagement in the activity (time always flies by when you're having fun!). In a world governed by time and where time is money, it is not surprising that activities that lead to a suspension of the time constraint are always going to be popular. Moreover, in a society that promotes convenience and easy options, it is possible to confuse a quick pleasure fix with activities designed to promote sustained happiness and enjoyment.

This is consistent with Freud's 'pleasure principle' which posits a basic human desire for instant gratification (and possibly self destruction!). The increasing drug culture and global club scene provides an interesting exemplar of this paradox. Moreover, Csikszentmihalyi argues that flow experiences are four times as likely during work than when watching television. Personal satisfaction is enhanced when activities are iterative and goal-directed. These conditions are more likely to be found within the work environment than within the more passive pursuit of watching television, although Csikszentmihalyi concedes that this is mitigated by the type of work and the type of programme under consideration. The leisure and entertainment industry is now attempting to imbue this immersion into a variety of previously passive leisure experiences, requiring little or no consumption skills. The media provides interesting examples of this trend with Sky Digital's *Interactive/Open TV* and the cable channel *Challenge TV* being cases in point. Museums are also recording increased visitor numbers to exhibits that encourage interaction and in some ways cultivate an ownership of the experience.

To some extent, moves towards deeper immersion necessitates the need for a more appropriate array of consumption skills. Roberts (1989) labels those who are consumption literate as 'leisure connoisseurs'. He argues that:

> *Collectively these leisure connoisseurs have little in common. Their interests are highly specialised. At the connoisseur level tastes are fragmented. Nevertheless, it is possible to discern a general bifurification in Britain's leisure markets, with the experts, who are growing in number, demanding a different standard of service to larger armies of dabblers who are content with mass-marketed goods and packaged experiences.* (Darton 1986:55)

The Leisure Experience

Neulinger (1980:9) argues that academic attempts to define leisure can be divided into three mutually exclusive categories: 'leisure as a period of time, leisure as an activity, and leisure as a state of mind.' Increasingly, there is a move in both academic and management circles to promote a more holistic view of leisure as 'experience' (see Toffler 1979). For the leisure consumer, this has positive benefits as organisations adopt a more integrated view of their market offerings. Narrow definitions of 'product' can stifle innovation. Instead, conceptualisations of leisure as merely 'product' or 'activity' are replaced by a more inclusive view of leisure as a psychological construct or experience.

The opening of 'Niketown' in central London during 1999 provides an example of this phenomenon where sports retailing and entertainment co-exist to promote brand awareness and customer loyalty. Similarly, Virgin have entered the health and fitness market by promoting a more inclusive approach to this area. Customers are invited to Virgin's 'Life Centres' to enjoy a healthy leisure experience that includes user friendly exercise equipment, a segregated adult and kids' pool, library, medical centre and most importantly *fun*.

Organisations that add value to the experience by promoting (in)direct communication with customers are likely to be more responsive to changing tastes and fashions. In the discerning world of the leisure consumer, it is important to develop relationships that recognise the centrality of the customer within the leisure production process. This represents an interesting departure from traditionally demarcated studies of consumer behaviour that focus upon either product or service. Wolsey and Abrams (1998) call for a re-conceptualisation of the product-service continuum. Gabbot and Hogg (1994) argue that services provide different challenges for both consumer and provider. Customer involvement varies to the extent that the service is people or product based. Leisure facility provision has both product and service components, the importance of which will vary for each customer. Some will demand personal attention while others would prefer to be left alone. Some will want to be entertained, while others will want to provide the entertainment! Saren and Tzokas (1998:458) argue the case for a 'pluri-signified' relationship between buyers, sellers and the product. They contend that '. . . new product ideas are essentially the *result of relationships*. This broadens the search for new product concepts from that of traditional theory which is based on the needs and expectations of the customer.' This relationship is three-dimensional and reflects the dynamic interplay of the product, provider and consumer through time. In order to promote an increased understanding of different customer groups, there should be recognition that relationships are fluid and that product/service perceptions will vary. If handled sensitively, an improved understanding of individual needs has the power to cultivate patronage by improving responsiveness.

Paradoxically, the alleged 'dumbing down' of many areas within society, reduces the likelihood of experiencing 'flow' during many leisure activities. As Scitovsky (1992:232) argues:

> *I have already mentioned a few forms of stimulation whose enjoyment requires virtually no skill and no effort on the recipient's part; there are many more. The entertainment industry provides much of it; for the rest, an open-eyed person can get a lot of stimulation out of just watching the world go by and following the change in political and economic fashions. Time-budget surveys and various sociological studies tell us that the main sources of stimulation in the United States are watching television, driving for pleasure, and shopping – all of which are stimulation requiring no skill.*

This trend is also reflected in the UK. Gershuny and Jones (1987) researched the changing nature of consumption patterns and found that the time devoted to shopping had doubled in the last 30 years. For some, this is a worrying development and undermines the ability of leisure to facilitate experiences that contribute to both individual and societal health (Driver, Brown and Peterson 1991). Such concerns are reflected in the growing body of literature surrounding ethical/societal marketing. To the commercial leisure industries, however, experiences that provide pleasure to the lowest common denominator merely increase the size of the potential market and thus profit. Leisure organisations have to operate within the legal boundaries laid down by the country within which they operate. However, in an investment climate dominated by short-term gain, it is rarely seen as the function of commercial leisure enterprises to engage in altruism without the lure of (in)direct profit. Moreover, it is incumbent upon the management of such organisations to exploit the symbolism that surrounds an increasing array of leisure purchases.

Western economies reflect a social, economic and political climate that promotes the virtues of individual responsibility and choice. In the UK the democratisation of culture, also leads to its dilution. Popular culture is all-pervasive and encouraged by a Labour government driven by soundbites and the image of 'Cool Britannia'. It is unlikely, therefore, that the impact of consumer culture will be significantly curtailed in the foreseeable future.

Leisure Lifestyles in the New Millennium

> *People no longer identify themselves as part of a mass: they want to express their difference through identity with subsets of the once homogenous conception. Now there are plural, multiple and niche-based sources of identity available to people, such as their sexuality, their culture, their ethnicity. Niche-based markets sustain these sources of identity.* (Clark and Clegg 1998:49)

In an increasingly individualistic society the construction of personal identity manifests itself in a number disparate ways. The concept of lifestyle is the marketing oriented buzzword of the late nineties. In a world of complexity, it represents a simplistic but convenient method of categorising individuals according to income, behaviour and psychographic variables. Such typologies have been popularised by the media and give marketers the opportunity to influence tastes and raise aspirations by allowing consumers a taste of more exciting and cosmopolitan lifestyles. The popularity of *Hello* and *OK* magazines provide a useful example of this voyeuristic phenomenon. You may not have been there but at least you've got the T-shirt. You may not be an Olympic skier, but you can buy into the 'image' through the purchase of expensive ski wear. You may have never been to Old Trafford, but you can share in the experience and trappings of being a Manchester United supporter by subscribing to its fledgling cable channel. Moreover, for the equivalent of £30, Tinseltown Studios in the United States will offer a virtual Hollywood experience, where customers attend the Oscars and act out acceptance speeches to the assembled audience of other paying customers!

Consumers engage in vicarious and virtual lifestyles by adopting the external signs without fully subscribing to the parent subculture. This allows producers the opportunity to create 'false needs' in an effort to increase profits. The music industry provides a useful example of this:

> *. . . the CD told your friends that you were a go-ahead sort of person. It was even more convenient for record companies, in that it meant they could sell your record collection back to you again with little effort and mega profit. Now that the late Nineties have turned into edited highlights of the Seventies, it's vinyl that's the lifestyle statement.* (Cox 1998:3–4)

The rapid and continued advancement of technology is a fundamental driver of future leisure choices. In an effort to balance the often competing needs of the consumer and producer there is an increasing ability, on the supply side, to cater for individual differences. Technology allows this to happen by presenting the consumer with a variety of choices from which the supplier provides a tailored offer to an increasingly heterogeneous and fickle market. Mini discs allow the recording and convenient playback of CD-quality sound from existing and personalised back catalogues. Satellite television brings increased viewing choice, whilst digital television will give the opportunity to instantly download programs, music and games on demand. This means that the armchair football supporter never has to miss another *Match of the Day*. Indeed, they will be able to fast-forward, freeze-frame and customise action replays within an improved and interactive viewing experience. With government guidelines for phasing out analogue television set at 2010, this will soon be reality not merely science fiction!

A Question of Balance

In an increasingly sedentary society the psychological demands of modern living are exacerbated by a confusing array of choices and consequences. For some there is the need for interior designers, personal shoppers or even astrologers to help negotiate the murky waters of consumerism. As discretionary spend continues to rise and competition for the leisure pound intensifies, it is important to more accurately target product/services. Technology provides the tools for this to happen, whilst simultaneously promoting the virtues of convenience and customisation. Drawing on the work of Sir Charles Hawtrey, Scitovsky (1992) talks of the duality between defensive and creative products. The former satisfies need, whilst the latter yields pleasure over and above the cessation of need alone. Whilst it is possible to satisfy the demand for life's necessities, Scitovsky (1992:110) argues that 'the desire for pleasure seems insatiable'. As expectations increase and the exciting of today becomes the mundane of tomorrow, Scitovsky (1992) argues that traditional models of consumer behaviour pay inadequate attention to the human need for novelty and variety.

Far from being stable, individual leisure choices will vary through time. Traditional perspectives of consumer behaviour would regard consumers as relatively passive and, hence, predictable in their responses. Change is something that is done to the individual who then reacts according to pre-ordained patterns. The individual has little control on this process and is motivated by the assumption of 'homeostasis'. This has been defined by Hjelle and Ziegler (1992:19) as an attempt 'to reduce tensions and maintain an internal state of equilibrium'. Interpretive and post-modern approaches assume that consumers are proactive when faced with changing environments. However, whereas interpretive approaches concede that some elements will be fairly stable, post-modern approaches are dismissive of anything that acts as a constraint to individual freedom. Personal identity is seen to be dynamic and fragmentary and thus governed by the assumption of 'heterostasis'. Individuals have multiple and transient personalities which change dependant on a plethora of internal and external variables. You may be one 'type' of person at work, another at home and yet another still when your parents are in the same room! However, although such arguments have some merit, rarely are individuals afforded the nihilistic luxury of free choice when faced with a variety of leisure alternatives.

The need for both comfort and stimulation are not mutually exclusive but symbiotic in their valences. In times of confusion and complexity, it is human nature to seek comfort. In times of comfort and stability, there is a search for excitement and new experiences. Similarly, in times of economic recession there is an increase in home-based leisure, whilst in times of relative affluence there is a tendency to leave the home environment in search of more exciting and frequently more expensive leisure experiences. Activities that yield fun and excitement are highly saleable commodities, as they raise consciousness to levels that cannot be achieved within habitual daily routines. Surely it's better to *live* rather than merely *exist*! In a money oriented society, the best things in life are rarely free. If leisure organisations could bottle the essence of flow activities, they would have a licence to print money as the desire for excitement becomes addictive and has the power to subvert rational choice; just ask the many 'consumers' who have lost their shirt in Las Vegas! The public get what the public want as long as they can afford to pay for it! As consumer sovereignty prevails and national governments concede power to the global markets, the leisure industries must attempt to cultivate demand by shaping the future. Paradoxically, the extrapolation of historical trends into the future shows early signs of a return to the original notions of leisure developed by Plato and Aristotle.

Back to Basics, Back to the Future

Whilst quiet contemplation and the search for personal fulfilment occupied the time of free men in Ancient Greece, contemporary society does not offer this luxury. Indeed, successive governments have taken little interest in questions of leisure, seeing this as essentially a *private* and not *public* matter (Roberts 1989). As national boundaries are increasingly bypassed by multinational conglomerates and the power of the Internet, there is a need for consumers to assert a higher degree of control over the choices they make. In a capitalist-driven economy, consumers not only get what they want; they also get what they deserve. This, in turn, impacts upon the time available for work, rest and leisure. As Bosserman (1989:175–176) argues:

> *To be sure there are enormous social forces and constraints upon this time, particularly from the economy, based as it still is on growth and the subsequent need for citizens to consume more and more. But this very growth is one of the factors producing the crisis we sense. We have reached the boundary of an economy dependent on consumerism. Crude material wealth does not bring fulfilment. There is a profound poverty in our abundance of things.*

Based on Elgin's (1981) notion of 'voluntary simplicity', Bosserman (1989) argues against the dominant capitalist ideology, in favour of 'personal communalism', where happiness is cultivated through simplicity and collectivism; co-operation not competition. Personal fulfilment can be found through a variety of activities. To this extent, in common with ancient civilisations, distinctions between work and leisure become artificial and blurred. Kotler (1997) also agrees that consumer attitudes are changing and sees the balance between work, leisure and consumption as holding the key to future levels of happiness. He argues that, in the future, consumers will 'work to live', not 'live to work'. However, in a world of infinite possibilities, how do we differentiate good leisure from bad? Anthropological research into the use of the Internet reveals increased levels of inactivity, insularity and, in some cases, anti-social behaviour. As Professor John Dory, of the University of Los Angeles, contends:

> *. . . those who use it at home for work can no longer tell the difference between work and their private life. This could have longer-term psychological problems.*
>
> (Harlow and Gadher 1999)

Capitalism and consumerism exist in a symbiotic state. There are both positive and negative externalities resulting from this marriage. However, there is a growing feeling that the effects on society are reaching unacceptable, parasitic levels. This particularly relates to the role played by capitalism in the perpetuation of societal inequalities and the increasing levels of stress, anxiety and depression found in every aspect of modern living.

Although it is in the interests of commercial leisure operators to adopt a more inclusive approach, this will only be for those with money and the requisite consumption skills. Others will be increasingly alienated. For example, despite general agreement of the importance of the 'grey market' (Kotler 1997; Gunter 1998), Brindle (2000) reports that, according to government research, 25 per cent of those aged over 50 would be unwilling to use the Internet for public services.

As a significant minority begin to question the very capitalist foundations upon which western society rests, the future looks increasingly uncertain. For Balmer (1979 in Mannell 1989:9–11):

> *New values will gradually take over as the dominant, decision-making values of our society. There will be a decline in values associated with materialism, private*

ownership, capitalism and unqualified economic growth. Increasing emphasis will be placed on concepts such as the quality of life, self-actualization, creativity, individualism and humanitarianism.

If Balmer is right, there will be a partial return to the earlier notions of leisure cultivated by ancient civilisations. However, this will be contexualised to reflect the demands of modern living. As Raymond (2000:12) argues:

. . . the clock is set to run for 24 hours, and in that time says Sean Pillot de Chenecey of trend analysts Informer, 'You work to rule, your own rules. This is not flexi-time (which still suggests a responsibility to others) but fulcrum time, i.e. the world revolves around your needs and responsibilities – family, friends, leisure, work – rather than everybody else's'.

Summary and Conclusions

Consumer behaviour is a black hole . . . We cannot predict consumer responses to marketing initiatives. The only thing we know with certainty is that we do not know very much at all. Not much of an outcome for 50 years' scientific endeavor. (Buttle 1994, quoted in Marsden and Little 1998:5)

In 300 BC, Aristotle argued that the pursuit of happiness is the fundamental driver of all human endeavour. However, as we approach the new millennium the concept of happiness is more difficult to define than ever. Studies have shown that to be successful and wealthy is not readily equatable with perceptions of personal well being. It is clear that happiness is an individual construct that is conditioned by a multiplicity of factors. It is the aggregation/balancing of such factors that provides insight into individual attitudes and behaviour. However, we are limited in this endeavour by a lack of consensus about the variables to be studied, their relative valences and the interplay of these through time and in changing circumstances. Historical lines of social and economic demarcation are being eroded and subjugated within a post-modern society that promotes 'the fragmentation of culture and the increased importance of symbol over substance' (Campbell 1995:99). Moreover, competing theories of consumer behaviour lead to what Deshpande (1984 quoted in Marsden and Littler 1998:5) calls 'theoretical myopia' as similar experiences are viewed through the lens of competing theoretical paradigms. Who are we to believe?

Sociological discourse, has tended to concentrate on consumption as a means of constructing social identity. Interpretive and post-modern approaches adopt an holistic view of the consumer through qualitative enquiry based on social psychology, whilst earlier theories favour elementalism and more positivistic approaches to psychological research. As the boundaries that bind society are increasingly eroded, the leisure consumer of the twenty-first century is likely to become more difficult to define. Whilst interdisciplinary work is to be encouraged, the lack of consensus within individual academic areas, combined with an increasingly dynamic consumer environment, simply adds to the complexity of this process. It is likely that the only way to define the leisure consumer of the future is to allow consumers to define themselves. This can only be achieved, however, if choices are both accessible and capable of being tailored to individual need. Technology must be embraced to deliver production and consumption synergies that facilitate a move away from

Summary and Conclusions continued

old Fordist paradigms of capitalism, towards the mass customisation of leisure experiences. As a consequence, fuelled by commercial pressures to compete, issues of convenience, choice, customisation and commodification are likely to dominate market relationships well into the next millennium.

Suggested Tasks for Further Study

1. Construct a table that firstly lists and then analyses the leisure choices made by you over a period of one month.
2. Which leisure choices did you deliberately avoid? Why?
3. Try to explain your choices in the context of the different approaches to consumer behaviour reviewed by the chapter, e.g. behaviourist, cognitive, trait, interpretive, postmodern.
4. In what ways do your choices for non leisure related products/services differ from those made above?
5. Compare your answers with others in a small group of two to four people.
6. Look at the marketing of a selective range of leisure products and services. Analyse how they are packaged and promoted. Discuss how their marketing is designed to appeal to different market segments. What do you think these segments are? How effectively do you feel they have been targeted?
7. What do you see as the principal dangers of a consumer-driven society? Identify any areas in which you feel that consumer sovereignty should not prevail.

References

- Allport G W 1968 'The historical background of modern social psychology' in Lindzey G and Aronson E (Eds) *The Handbook of Social Psychology* (2nd Ed) 1968 pp.1–80 Reading
- Belk R W 1995 'The sociology of consumption' in Miller D 1995a *op. cit.* pp.58–95
- Bosserman P 1989 'The USA: Modern Times and the New Solidarity' in Olszewska and Roberts 1989 *op. cit.* pp.162–177
- Brindle D 2000 'Over-50s suspicious of Internet' in *The Guardian* 15 January 2000 p.7
- Bull A 1997 *Downshifting* Harper Collins, London
- Campbell C 1995 'The Sociology of Consumption' in Miller D 1995a *op. cit.* pp.96–126
- Clarke T and Clegg S 1998 *Changing Paradigms, the transformation of management knowledge for the 21st century* Harper Collins, London
- Cox T 1998 'Full Circle' in *The Guardian* 20 October 1998 G2 section pp.4–5
- Crace J 1999 'Secrets of the time lords' in *The Guardian* Jobs and Money Section 9 January 1999, p.18
- Csikszentmihalyi M 1992 *Flow, The Psychology of Happiness* Harper and Row, London
- Dower M 1965 'Fourth Wave: The Challenge of Leisure' reprinted from *Architects' Journal* 20 January 1965
- Driver B L, Brown P J and Peterson L (Eds) 1991 *Benefits of Leisure* Venture Publishing Inc, PA

- Earl P 1986 *Lifestyle Economics; Consumer Behaviour in a Turbulent World* Wheatsheaf Books Ltd, Brighton
- Elgin D 1981 *Voluntary Simplicity* William Morrow, New York
- Evans M J, Moutinho L and Van Raaij W F 1996 *Applied Consumer Behaviour* Addison Wesley, Harlow
- Forgas J (Ed) 1991 *Emotion and Social Judgements* Pergamon Press, Oxford
- Frank R H 1999 *Luxury Fever: Why Money Fails to Satisfy in an Era of Excess* Penguin
- Gabbott M and Hogg G (Eds) 1997 *Contemporary Services Marketing Management; A Reader* Dryden Press, London
- Gates M 1989 'VALS Change With the Times' *Incentive* 163(3) pp.27–30
- Gershuny J and Jones S 1987 'The changing work leisure balance in Britain 1961–1984' in Horne J, Jary D and Tomlinson A (Eds) 1987 *Sport Leisure and Social Relations* Routledge and Kegan Paul, London
- Gibson R 1997 *Rethinking the Future* Nicholas Brealey Publishing, London
- Govaerts R 1989 'Belgium: Old Trends, New Contradictions' in Olszewska and Roberts 1989 *op. cit.* pp.62–84
- Gunter B 1998 *Understanding the Older Consumer; The Grey Market* Routledge, London
- Haim A and Schewe C D 1992 *The Portable MBA in Marketing* John Wiley and Sons Inc, New York
- Handy C 1997 'Finding Sense in Uncertainty' in Gibson R 1997 *op. cit.* pp.16–33
- Harlow J and Gadher D 1999 'The Second Internet Revolution' in *The Sunday Times* 17 October 1999 p.16
- Hjelle L A and Ziegler D J 1992 *Personality Theories: Basic Assumptions, Research and Implications* (4th Ed) McGraw-Hill, New York
- Iso-Ahola S E (Ed) 1980 *Social Psychological Perspectives on Leisure and Recreation* Charles C Thomas Publisher, Springfield, Illinois US
- Jenkins C and Sherman B 1979 *The Collapse of Work* Methuen, Fakenham
- Kotler P 1997 'Mapping the Future Market Place' in Gibson R 1997 *op. cit.* pp.196–210
- *Leisure Opportunities* Issue 222 Nov/Dec 1998
- Linder S B 1970 *The Harried Leisure Class* Columbia University Press, New York
- Mannell R C 1980 'Social Psychological Techniques and Strategies for Studying Leisure Experiences' in Iso-Ahola 1980 *op. cit.* pp.62–88
- Marsden D and Littler D 1998 'Positioning Alternative Perspectives of Consumer Behaviour' in *Journal of Marketing Management* 14 Westbury Publishers Ltd pp.3–28
- Maslow A 1968 *Toward a Psychology of Being* (2nd Ed) Van Nos Reinhold, Toronto
- Miller D (Ed) 1995a *Acknowledging Consumption: A Review of New Studies* Routledge, London
- Miller D 1995b 'Consumption in the Vanguard of History' in Miller D (Ed) 1995a *op. cit.* pp.1–57
- Miller D 1995c 'Consumption Studies as the Transformation of Anthropology' in Miller D (Ed) 1995a *op. cit.* pp.264–295
- Murray K B and Sclacter J L 1990 'The impact of services versus goods on consumers' assessment of perceived risk and availability' in *Journal of the Academy of Marketing Science* 18(1) pp.51–65 in above pp.96–118
- Neulinger J 'Introduction' in Iso-Ahola 1980 *op. cit.* pp.5–18
- Olszewska A and Roberts K (Eds) 1989 *Leisure and Lifetsyle, A Comparative Analysis of Free Time* Sage Publications Ltd, London
- Raymond M 2000 'Time to Change Your Life' in *The Guardian* The Editor (Supplement) 7 April 2000 pp.12–13
- Roberts K 1989 'Great Britain: Socioeconomic Polarisation and the Implications for Leisure' in Olszewska A and Roberts K (Eds) 1989 *op. cit.* pp.47–61

- Petty R E, Faith G and Baker S M 1991 'Multiple Roles for Affect in Persuasion' in Forgas J 1991 *op. cit.* pp.181–200
- Saren M and Tzokas N 1998 'The Nature of the Product in Market Relationships: A Pluri-Signified Product Concept' in *Journal of Marketing Management* 1998 14 pp.445–464
- Schor J B 1993 *The Overworked American: The Unexpected Decline of Leisure* Harper Collins
- Schor J B 1999 *The Overspent American: Upscaling, Downshifting, and the New Consumer* Harper Collins
- Scitovsky T 1992 *The Joyless Economy; The Psychology of Human Satisfaction* (Revised Ed) Oxford University Press, Oxford
- Simon H A 1955 'A behavioural model of rational choice' in *Quarterly Journal of Economics* 69 pp.99–118
- Simon H A 1957 *Models of Man* Wiley, New York
- Smith D and Barot T 2000 'Boom makes Mr Average worth £7200' in *The Sunday Times* 9 January 2000 p.1, 7
- Toffler A 1979 *Future Shock* Random House, New York
- Veblen T 1925 *Conspicuous Consumption: The Theory of the Leisure Class* George Allen and Unwin, London
- Vogel H L 1990 *Entertainment Industry Economics: A guide for financial analysis* (2nd Ed) Cambridge University Press, New York
- Wolsey C and Abrams J 'A Critical Approach to Quality Initiatives within Sport and Leisure Organisations' in Conference Proceedings 'Service Quality and Sport' *European Association for Sport Management* Madeira Portugal 30 Sept–4 Oct 1998 Section 3 pp.1–8

Chapter 6

Strategy, Competition and the Commercial Leisure Markets

Chris Wolsey
Leeds Metropolitan University

Chapter Content

Abstract

This chapter provides a selective review of the strategy and competition literature. This is not intended to be comprehensive, as this is better accomplished outside of the expressed aims of this book (see, for example, O'Shaughnessy 1992, Chisnall 1995, McDonald 1996, Atkinson and Wilson 1996, Harding and Long 1998). This chapter provides a critical analysis of both theory and practice, as these apply to contemporary examples from the health and fitness market to the 'club scene' to the record industry. It is clear that the future is no longer predicated on the models and formulas that were successful in the past. Market structures are changing and, in the future, are likely to be governed by a mutually dependant network of partnerships, alliances, joint ventures, mergers and acquisitions. Leisure and sport organisations must seek to mould their own future in a way that is seen to be sustainable by the principal stakeholders. These include shareholders, customers, employees and other interested parties, such as local and national government agencies. Although there is still a place for the large leisure conglomerates, they must cultivate corporate parenting skills that promote synergies and add value, as defined by the customer. More importantly, perhaps, they should not be afraid to make strategic decisions that promote more specialisation, autonomy and innovation within both the organisation and the industry. Co-operation and competition are no longer mutually exclusive. Leisure and sport organisations must rationalise the competing pressures for change and continuity in a way that is proactive to a more complex and chaotic market environment. This not only requires a realistic business mission, or 'strategic intent', but a coherent approach to both inter and intra organisation relations. Ultimately, however, it will be the customers that will dictate future success or failure in this rapidly expanding and important area of the economy.

Related Chapters

Chapter 1: The Public Sector, Best Value and Local Authority Sports Development: Both chapters review the need to develop strategic partnerships and cultivate relationships with key stakeholders within a supply network designed to add value to the customer. The importance and approach of both the public and commercial sectors could be reviewed.

Chapter 2: Commercial Leisure – an International Perspective: Both chapters provide complementary analysis/examples with reference to the establishments of strategic networks within the commercial leisure sector.

Learning Outcomes

- to provide a critical review of related literature
- to apply related theory to contemporary leisure and sport practice
- to provide a critical evaluation of organisation rhetoric and reality
- to suggest future scenarios and strategies for commercial leisure and sport

Introduction

> *. . . strategy is a plan – some sort of* consciously intended *course of action, guideline (or set of guidelines) to deal with a situation.* (Mintzberg and Quinn 1991:12)

Strategy pervades all business activity and yet is still viewed by Porter (1997) as an emerging academic discipline. It may be informal in nature or reflect a highly structured and intricate process of corporate planning and control. The literature surrounding strategy provides a plethora of definitions, models and critiques. 'Strategic planning' is seen by many to reflect the conventional view of strategy, where the future is relatively stable and planning activities merely represent the linear extrapolation of future scenarios based on historical precedent (Mintzberg 1987/1994; Porter 1997). Some organisations, particularly in the public and voluntary leisure sectors, still engage in this form of strategy formulation. However, the increasing dynamism and complexity of the business environment militates against relatively prescriptive approaches in favour of more progressive ways to understand and develop strategic praxis. This is particularly true of the commercial leisure sector. According to Gratton and Taylor (1987:16):

One of the major characteristics of the demands for leisure goods and services is the volatility of such demands . . . Leisure is an area of consumer demand which as a whole grows slowly over time. But within that leisure sector, there will be areas of rapid expansion and rapid decline.

This creates uncertainty and risk in decisions taken about future strategy and thus investment.

For Mintzberg (1994:107):

. . . strategic planning is not strategic thinking. Indeed, strategic planning often spoils strategic thinking, causing managers to confuse real vision with the manipulation of numbers. And this confusion lies at the heart of the issue: the most successful strategies are visions, not plans.

Furthermore, Mintzberg (1987:13) draws distinctions between 'deliberate' and 'emergent' strategies, arguing that strategy should be viewed as 'a pattern in a stream of actions (Mintzberg and Waters 1985) . . . *consistency* in behaviour, *whether or not* intended'. Thus the emergent strategy is contingent upon the original planned strategy and the subsequent reaction of the organisation to it. This, in turn, is dependent upon the environmental opportunities viewed by the company and their response to them at any moment in time. Whilst some companies adopt a myopic view of strategy within existing market paradigms, others adopt a more creative approach to growth by pushing the envelope of traditional management wisdom within acceptable levels of risk. Porter (1997) argues that this reflects the distinctions between operational effectiveness (strategy based on incremental change within defined market boundaries) and true strategy. Similarly, Clarke and Clegge (1998:3) maintain that:

Increasingly, incremental change in industry is displaced by discontinuous change . . . standard answers and structured processes can no longer cope with the complexity of the new demands. New problems are confronted requiring new solutions that often involve fundamental transformation of business thinking and practice.

For Piercy (1997) traditional textbook approaches are of limited use and belie the fluidity of contemporary market fluctuations. Piercy argues that it is important to recognise the pragmatic realities of delivering customer focus and value. These include the erosion of traditional departmental boundaries through effective teamwork and the development of new relationships with key stakeholders. For Gronroos (1994), such attributes are more likely to be found within service organisations than within the adversarial intra/inter organisational relations traditionally cultivated within the manufacturing sector.

Prahalad (1997:70) argues that: 'Strategic intent is not an articulation of means, but of goals. Means have to be discovered as we go along.' Figure 6.1 illustrates the need to operationalise the business mission, or 'strategic intent', through the integration of both inter and intra organisational relationships. This is an iterative process, which seeks to proactively search for a workable compromise between necessary change and sustainable continuity. This requires a coherent approach to strategy. This is much easier said than done!

As far as customers are concerned, organisations are coherent entities. The bricks and mortar, the corporate logo, the quality assurance programmes, the words of the chief executive officer are all designed to reinforce this myth. In reality, organisations are formed by a myriad of groups, coalitions and agendas which collectively conspire against the utopian view of conventional strategic planning. Whilst the rhetoric of one organisation, one strategy, one voice continues to prevail in certain areas of the literature, a more critical approach is required. Organisations are abstract entities, glued together by the relationships

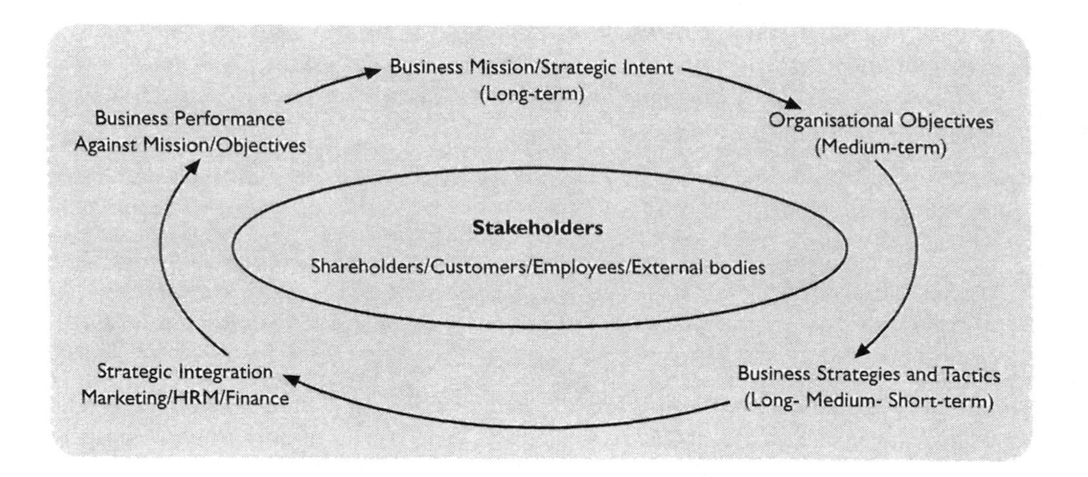

Figure 6.1 The virtual circle of business strategy

developed by those delegated to fulfil the corporate mission. Putting the corporate dream into action requires more than the series of prescriptions and off the shelf approaches to strategy that are sometimes promulgated by writers and consultants in this area.

The search for 'competitive advantage' is seen as a key function within the theory and praxis of strategy. Bharadwaj, Varadarajan and Fahay (1993) argue that this can be found in two areas, namely the tangible assets and intangible capabilities of the company. For Tofield (1998:21), the latter is critical:

> *Different consultants produce different analyses and panaceas, but whether we look at small businesses or big arts, there is one critical theme these reports largely ignore: it is people who create success.*

Competitive Advantage and the HR Function

The importance of nurturing employees to produce appropriate outcomes is now fundamental to business success. Pemberton (1998:17) reports on research conducted by the University of Sheffield and the London School of Economics that concluded from a ten-year study of 42 UK companies, 'that overall job satisfaction was a better predictor of the company's economic performance than competitive strategy, market share, or spend on research and development.' Slack (1997:233) argues that the '. . . central purpose of the human resources management function is to provide a sport organization with an effective and satisfied work force'. However, for typically staff-intensive sport and leisure organisations, there are often very real differences between organisational rhetoric and reality (Legge 1995; Gratton 1997; Barney and Wright 1998). For example, the international hotel chain that develops impressive staff development literature but then marginalise the training of part-time and casual staff; the public sector leisure department that develops a revised career development structure that effectively alienates the majority of the workforce; the leisure conglomerate that institutes a review of its employment practices which has a deleterious effect upon the terms and conditions of employment; and the national fitness chain where some managers coerce employees into washing the shower curtains, at home, in order to save costs! These are all real examples, involving real people, with real consequences. As Gratton (in Cowe 1997:23) argues:

We have been hearing managerial rhetoric about people being at the core of the business for years. It has been a load of bullshit. But there is now a growing awareness that people are the source of sustained competitive advantage.

For leisure and sport organisations, all employees play a crucial role in the virtual circle that links business mission to business performance. The real key to business success lies in the ability to match the resources of the organisation to the transient needs of its principal stakeholders. However, Cole (1997) argues the desire to satisfy customers may result in the marginalisation of employee needs and thus work against employee friendly definitions of HRM, such as that previously offered by Slack (1997). As Gratton (1997:251) argues:

Corporate mission statements extol customer satisfaction or product innovation. But when the communication fanfare is over and the customer-focus workshops have been completed, what is left? Groups of people trying to make sense of the paradoxes and mixed messages with which they are faced, who try to understand the underlying message of customer delight when no attempt is made to provide them with the skills necessary to deliver it, who are rewarded and promoted for delivering short-term financial targets and see the people who try hardest to understand customers' needs penalised for the time they take to do so.

A continued preoccupation with short-term profit is likely to lead to longer-term difficulties as corporate learning is limited by current operational imperatives. According to Hunter (1997), the expediency with which systems and people are matched should be guided by an understanding of customer needs and the external environment. As Kotler (1988:486) argues:

Excellently managed service companies believe that employee relations will reflect on customer relations. Management creates an environment of employee support and rewards for good service performance. Management regularly audits employees' satisfaction with their jobs.

Unfortunately, all too often such platitudes do not reflect the stresses and micro-politics of organisational reality. As Tofield (1998:21) reports:

Spreadsheet culture is short-term and superficial . . . Sir Colin Southgate, the businessman brought in to turn around the ailing Opera House, seems to have shown the characteristics of spreadsheet leadership. Bernard Haitink resigned as music director having got to hear about the cancellation of the entire 1999 season by fax.

Barney and Wright (1998) provide a useful way to conceptualise this important dynamic. They argue that:

. . . aspects of human resources that do not provide value can only be a source of competitive disadvantage. These resources or activities are ones that the HR executives should be discarding from the HR function. Aspects of human resources that provide value but are not rare, are sources of competitive parity. These resources are not to be dismissed as useless; not to have them is a source of competitive disadvantage, but because other firms possess them, they cannot provide an advantage in the competitive arena. Temporary competitive advantage stems from resources that provide value and are rare but are easily imitated. If these resources do serve as a source of competitive advantage, then other firms will soon imitate them, resulting in competitive parity. Finally, aspects of human resources that are valuable, rare, and not easily imitated, can be sources of sustained competitive advantage, but only if the firm is organised to capitalize on these resources.

Furthermore, Barney and Wright (1998) argue that the successful operation of strategic HR practices is contingent upon the coherency with which the differing functions are co-ordinated and thus perceived by the workforce. In purely commercial terms, it is of limited use having excellent incentives for the sales force, if it undermines the morale of the other employees, unless the sales force provide the key competitive advantage for the company. Whilst it is not the intention of this chapter to provide a detailed analysis of this area, the framework espoused by Barney and Wright (1998) provides a useful model with which to investigate other aspects of competitive behaviour within the leisure and sport industry.

The Need for Innovation

Many commentators argue that innovation is essential to remain competitive in today's commercial environment. Innovation is seen as existing on a continuum between completely new ideas/inventions and modifications to existing products (Chisnall 1995; Clarke and Clegg 1998). Tomorrow's businesses must dare to be different. Even in Japan, a recent report claims that 'Japan must abandon its obsession with conformity and equality' (Watts 2000:16). According to Hammer (1997) it is the ability of the organisation to innovate and demonstrate entrepreneurship that will be the arbiter of continuing success. The same can be said for the thinking that underpins contemporary market structures. Chan Kim and Mauborgne (1997) provide a particularly useful method of conceptualising the actions of more progressive and innovative organisations. Reflecting on a five-year review of high growth companies, they argue that:

> *The difference was in the companies' fundamental implicit assumptions about strategy. The less successful companies took a conventional approach: Their strategic thinking was dominated by the idea of staying ahead of the competition. In stark contrast, the high-growth companies paid little attention to matching or beating their rivals. Instead, they sought to make their competitors irrelevant through a strategic logic we call* value innovation. (Chan Kim and Mauborgne 1997:103)

Table 6.1 clearly establishes the key dimensions of strategy and demonstrates the differences between 'conventional' strategic planning and the approach adopted by companies such as Rupert Murdoch's News Corporation (owners of BSkyB), Virgin, America On-Line and Amazon.com.

The lessons of the above research are reminiscent of earlier work by Ohmae (1982), who argued that organisations may be better concentrating on their strengths and satisfying customers rather than paying too much attention to the competition. He argues that companies should identify the key factors for success (KFS) and allocate resources accordingly. The Virgin brand, for example, stands for quality, value, innovation and fun. It affords Virgin the competitive luxury of operating in a number of disparate areas, usually by challenging the dominant market paradigm in ways that add customer value. This gives Virgin an instant competitive advantage which is frequently unnerving for competitors when they enter a new market arena. This is equally true of Amazon.com, the Internet bookseller. As Jeff Bezos (quoted in Rushe 1999:9), the founder and CEO argues:

> *If you do a good job in one area then you get permission and encouragement from customers to do it in another area. What we won't do is go into an area we don't think we can dramatically improve the customer experience.*

Ohmae (1982) would categorise this as the 'strategic degrees of freedom' available to a company or the ability and flexibility to innovate, particularly in areas where no competition exists. Most companies would seek to leverage existing capabilities to provide strategic fit

Table 6.1 Differences between conventional logic and value innovation logic

The five dimensions of strategy	*Conventional logic*	*Value innovation logic*
Industry assumptions	Industry's conditions are given.	Industry's conditions can be shaped.
Strategic focus	A company should build competitive advantages. The aim is to beat the competition.	Competition is not the benchmark. A company should pursue a quantum leap in value to dominate the market.
Customers	A company should retain and expand its customer base through further segmentation and customisation. It should focus on the differences in what customers value.	A value innovator targets the mass of buyers and willingly lets some existing customers go. It focuses on the key commonalities in what customers value.
Assets and capabilities	A company should leverage its existing assets and capabilities.	A company must not be constrained by what it already has. It must ask, 'what would we do if we were starting anew?'
Product and service offerings	An industry's traditional boundaries determine the products and services a company offers. The goal is to maximise the value of those offerings.	A value innovator thinks in terms of the total solution customers seek, even if that takes the company beyond its industry's traditional offerings.

Source: Chan Kim and Mauborgne (1997:106)

between the resources of the company and current market boundaries. This usually translates to a narrowing of market segments as niches are identified and subsequently targeted as sources of additional profit.

There has been rapid growth in the health and fitness market over the last five years. In monetary terms it is worth approximately £1 billion per annum to the UK economy (Batram and Sahil 1999). It is now characterised by high levels of competition in an increasing number of geographical areas. In a recent review of the market, city analyst Granville plc offer an optimistic view of the market, with an anticipated 40 per cent increases in new openings during 1999, as both existing and new entrants seek to capitalise on the large growth in demand and thus profit potential (Batram and Sahil 1999).

The structure of the market is also changing. Whilst Granada, and others, continue to operate from a base of divested leisure interests, there is a move among other key players to consolidate. Greenalls, for example, have completed disposal programmes that allow specialisation in this area. Similarly, Vardon Leisure have systematically divested their interests in a number of other leisure areas, raising £110 million, to focus on the health and fitness market. During January 1999, Vardon Health and Fitness was rebranded to become the Cannon's Group. As Nick Irens (quoted in *Leisure Opportunities*, January 1999) contends:

> *Focused purely on health and fitness, and supported by minimal gearing with a strong balance sheet, we are well placed to take advantage of our position as one of the market leaders in this industry. The prospects for health and fitness are excellent and we will continue to invest in this fast growing market.*

This runs counter to claims by Gratton and Taylor (1987) that concentration without diversification is a short-term tactic of recessionary caution. Clearly, for some leisure organisations, specialisation is now viewed as a very real and necessary long-term strategy.

Early marketing literature suggests a strong correlation between market share and profitability and between relative product quality and return on investment. Whilst some of the assumptions underpinning this hypothesis are now dated, it did provide the early basis for the development of Porter's (1980) model of competition within markets. This is predicated on the five forces of buyers, suppliers, competitors, potential entrants and substitutes which yield the three generic strategies of lowest cost, differentiation and focus. However, in the increasingly competitive environment of the late 1990s, it is clear that organisations must offer value for money, which often means a balancing of all three strategies. Moreover, this frequently leads to lower profit margins and product differentiation strategies that meet the needs of more disparate and discerning leisure consumers. This requires organisations to concentrate on the appropriate juxtaposition of all of Porter's three strategy alternatives within the context of the prevailing market structure and strategic capabilities. The current movements in the health market are merely a reflection of this dynamic.

As the generic market becomes increasingly saturated, there is a need to differentiate the product to better reflect individual preferences by searching for profitable market niches (Ries and Trout 1997). For example, in the health and fitness market, 'Lady in Leisure' specialise in the female market, whilst 'Pinnacle' clubs target the family. Kotler (1988) argues that market niches should be profitable, have growth potential, be of negligible interest to competitors, reflect existing skills and be capable of defence from competition. Mercer (1998:265) argues:

> *Many marketers would, however, question the practical worth of either sort of (theoretical) gap analysis. As with most management techniques it has too often been oversold by its supporters. Instead these practicing managers would adopt a more pragmatic approach to development. They would, for instance, immediately start to* proactively *pursue a search for a competitive advantage! . . . In this context, the best R & D of all is to let the* customer *or consumer tell you how the existing product or service should be developed.*

This can be seen in the health and fitness market where Granada attempted to introduce a new 'Go-Fitness' brand targeted at the young and upwardly mobile, only to see it fail within the first 18 months through a combination of spurious research and inappropriate marketing strategies. Conversely and paradoxically, after extensive research, Virgin Active decide to enter the market by moving decisively in the opposite direction. Rather than looking towards the 'conventional logic' of existing market boundaries, Virgin looked to leverage the strength of the brand by promoting market expansion. They accomplished this by deliberately and successfully targeting traditional non users and adopting a more inclusive approach in its marketing concept and operational practice. For example, each new member is issued with an electronic key to be used with every piece of equipment in the club. The key stores the personalised workout details of each member and irradicates the need to carry a written fitness programme listing the individual requirements for each piece of equipment. Not surprisingly, given the target market, the Virgin 'offer' has attracted a substantial number of first-time users into the world of commercial health and fitness provision. However, the real test for Virgin will be the ability to maintain the momentum and retain existing customers as the initial promotional hype begins to fade.

This will, in part, be conditional upon the continued distinctiveness of the Virgin offer. Nick Varney (1998), speaking as the Managing Director of Vardon Attractions, argues that there is a 'commercial war' between brands: 'You have to deliver what you communicate otherwise customers will feel short changed.' If competitive advantages are easily copied then any advantages will be short term as their benchmarking returns the market to competitive parity. It is the need to offer sustainable competitive advantage that has led the literature to an examination of core competencies.

Core Competencies

Core competencies are defined by Johnson and Scholes (1999:160) as 'those competencies which critically underpin the organisations' competitive advantage'. Whilst they are fundamental to the critical success factors previously identified by Ohmae (1982), they are not exclusively predicated upon existing market paradigms, but are also used as a vehicle towards future growth. Prahalad and Hamel (quoted in Atkinson and Wilson 1996:20) argue that core competencies should provide access to a wide variety of markets, make a significant contribution to perceived customer benefits and be difficult to imitate. In other words they should be the identifiable factors that lead to sustainable competitive advantage, as previously defined by Barney and Wright (1998). Furthermore, Prahalad and Hamel (1990) argue that strategic business units (SBUs) are of limited use for planning purposes. Instead the organisation should view their structure as a portfolio of related core competencies, that should be leveraged within existing and new market areas. Again, Virgin provide a good example of this within a number of markets, including leisure, by pursuing strategies based on 'value innovation'.

Gratton and Taylor (1987:27) argue that: 'It is not surprising, then, to see leisure firms diversifying into other leisure markets, because these firms have specialist knowledge of leisure demands.' However, whilst this may have been true in the 1980s, the subsequent increase in commercial leisure provision, and thus competition, mediates a re-evaluation of such claims. For example, in the 1980s Wembley plc diversified into a number of leisure related areas, both in the UK and overseas. Expanding markets yield growth potential for both existing companies and new entrants, attracted by the lure of additional profits and the perception of related corporate capability. However, the recessionary pressures of the early 1990s and subsequent market contraction, usually favours the more experienced players. Such organisations have more knowledge of the market and are usually more motivated and better placed to defend their market position. Wembley plc have now gone 'back to basics' and are now a much leaner company specialising in event management; their area of true expertise. Indeed, having identified their core competencies in this area, they have recently sold Wembley Stadium to the English Sports Council, whilst securing the exclusive right to manage the facility.

This highlights the importance of 'strategic fit'. This is predicated on the ability of leisure organisations to understand their strengths and weaknesses and to match these with a clear knowledge of the markets in which they choose to operate. Johnson and Scholes (1999) (see Figure 6.2) provide a development of Ansoff's (1968) matrix by adding the competence dimension.

Any attempt to move out of current areas requires a judgement to be made about the nature of the market and the competencies required to ensure a competitive position within that market. When product development and diversification are incorrectly predicated upon existing competencies, companies such as Wembley plc become exposed, particularly when competition intensifies.

Figure 6.2 Directions for strategy development

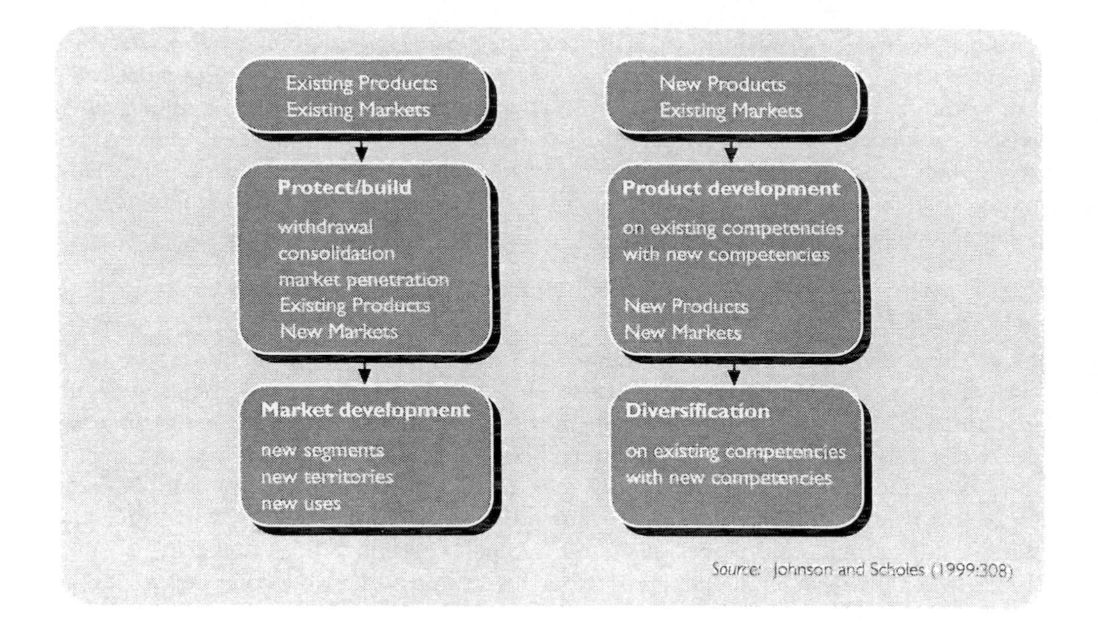

Think Global, Act Local

Whilst it remains true that size and diversification insulates organisations from market fluctuations and the volatility of leisure demands, there is evidence to suggest that the expertise developed through specialisation is now a crucial ingredient to success in a variety of leisure markets. *Think Global, Act Local* is one of the key corporate mantras for the foreseeable future. Bricks and mortar are no longer the guarantors of future success. We are now living in an era in which the combined, accumulated and developing knowledge of organisations is the key source of sustainable competitive advantage. Where attention to detail and personal vision/autonomy is stifled by the requirements of corporate parenting, there are likely to be a number of very successful smaller players who cultivate demand in ways that larger leisure organisations find difficult to imitate. For example, the vibrant club scene is increasingly likely to be found away from the direct control and influence of larger leisure conglomerates such as Rank and First Leisure. The success of Cream and Ministry of Sound on the local, national and now international club scene is a case in point. This example is replicated, on a more localised level, within practically every major city in the UK, where monopolistic competition prevails (i.e. competition based on a large number of companies offering differentiated products and services). For leisure conglomerates, more accustomed to oligopolistic competition (i.e. competition where a few companies dominate the market), there is a need to provide corporate parenting skills that add value to, rather than stifle innovation, in this and other areas.

Handy (1997) argues that organisations need to separate the core (important and centrally controlled), from the periphery (less important and better left to those who specialise in such areas). Corporate parenting skills should be based on the concept of federalism which accentuates the positive, whilst facilitating flexibility within the partnerships and outsourcing arrangements entered into by the firm (Handy 1997; Bennis 1997). Moreover, Prahalad (1997:71) argues that:

> *. . . management needs to start thinking differently about the organisation. It must become synergistic. We cannot mobilize the energies of a whole company around*

a strategic intent using the old ways of managing. The first things challenged by the new ways of managing are the role and value added of top management.

In a consumer-driven society, boardrooms that prioritise profits and shareholder value, whilst simultaneously proclaiming customer focus, will be exposed and punished. Markets driven by technological innovation are beginning to re-write the competitive landscape of both strategic theory and strategic practice. Despite this, Bob Monks (in Caulkin 2000), the US corporate expert, argues that shareholder value is still the driving force for British business. Perhaps one of the key functions of strategy is to be instrumental in the charting of future market characteristics and thus organisational direction. Schumpeter (1934) (quoted in Clarke and Clegg 1998:12), argues that business cycles drive macroeconomic growth where there are a cluster of innovations that fundamentally effect trade. Similarly, Kondratiev's (1935) Long Wave theory (quoted in Clarke and Clegg 1998:11) posits economic cycles of around 50 years fuelled by investments in new forms of infrastructure. Such thinking is also reflected in the work of Alvin and Heidi Toffler (in Gibson 1997), who advocate the need to move 'beyond bureacracy' and 'homogeneity' in favour of 'adhocracy' and 'de-massification'. Whilst the lessons of the past should not be ignored, it is clear that the future will not be charted based on linear thinking and the previous ingredients/formulas of business success (Handy 1997; Senge 1997; Hammer 1997; Prahalad 1997). This is particularly true of the digitally-driven markets of the new millennium.

The Future's Bright, the Future's . . .

The task of coming to an agreement on what strategy is, or should be, is complicated by the fact that the phenomena under study are changing faster than they can be described. (Hamel and Heene 1994:2–3)

Prahalad (1997) argues that the traditional assumptions that underpin competition are no longer valid. No longer do industries have clear boundaries with distinct characteristics. Moreover, the assumption that you can plan for the future is considered misguided. However, in a business environment that still covets material wealth, the Internet is seen, by many, as the new Jerusalem. Indeed, there is a growing realisation that technology, far from being simply a part of the strategy for growth, in many instances is rapidly becoming the key strategy (Piercy 1997; Jackson 1998). In a world where processing speeds are increasing exponentially, there are fundamental implications for the nature of business and the underlying principles of management.

For some, the leisure industry remains relatively insulated from the Internet revolution. Commenting on the increasing influence of the dot.com companies, Cannon (2000:13) argues that: 'Other sectors will be less affected. We will never be able to buy beer or a restaurant meal over the Internet.' Whilst this may be true, it would be wrong to underestimate the power of the digital revolution for the leisure industries. As issues of choice, customisation and convenience begin to govern market relationships, the Internet provides a means of mass customisation to an increasingly sophisticated 'cynical and hostile' consumer, with variable levels of loyalty (Piercy 1997). This is particularly important for home based entertainment activities that can be digitised and thus provided directly through the Internet.

Satellite and cable television has had a profound effect upon televised sport throughout the world. Although the most notable differences in the UK can be seen through televised football, its pervasive influence is now spreading into the world of horse racing, with fears of a similar style division between the have's and have not's in the racing fraternity (Knowsley and Hastings 2000; Doward 2000). This has very real consequences for traditional turf accountants such as Coral who are currently investing heavily in off-shore

Internet betting, in order to enhance their strategic capabilities in this area (Finch 2000). Similarly, Daneshlhu (2000) reports moves by Stanley Leisure (the casino and betting shop group), to launch a virtual casino based outside the UK, combined with Internet sports betting specialising in horse racing and football. The changing digital landscape requires existing organisations to search for new ways of 'stretching' their existing core competencies. If this is not possible through organic growth, or time and commercial imperatives negate this option, there is a need to leverage competencies through partnership, strategic alliance, merger or acquisition.

The January 2000 announcement of a merger between AOL and Time Warner, provides a particularly useful example of the need to leverage strategic capabilities in this way. Porter (1997) argues that 'me-too' strategies are now mercilessly punished, thereby increasing the importance of clear strategic intent. He argues that there is a need for organisations to position themselves in unique market segments. This requires strategic choices and 'trade-offs' to be made that are 'inconsistent with delivering other types of value to other customers' (Porter 1997:52). This builds upon the earlier literature dealing with core competencies (Prahalad and Hamel 1990; Johnson and Scholes 1999) and sustainable competitive advantage (Barney and Wright 1998). It also reflects the increasing moves towards specialisation in some areas of the leisure industry, such as the previously reviewed health and fitness market. However:

> *The trouble is that companies hate making choices, because doing so always looks dangerous and limiting. They always want the best of all worlds. It's psychologically risky to narrow your product range, to narrow the range of values you are delivering or to narrow your distribution. And this unwillingness to make choices is one of the biggest obstacles to creating a strategy.* (Porter 1997:52)

In this sense, Chesbrough and Teece (1996) argue that strategic alliances represent a compromise between the need to innovate and need to retain control. For Hamel (1997) the future is made up of a series of 'opportunity arenas'. The AOL and Time Warner merger is an attempt to promote the structural evolution of the industry in a way that affords the protagonists a considerable presence and thus power/competitive advantage in the future landscape of entertainment provision and e-commerce.

According to Prahalad (1997:74) companies that survive successfully:

> *are continually looking forward, not backward. They are continually changing the rules of competition, rather than following accepted rules. They are regularly defining new ways of doing business, pioneering new product concepts, building new core competencies, creating new markets, setting new standards and challenging their own assumptions. They are taking control of their future.*

Teece (1986) offers a more structured view to competitive strategy in an environment of technological innovation, by arguing for three main considerations to be taken into account:

1. *Appropriability*: Environmental factors, excluding firm and market structure, that affect the ability to capture benefits from the innovation. Most importantly is the nature of technology and legal protection. Appropriability regimes are said to be tight or weak. For example, the source code for the Microsoft Windows software has been subject to tight appropriability, but may be compromised by the current anti-trust litigation in the United States.
2. *Dominant design paradigm*: The dominant infrastructure, framework or platform that governs the market. For example, the battle between Betamax and VHS (now video and DVD), vinyl and CD (now CD/Minidisc and MP3 technology).

3. *Complementary assets (three types)*: These are products or services that are complementary to the innovation.

   - *Generic assets*: These are universally available and require no/few specialised skills. For example, the manufacturing of Nike's footwear.
   - *Specialised assets*: There is unilateral dependence between the innovation and the asset, i.e. the asset is dependent upon the innovation, but the innovation is not dependent upon the asset. For example, the licensing of games software for the Sony Playstation games console.
   - *Co-specialised assets*: There is a bilateral dependence between the innovation and the asset, i.e. you cannot have one without the other. For example, the Internet and computers (although this is rapidly changing as the Internet will increasingly be made available through televisions and WAP mobile phones). This has prompted Microsoft to amend its mission statement which previously advocated a vision of a computer on every desk.

The mutual interdependencies of companies will ultimately dictate the extent to which relationships are governed by tacit agreement, contractual arrangements, strategic alliance, merger or acquisition. Nike, for example, hold all the cards when dealing with manufacturing organisations. Moves to cement existing outsourcing arrangements, through vertical integration, would limit flexibility and would be completely unnecessary given the inherent power imbalances that exist. Teece (1986:238) argues that distribution systems are likely to hold the key power in networked markets. This explains why Manchester United have their own dedicated cable channel (MUTV) and why David Beckham's website (containing exclusive interviews and insight!) is reportedly worth £8 million to the football icon (Kelso 2000). Similarly, BSkyB have bought a 9.9 per cent stake in Chelsea FC, Leeds United, Sunderland, Manchester United and Manchester City in return for the exclusive right to negotiate the media rights on behalf of the football club. They are not alone as Granada hold a 9.9 per cent stake in Liverpool FC; NTL, the French telecommunications company, have 9.9 per cent stakes in Aston Villa and Newcastle United. The modality of commercial business is based upon securing profits over the short-, medium- and long-term. As the premier league announce plans to offer 40 pay-per-view matches each season, the importance of securing a presence in this area becomes all the more obvious (Millward 2000). Moreover, Teece (1986:238):

> *In rare instances where incumbent firms possess an airtight monopoly over specialised assets, and the innovator is in a regime of weak appropriability, all of the profits to the innovation could conceivably accrue to the firms possessing the specialised assets, which should be able to get the upper hand.*

Herein lies the strategic logic to the AOL/Time Warner merger and helps to explain why CISCO Systems, which develops both hardware and software for the Internet, has recently eclipsed Microsoft as the world's most valuable company.

Whilst it remains a truism to argue that the Internet cannot be owned by any one person or company, the economics of the information age necessitates that organisations critically examine the very value chains that have historically driven competitive advantage and thus profit. Encyclopaedia Britannica nearly went into liquidation following their inability to come to terms with the influence of CD-Rom based alternatives. Similarly, there are lots of current examples to be found from within the leisure and sports industry. William Hill, (the turf accountants), have been slow to respond to the very real competitive pressures from the Internet. Thomsons (the travel company), who dominated the market during the

1980s and 1990s, have failed to embrace the Internet and competition from such fledgling companies as Ebookers and LastMinute.com. Following boardroom disagreements and a poorly performing share price, Parsley (2000) reports that they are now facing a takeover bid from a German rival. Similarly, the record companies have, until now, failed to react to the technological threat of downloaded music from the Internet. This has clear and fundamental implications for 'appropriability' and thus the future copyright, royalties and revenues of both record companies and record retailers. Indeed, Virgin are so concerned with this development that they are seriously considering re-positioning their 'Our Price' music stores, as dedicated mobile phone outlets (O'Connor 2000). Sullivan (2000) reports on the freely available Napster software, which networks computers containing MP3 files. This facilitates free access to practically the entire back catalogue of worldwide recorded music. Similarly, Peoplesound.com provides for the free download of material submitted by new bands, whilst offering tailored CD albums, specifically 'burned' to order. Appropriability is a key issue, as music and media organisations must look to technology in order to maintain their future copyright security. If companies fail to embrace this new technology, the very basis of their competitive advantage will be very quickly and fundamentally undermined!

According to Chesbrough and Teece (1996) the economics of the information age dictate that organisations must find an acceptable trade-off between 'richness' (quantity and quality of information) and 'reach' (the number of people available to target). The AOL/ Time Warner merger represents a clear and decisive move towards symbiotic vertical integration. This combines both richness and reach whilst, temporarily perhaps, ensuring market leadership in both digital distribution networks (AOL has 23 million users in Europe alone) and the quality of the content (supplied by Time Warner). However, in order to compete in a consolidating world, it is necessary to have more than size advantages. Economies of scale are just one competitive advantage in the emerging networked global economy.

A Networked Economy

Porter (1997:55) regards cross-functional integration, as the 'essential core of strategy'. This builds upon the previously reviewed work of Barney and Wright (1998) and represents 'the capacity to link and integrate activities across the whole value chain and to achieve complementarities across many activities. It's where the way you do one thing allows you to do something else better' (Porter 1997:55). This represents a more inclusive and holistic approach to strategy as management functions, such as HRM and marketing, are considered in the context of the whole organisation. How this is achieved impacts on organisational culture and has the potential to build important core competencies, based upon the unique configuration and subsequent organisation learning. Crucially, the success of the merger between AOL and Time Warner will rest upon the operationalisation of the boardroom's strategic vision. The two companies must work to ensure that the synergies sought through the merger are carefully nurtured in a way that adds value to the customer, and is difficult to imitate by competitors. As Jay (2000:2) argues:

> *. . . executives at the top of media companies such as Bertelsmann, Disney, News Corporation . . . and Viacom are anxiously reviewing their strategies, wondering what the deal means for their already rapidly changing industry. Should they turn sellers or should they take on the AOL Time Warner men and build lookalike megaliths?*

For Ries and Trout (1997), the merger may represent a move in the wrong direction. They argue that the convergence of markets should not prove the driving force of strategic decisions. Instead, organisations should recognise the inalienable truth, that industries divide, not converge. Time Warner have tried and failed to previously make the crossover into interactive media. The ability of the newly formed company to think global and act local is critical. They will need to combine their corporate strength with a strategic and operational coherency that is sensitive to the future needs of an increasingly disparate consumer. Prahalad (1997:67) calls this the strategic architecture of the organisation, which he defines as:

> *. . . the big picture. It's the broad agenda for deploying new functionalities, acquiring new competencies, leveraging existing competencies and reconfiguring the customer interface.*

The ability to both combine and 'stretch' the existing core competencies, will undoubtedly impact on their future position in this rapidly changing competitive arena. Naisbitt (1997:213) claims that '. . . there's a new kind of bigness. And that's big networks, rather than big main-frames.' This reflects a growing realisation that, as competition intensifies, it is increasingly difficult to find all the necessary resources and competencies within the same organisation. Organisations are inextricably linked to the macro environment. There is a need to look into the value chains of other companies and enter into strategic relationships based on co-operation and mutual self interest, within a networked chain of supply. Amazon.com have over 30,000 affiliated sites that work on commision, whilst LeisureHub.com provides the first e-commerce site for the leisure industry by providing a one stop supermarket that links leisure providers and suppliers. Gilson *et al.* (2000) call this 'co-opetition' and uses competitive sport as a conduit to explain the concept further:

> *In business, players must co-operate to increase the scope and value of a game . . . basketball teams co-operate in the development of the National Basketball Association to create a valuable entertainment industry, and then they compete intensely within the industry to extract value from it.* (Gilson *et al.* 2000:247)

Similarly, the auction for the five UK licences to operate the next generation of mobile phones was dominated by a series of consortia, not individual companies (Hamilton 2000). The laws of demand and supply, combined with the competitive and commercial imperative of securing future capacity/bandwidth, have fuelled the bidding war to a staggering £22.5 billion. This was a competition that the established players simply could not afford to lose.

In order to secure a dominant position, in the digital markets, organisations must have deep pockets. For example, BSkyB announced losses of £13.6 million in 1999 in order to fund the rapid expansion of digital television, through the provision of free set top boxes. Thal Larsen (2000:31) reports that Sega are giving away their Dreamcast games console, if customers agree to be locked into a two-year contract that establishes the company as an Internet Service Provider (ISP). This buys the company a degree of loyalty ('stickiness') in the on-line gaming market which is set to expand during the next few years. Thal Larsen (2000) also reports that Sega are in negotiations with MP3.com (the on-line music group) with a view to forming an alliance which would allow subscription customers the option of downloading music. In response, Microsoft, attempting to regain a degree of control in this area, have announced the development of their X-box, a future games console that is said to be three times more powerful than the recently launched Playstation2 (Kelso and Schofield 2000). The X-box is designed to provide both access to the games market and also to act as a 'portal', allowing the playback of DVD movies and the use of peripherals such as digital cameras. In other words, like Sega's Dreamcast console, it is designed to provide access to the digital world, through a user friendly and relatively inexpensive alternative to the computer. Not surprisingly, Microsoft will face stiff competition from the established Sony and Sega offerings, and the forthcoming Nintendo Dolphin and Sega's Dreamcast2.

The key to the future networked economy will be the control of the strategic access points or 'portals'. However, it is clear that being first to the market is not enough. There is a need to ensure future competitive advantages through the control and commercial exploitation of such portals, within the limits of the market and existing legislative frameworks. However, organisations must be careful here. When competitive advantages are secured in ways that exploit the consumer, there may be dire consequences for the organisation(s) involved. In the US, Microsoft are currently embroiled in a distracting anti-trust legal battle, whilst in Europe, Nintendo are facing similar allegations concerning, alleged, price fixing in the video games market. As we enter the new milennium, it is clear that there are an increasing number of banana skins waiting for companies who fail to rationalise the chaos and complexity found within the local, national, international and global marketplace.

Summary and Conclusions

The digital revolution opens up a new Pandora's box for both organisations and consumers. As e-commerce increasingly represents a more value driven and convenient option to the choice hungry consumer, existing businesses based upon personal service must respond or face extinction. Size can only insulate organisations from the Internet revolution, up to a point. As the virtual world of e-commerce has a deleterious effect upon traditional barriers to market entry, industries will be increasingly dominated by smaller, more responsive competitors.

Whilst markets are still dominated by the prevailing capitalist orthodoxy, there is a need to adopt strategies that balance the disparate needs of all principal stakeholders, whilst simultaneously responding to the volatile needs of the external environment. It is likely that the future competitive landscape will be governed by a series of mutual alliances, that together offer a unique bundle of benefits for a more targeted, discrete and discerning consumer.

Organisations must seek to cultivate new markets based on co-opetition. This requires the nurturing of both current and future inter/intra organisational relationships based on mutual dependency and value added, as measured by the customer. The future configuration of a networked series of value chains will offer either competitive disadvantage, competitive parity or competitive advantage. However, in order to offer more sustainable growth, leisure and sport organisations must seek to find a more coherent and synergistic balance between organisation rhetoric and reality, between theory and practice.

There is no pre-ordained future. There is no magic formula yielding success in the short-, medium- and long-term. At any moment in time there are a series of multiple future realities. Moreover, as predictions are increasingly based upon forces that are outside the (in)direct control of organisations, the natural selection of dominant consortiums will be based upon both luck and judgement. What there is, however, is a series of choices, each requiring logical and lateral extrapolation. An understanding of the forces and changing dynamics within existing market structures will facilitate more informed strategic decisions. As the future becomes increasingly difficult to predict, it is incumbent upon organisations to mould the future based not only upon their own image but one that mirrors a landscape familiar to a sustainable number of stakeholders. Ultimately, however, commercial, public and voluntary leisure organisations cannot exist without customers. As Bezos (quoted in Rushe 1999:9) argues:

> *I want my people to wake up in the middle of the night dripping with sweat and fear. But I don't want them to be scared of the competition. It's the customer I want them to be scared of.*

Suggested Tasks for Further Study

1. Review the wider literature in the area of strategy and competition. As a starting point, readers could look to O'Shaughnessy 1992, Chisnall 1995, McDonald 1996, Atkinson and Wilson 1996 or Harding and Long 1998. This is not an exhaustive list. Any general 'strategy' textbook from around 1990 onwards will be able to provide a useful synopsis of the main theories and models in this area.
2. Look to the bibliography of the 'strategy' textbooks selected and further develop your knowledge in areas of particular interest by consulting the original references. These would usefully include journals such as the *Harvard Business Review* and the *Journal of Marketing Management.*
3. Type *strategy* into any Internet search engine and see what you get. More useful sites include those of the Harvard Business School and the Institute of Management. Both FT.com and Bloomberg.com provide excellent starting points for the background narrative and financial performance of many listed leisure companies.
4. For a selected leisure market, review the most recent reports in the national and leisure press for the last six months. The *Financial Times* contains articles every week that have direct relevance to the leisure and sport industries. You should easily be able to find at least 20 articles that have direct/indirect relevance to the area you have selected.
5. Compare, contrast and critique the knowledge you have gained from activities 1, 2, 3 and 4.
6. Produce a simple spreadsheet mapping the weekly fluctuations of the share prices of organisations with an interest in leisure and sport. Prices can be found daily in the national quality papers and usually cover areas such as Leisure and Hotels, Telecoms, Beverages, Media, Restaurants and Pubs.
7. Try to match significant weekly share movements (+/– 10 per cent) with the reports contained on television news bulletins/programmes and the daily/weekly business press.
8. Look to the *Annual Reports* for information that helps explain the current direction and/or actions of selected leisure/sport companies.

References

- Ansoff I 1968 *Corporate Strategy* Penguin, London
- Atkinson J and Wilson I 1996 *Strategic Marketing, Cases, Concepts & Challenges* Harper Collins, London
- Barney J B and Wright P M 1998 'On Becoming a Strategic Partner: The Role of Human Resources in Gaining Competitive Advantage' *Human Resource Management* Spring 1998 Vol.37 No.1 John Wiley and Sons Inc. pp.31–46
- Batram N and Sahil S 1999 'Fortune Telling' *Health Club Management* January 1999 Leisure Media Company, Hitchin pp.24–25
- Bennis W 1997 'Becoming a leader of leaders' in Gibson R 1997 *op. cit.* pp.148–163
- Bharadwaj S G, Varadarajan P R and Fahay J 1993 'Sustainable competitive advantage in service industries: a conceptual model and research propositions' *Journal of Marketing* 57 (October) pp.83–99
- Cannon H 2000 'Old economy in the new paradigm' in *The Observer* Cash Supplement 26 March 2000 p.13
- Caulkin S 2000 'Governance is its own reward' in *The Observer* 26 March 2000 p.11
- Chan Kim W and Mauborgne R 1997 'Value Innovation: The Strategic Logic of High Growth' *Harvard Business Review* Jan–Feb 1997 pp.103–112
- Chesbrough H W and Teece D J 1996 'When Is Virtual Virtuous? Organizing for Innovation' in *Harvard Business Review* Jan–Feb 1996 pp.65–73
- Chisnall P M 1995 *Strategic Business Marketing* (3rd Ed) Prentice-Hall, London
- Clarke T and Clegg S 1998 *Changing Paradigms, the transformation of management knowledge for the 21st century* Harper Collins, London
- Cole G A 1997 *Personnel Management* Letts Educational, London
- Cowe R 1997 'A fresh focus on the human factor' *The Guardian* Jobs and Money Section 15 November 1997 p.23
- Daneshlhu S 2000 'Stanley to wheel out virtual casino' in *The Financial Times* Companies and Finance Section 14 January 2000 p.21
- Doward J 2000 'Two-horse TV could leave 47 also-rans' in *The Observer* Business Supplement 26 March 2000 p.1
- Finch J 2000 'Coral prepares £1 bn stock market return' in *The Guardian* 26 January 2000 p.30
- Gibson R 1997 *Rethinking the future* Nicholas Brealey Publishing Limited, London
- Gilson C, Pratt M, Roberts K and Weymes E 2000 *Peak Performance: Business Lessons from the World's Top Sports Organizations* Harper Collins, London
- Gratton C and Taylor P 1987 *Leisure Industries: An Overview* Comedia, Old Woking
- Gratton L 1997 'The art of managing people' in Dickson D (Ed) *Mastering Management* Pitman, London pp.251–258
- Grönroos C 1994 'From Scientific Management to Service Management: A Management Perspective for the Age of Service Competition' *International Journal of Services Industry Management* 5(1), 5–20 in Gabbott M and Hogg G (Eds) 1997 *Contemporary Services Marketing Management; A Reader* Dryden Press, London pp.345–360
- Hamel G and Prahalad C K 1989 'Strategic Intent' *Harvard Business Review* May–June 1989
- Hamel and Heene 1994 quoted in Clarke and Clegg 1998 *op. cit.*
- Hamel G 1997 'Reinventing the basis for competition' in Gibson R 1997 *op. cit.* pp.76–92
- Hamilton K 2000 'A defining deal that changes our media landscape forever' in *The Sunday Times* Business Section p.3.4
- Hammer M 1997 'Beyond the end of management' in Gibson R 1997 *op. cit.* pp.94–105
- Handy C 1997 'Finding Sense in Uncertainty' in Gibson R 1997 *op. cit.* pp.16–33

- Harding S and Long T 1998 *MBA Management Models* Gower Publishing Ltd, Aldershot
- Hunter L W 1997 'Choices and the high performance workplace' in Dickson D (Ed) *Mastering Management* Pitman, London pp.267–273
- Jackson T 1998 'The machines are taking over' in *The Financial Times* 23 February 1998
- Jay J 2000 'Day of reckoning looms for cyberspace emperors' in *The Sunday Times* Business Section 16 January 2000 p.3.2
- Johnson G and Scholes K 1999 *Exploring Corporate Strategy Text and Cases* (5th Ed) Prentice Hall, Harlow
- Kelso P and Schofield J 2000 'Playtime: Microsoft enters the games console market' in *The Guardian* 11 March 2000 p.10
- Kelso P 2000 'A further £8m in the pipeline for Beckham on the net' in *The Guardian* 25 March 2000 p.2
- Knowsley J and Hastings C 2000 'Murdoch's £12m gamble on the horses' in *The Sunday Telegraph* 30 January 2000 p.19
- Kotler P 1988 *Marketing Management: Analysis, Planning, Implementation and Control* (6th Ed) Prentice Hall, New Jersey
- Legge K 1995 *Human Resources Management Rhetorics and Realities* Macmillan Business, London
- *Leisure Opportunities* 1999 'Leaner Vardon set to focus on fitness' Issue 225 January 1999 p.1
- McDonald M 1996 *Strategic Marketing Planning* (2nd Ed) Kogan Page, London
- Mercer D 1998 *Marketing Strategy, The Challenge of the External Environment* Sage Publications, London
- Millward D 2000 'Premier clubs offer pay-per-view football' *The Daily Telegraph* 4 April 2000 p.4
- Mintzberg H 1987 'Five Ps for Strategy' in *California Management Review* Fall 1987
- Mintzberg H and Quinn 1991 *The Strategy Process* Prentice-Hall, Englewood Cliffs, N.J.
- Mintzberg H 1994 'The Fall and Rise of Strategic Planning' in *Harvard Business Review* Jan–Feb 1994 pp.107–114
- Naisbitt J 1997 'From nation states to networks' in Gibson R 1997 *op. cit.* pp.212–227
- O'Connor A 2000 'Virgin closer to deal on debts to music companies' in *The Financial Times* 4 April 2000 p.26
- Ohmae K 1982 *The Mind of the Strategist (The Art of Japanese Business)* McGraw-Hill, New York
- O'Shaughnessy J 1992 *Competitive Marketing* (2nd Ed) Routledge, London
- Parsley D 2000 'Thomson ready to talk – at a price' in *The Sunday Times* Business Section 9 April 2000 p.3.6
- Pemberton C 1998 'From the top' in *The Guardian* Jobs and Money Section 12 December 1998 p.17
- Piercy N 1997 *Market-Led Strategic Change; Transforming the Process of Going to Market* (2nd Ed) Butterworth Heinmann, Oxford
- Porter M E 1980 *Competitive Strategy: Techniques for Analysing Industries and Competitors* The Free Press, New York
- Porter M E 1985 *Competitive Advantage: Creating and Sustaining Superior Performance* The Free Press, New York
- Porter M 1997 'Creating tomorrow's advantages' in Gibson R *op. cit.* pp.48–61
- Prahalad C K 1997 'Strategies for Growth' in Gibson R 1997 *op. cit.* pp.62–75
- Ries A and Trout J 1997 'Focused in a fuzzy world' in Gibson R 1997 *op. cit.* pp.180–195
- Rushe D 1999 'Amazon aims to flood Britain' in *The Sunday Times* Business Section 7 November 1999 p.3.9

- Senge P 1997 'Through the Eye of the Needle' in Gibson R 1997 *op. cit.* pp.122–146
- Slack T 1997 *Understanding Sport Organisations* Human Kinetics, Leeds
- Sullivan A 2000 'Net music is the food of world revolution' in *The Sunday Times* News Review Section 9 April 2000 p.5.5
- Teece D J 1986 'Profiting from Technological Innovation: Implications for Integration, Collaboration, Licensing, and Public Policy' in *Research Policy* No.15 1986 pp.285–315
- Thal Larsen P 2000 'Sega goes online to shift Dreamcast' in *The Financial Times* 4 April 2000 p.31
- Toffler A and Toffler H 1997 in Gibson R 1997 *op. cit.* pp.viii–x
- Tofield B 1998 'Why bosses must know the score' in *The Guardian* Jobs and Money Section 5 November 1998 p.21
- Varney N 1998 'Market forces' in *Leisure Opportunities* Issue 222 Nov/Dec 1998 pp.11–12
- Watts J 2000 'Dare to be different, Japanese are urged' in *The Guardian* 19 January 2000

Chapter 7

Access and Leisure Policy

John Spink & Peter Bramham
Leeds Metropolitan University

Chapter Content

- Introduction
- Access to the Countryside
- Access to Televised Sport
- Summary and Conclusions
- Suggested Tasks for Further Study
- References

Abstract

The context of policy-making and the relevant ideological ethos is explored in relation to the dominant political ideas of post-war Britain, social reformist Labour and neo-liberal New Right Conservative governments. Both approaches have been influential in shaping recent leisure and sports policy. Managers are introduced to the impact of these ideas, both in the recent past and in relation to contemporary access case studies of freedom to roam and the freedom to view televised sport. The role and limitations of public policy-making are examined in an age of private consumers and the effectiveness of public policy considered. The impact of power and pressure groups on policy through the policy-making process is explored as a key feature of decision-making in a pluralist democratic state.

Related Chapters

Chapter 1: The UK Public Sector: Public policy is the driving force for development and change within the public leisure sector. The main changes faced by public providers are often driven by public policy decision-making.

Chapter 11: Service Quality: The paradigm for organisational effectiveness in the 1990s was that of service quality within public sector organisations. Public ▷

policy was often the driver of these changes. The need to do more with less, to compete with the private sector and at the same time to maintain and improve service quality were all part of this thinking.

Learning Objectives

- to contextualise changing political ideologies behind politics, policies and power
- to introduce models for the analysis of power within the policy process
- to explore access case studies regarding both 'freedom to roam' rural areas and 'freedom to view' sport on TV
- to evaluate the changing rationale of leisure policy and its role in government agendas

Introduction

The 1980s and much of the 1990s were dominated by versions of New Right governments over much of the developed world. Leaders like Thatcher and Reagan embodied a neo-liberal agenda which emphasised belief in free markets, privatisation of public functions, reduction of restrictions on flows of capital and labour, along with encouragement of individualism and self reliance (Heywood 1997a). This era marked the end of the long post-war consensus around state welfarism and represented an altogether radical and challenging break with the past. Leisure and sport were not immune from these political and intellectual challenges as policy increasingly came to reflect its political context (Henry 1993).

In the UK, market-driven approaches to efficiency, value for money, privatising and contracting of service delivery dominated the public sector of leisure provision. A new managerialism came to challenge the power of producer groups, particularly within local authorities and public sector trades unions, as the emphasis shifted to customer care, income generation and to associated issues of quality of provision and entrepreneurial responses to niche markets. Constraints on public spending, particularly within local government, ensured that expansion and investment came almost exclusively from within the commercial sector.

This high tide of New Right economic realism in the UK appeared to ebb with the election of a New Labour government in 1997. However, despite its social reformist and social democratic roots, New Labour has continued many of the policy initiatives of previous Tory regimes. Dominant ideologies, those sets of ruling ideas of every age, propagated by the media and held unconsciously as 'natural' common-sense by the majority of the population, once displaced, usually demonstrate an intellectual continuity and political tenacity. Accordingly, Prime Minister Tony Blair's approach to various leisure and sports policies reflects many of the concerns of his predecessors. Elements of neo-liberalism thus show every indication of continuing to influence UK policy through initiatives like those of 'Best Value', however linked with more social democratic concerns towards social equity and exclusion. It is this mixture of political ideas, some coherent and rationally based, some bureaucratically convenient, while others are simply historical accretions due to institutional inertia and dating from previous administrations, which constitutes UK leisure and sports policy. It forms the complex historical and intellectual environment which this chapter seeks to explore, since it represents the essential political context for contemporary leisure and sports management.

Social reformist Labour governments have historically been associated with policies aimed at furthering core values of equity and social justice. As such, a New Labour regime, despite apparently residual elements of neo-liberalism, would still be expected to focus on a variety of leisure and sports policy issues linked to:

- ensuring mass access to leisure, recreational and sport resources;
- combating forces increasing social exclusion, polarisation and disadvantage with their inevitable constraints on equal participation for all;
- maintaining national cultural identity both through arts and heritage subsidies and also through support for elite sporting success, nationally and internationally;
- regulating commercialism and commodification of leisure, with particular emphasis on reducing monopolistic dominance, whether of satellite broadcasting, pub chains or package holidays.

This wide-ranging agenda would be augmented by continuing and usual governmental concerns over young people and social disorder, either raised in issues like crime, drugs on the streets or in sport, moral panics about hooligans, concerns over teenage sex, or worries over increasing tobacco and alcohol consumption.

Leisure, sports and tourism policies have also recently grown in significance within economic policy domains, representing valuable opportunities for urban partnership, civic boosterism and prospects of economic regeneration for many areas and groups experiencing real hardship. So, along with increased prominence in society, partly through the growing importance of leisure lifestyles to citizens, but also because of this economic rationale, leisure and sports policies have also grown in salience within government and now form an important aspect of domestic policy-making, as ministers like Chris Smith, Tony Banks and later, Kate Hoey, have demonstrated.

Within this chapter we wish to focus initially on an issue which reveals many of the processes behind public policy-making and which represents the relative power of groups and organisations involved in politics and practical policy formulation, that of 'freedom to roam'.

Access to the Countryside

The whole issue of freedom to roam is a suitable topic as it illustrates many of the elements involved in development of leisure policy in the UK and the influential groups involved, but also it represents an historically significant issue within social reformist tradition. Even in the nineteenth century there were attempts to obtain access to upland wilderness and mountain moorlands. Bills introduced from 1884 onwards were lost in a landowning parliament, but the notion of the mass populace of urban centres, many of them recent landless rural migrants, having rights of access to countryside, despite its enclosure, continued to attract the radical conscience.

Conflicts continued throughout the 1930s with the mobilisation of mass trespass movements (see Marion Shoard's 1997 *This Land is Our Land* for details of the evolving struggle). The importance of the issue for British Labour Party politics is reflected in the title of the 1949 National Parks and Access to the Countryside Act, as a keynote element of rural recreation policy for Atlee's post-war government.

More recent controversy over countryside access has in part been related to growing privatisation of land, formerly owned by public water authorities or the Forestry Commission, and the consequent threat caused to public access as some of these substantial tracts of land were sold. These sales have continued even under New Labour, as the various quangos and private companies have striven to achieve Treasury performance targets or enhanced profits. The sales led to a series of 'Forbidden Britain' days of action in the 1980s and resurrected the old campaign issues of rural access and trespass during the Thatcher Conservative regime with its moves to further land privatisation and to redefinitions of trespass, culminating in its criminalisation in the Criminal Justice and Public Order Act of 1994 (Shoard 1997)

It is the contemporary situation which is analysed here. 'Right to Roam' usefully illustrates several aspects of the subtle interplay between power and policy-making in the UK, and illuminates the influence of the political ideological context. A relevant theorist in any analysis of political power is Stephen Lukes (1974, and later reinterpreted in Coates 1993) who explored three dimensions of power. Political power is the ability to achieve intended ends and to reach political goals despite resistance (Heywood 1997b, pp.10–12). Achieving power is related to the way in which decisions are made and the dimensions of power articulated. In Lukes' analysis a one-dimensional study of power merely explores policy outcomes, as to who has won and who has lost in achieving their desired goals. This represents power manifested in acts of Parliament or victories within the political sphere, either nationally or locally, in clear conflicts which are resolved in favour of one participant or another, as a result of their exercise of power.

More subtle, however, are two-dimensional analyses which recognise the importance of non-decisions and the determination of what is discussed or included to form part of the political agenda. This represents latent power as elites seek to shape agenda or to effectively silence political opponents. Agenda-setting in an age of multimedia publicity and heightened public awareness may well be all important. In a pluralist democracy this is very much the policy-influencing domain of a range of pressure groups. Some represent a vested financial interest in topics under discussion and may be seen as such (see Figure 7.1).

Others are much more concerned with promoting a single issue or cause and represent a series of values or ethical stances in attempting to place their perspective on the agenda. Orienting the focus and topic of debate or the nature of the discourse may thus be a crucial dimension of the eventual outcome. Importantly, the pressure groups involved differ in their access to the media and to the executive institutions of government. Some are so powerful, due to media resources or nearness to government, that they are recognisably 'insiders', while others are so distant from the direct levers of institutional power and influence that they are forced to operate as 'outsiders'. In the pursuit of high profile publicity being 'outside' may be no bad thing. However, the need for direct action, street riots, or publicity stunts, generally correlates with a relative absence of direct political power. The well-connected, financially well-endowed and central decision-making institutions do not have to attract attention to themselves to get their voices heard. Their latent power may well become apparent in what is not included on the agenda for discussion, or in the way the debate or discourse is structured and the argument developed. This second dimension of power is entirely about influencing how debate proceeds, what concepts and language are used, and the way issues are presented within public, and hence democratic, arenas.

The third dimension to consider in any political conflict is that of in-built structural constraints and implicit resource bias. The extent to which property, law, ideology and economic or social circumstances may affect policy outcomes is a significant element. To pluralists the debate between interested parties may be seen as open and on a fairly level playing field, while for others, especially those following Marxist or elitist critiques, the whole process may be little more than an unequal charade, disguising the alliances of vested interests which ensure particular outcomes to the advantage of the wealthy or powerfully connected.

Figure 7.1
Access pressure groups

	Insiders	*Outsiders*
Interest groups	National Farmers' Union Country Landowners' Association	Hill farmers
Promotional groups	National Trust Countryside Agency	Ramblers' Association Friends of the Earth

Source: Adapted from Spink (1994:68)

It is these three elements which analysis of the Right to Roam conflict needs to encompass:

1. The relative powers of activists involved in securing particular outcomes.
2. The way in which topics are addressed, presented and structured.
3. The structural forces at work which combine to favour one side more than the other in any political power struggle.

As Figure 7.1 shows, the various parties involved can be clearly identified. Those favouring greater rights of access have been groups like the Ramblers' Association, large numbers of the articulate middle classes who as walkers or naturalists form part of the 20 millions or so who regularly head for the hills as part of their leisure time, along with a substantial proportion of members of the Labour Party for historic and ideological reasons. Opposing them have been landowning and farming interests, formally represented by bodies like the Country Landowners' Association and the National Farmers' Union. These are the elements comprising the first dimension of power to be considered in this case. Historically, the landed and farming interests, with their links to the relevant Ministries of Agriculture, and for Environment and their access to finance and hence to the media, must be considered to represent 'insiders' in any battle over access rights.

The Ramblers' Association and others within the access coalition recognised that only through mobilisation in the second of Lukes' dimensions of power could their concerns be raised and placed on the public's agenda. Accordingly, beginning in the 1980s with regular 'Forbidden Britain' days, these groups revived the mass trespass campaigning idea of the 1930s and used it to secure useful recognition of the access issue by the media and subsequently by the general public. At that time, within the then current New Right context of neo-liberal privatisation and defence of property rights, the action was largely a defensive response to loss of ramblers' rights through government sales and landowner action. But increasingly in the 1990s this publicity came to recast the debate around a much more positive and favourable discourse; that of personal 'freedom' in the guise of a Freedom to Roam campaign.

Lukes' second dimension is thus particularly important to the extent to which shaping of public perception is decisive. It reinforces the significance of discourse and discourse analysis in examining the development of public and political ideas. In a media-dominated age, positive presentation of ideas and informing the voting public serves to reinforce the link between electoral knowledge and political power. Expression of *rights* and *freedom* are subtly different in their emphases on *duty*, *citizenship* and *responsibility*. But the growing confidence of the pro-access lobby increasingly came to mirror a national mood and thus sustained a shift towards pro-access terminology. At the more radical extreme, promotion of the 'Right to Trespass' idea demonstrated the diversity of agendas, policies and ideologies within any terrain contested by very diverse interest groups.

On the other side, the Country Landowners' Association continued to provide journalists with copy and to use their *friends* in the media to promote a case aimed towards electorally all-important middle England voters, much as the Countryside Alliance did to defend fox hunting. Stories and headlines along the lines of 'Duke makes last stand against right to roam' (*Times* 21 October 1997); 'Owners back voluntary route for access' (*Yorkshire Post* 3 June 1998); 'Right to roam law is on the wrong track' (*YP* 12 April 1999); 'Right to roam law will harm wildlife' (*YP* 28 April 1999); frequently presented and promoted the landowners' case.

To rebut these ideas and seize the agenda-setting battleground the pro-access coalition responded with media attractive stunts, like trespasses and also by highlighting particular cases where landowners wilfully blocked established and legal paths. ('Bullies and Blockers: Back Off!' national campaign advert by The Ramblers, *Observer* 31/1/99.) This was a crucial element in determining the impact of the second dimension of power. However, it is important not to neglect the third dimension; those structural elements which affect all policy struggles. Certainly the CLA and NFU landowning forces represented not only landed capital and legal rights of property, but also considerable financial assets and also some degree of media ownership. Compared with this structural advantage, the resources of the Ramblers' Association or groups like Friends of the Earth, came only from subscriptions and voluntary donations given by members and supporters. Certainly, in the 1980s this pro-access alliance would have found the structural obstacles to change great indeed, given the New Right private property ownership ethos of the times. However, perhaps one of the most important shifts facilitating Right to Roam in the 1990s was national political change.

The ideological dominance of the Conservative Party New Right over the 1980s and early 1990s gave way in 1997 to the somewhat enigmatic social reformism of New Labour. While the latter may have been far from revolutionary, it did at least end executive government dominance by an individualistic and landowner dominated Cabinet. It also perhaps reflected a changing balance of power between the more urban based ideology of New Labour and the more rural basis of traditional Conservative thought on issues like countryside access, or attitudes towards deer and fox hunting. Importantly for the new Labour Government, Right to Roam was essentially a cheap yet highly symbolic opportunity to maintain reformist credentials at a time of introduction of other more conservative economic and welfare policy changes, when its radical credentials were being seriously questioned by Labour back-bench MPs and activist party members.

Perhaps this was a key aspect of the policy-making process involved in this example. Despite many media 'leaks' about a likely reliance on voluntary access agreements with landowners, it then came almost as a complete surprise when on March 8th 1999, Michael Meacher as Minister for Environment announced, to cheers from the Labour benches in Parliament, that the government proposed statutory legislation protecting individual 'rights' to ramble over designated uncultivated land and upland areas. It may well have been the need to avoid a likely confrontation with the influential pressure groups of Labour Party members and its MPs which finally precipitated this largely unexpected decision to support statutory rights. However, the necessary legislation was drafted, and by March 2000 the Countryside and Rights of Way Bill had its second reading in the Commons, promising public access on a scale, in Meacher's words, 'never before seen', opening up about one-ninth of the land in England and Wales.

For leisure managers, the Right to Roam issue reflects the interaction of various dimensions of power in policy-making; from who is involved as activists and agencies, to how the debate is addressed, developed and presented on the political agenda; to how it relates to existing structural forces at play, whether political, ideological, financial or social. Perhaps the changed national political context of a new administration more than any other factor reduced the power of historic 'insiders' and also gave due recognition to traditional forces of 'outsiders' in promoting wider access. Thus, in policy-making not only must the structural forces of Whitehall and departmental inertia be considered, but also the ethos of the age, which in a media-dominated politics may well prove an all important factor.

Access to Televised Sport

Another aspect of recent intervention fits our earlier designation of regulation of free markets as a key element of social reformist government policy. Leisure policy at the end of the twentieth century was forced to address issues of access to televised sports events.

Since the 1950s, with the massive growth in television ownership, the UK developed to be a nation of TV sports spectators. Secured by the 1966 World Cup and access to colour broadcasts and regular diets of snooker, horse jumping, cricket Test matches and soccer *Match of the Day*, sports television became an integral part of citizen expectation and consumption. Licence fee payers expected to be able to receive key sports events at home and domestic television viewing encouraged the growth of weekend and even mid-week sports match coverage. For post-modern theorists, mass media and mass communications symbolised a figural culture in which many individuals spent increasing free time watching sport and spectating via the TV 'gaze' (Haywood *et al.* 1995).

From a political, and hence a leisure policy perspective, access was not a problem in the 1960s and 1970s when competition for live sports coverage was between the terrestrial broadcasting duopoly of the BBC and ITV. From 1956 they had voluntarily agreed not to seek exclusive broadcasting rights for the following listed events:

- The FA Cup Final
- The Scottish FA Cup Final (in Scotland)
- Wimbledon (the whole Championships)
- All cricket Test matches
- The Derby
- The Grand National
- The Boat Race
- The Olympic and Commonwealth Games (when held in the UK)

The list was reinforced further by legislation in 1981 and 1984, while the FIFA World Cup Finals were added in 1985. Trouble only came with the growth of satellite subscriber viewing in the late 1980s as part of the New Right agenda of deregulating broadcasting from much existing state control.

The historic cosy consensus about sports broadcasting was disturbed by the Broadcasting Act 1990, which in a neo-liberal spirit of deregulation lifted restrictions on the televising of some six national sporting events, allowing bids from satellite TV companies. The consensus was effectively ended by the entrepreneurial initiative of Rupert Murdoch and his 1992 BSkyB purchase of television rights to screen live Premier League soccer games. This was followed by expensive 'captures' of golf, cricket, snooker, darts, a recent bid for horse racing, and most symptomatically, by the summer restructuring of Rugby League to fit his Australian concept of Super League.

This was an important policy challenge to terrestrial broadcasters and governments. To sports governing bodies it gave prospects of huge increases in fees linked to television rights for their competitions to a scale far beyond that encompassed by the historic duopoly. (The current bidding round in April 2000 for the Premier League's package of 66 live games, with an additional 40 matches covered via pay-per-view, should raise well over £1 billion for a three year contract.) It was successful, in that sport above all, drew in millions of viewers to invest and subscribe to Sky TV via satellite and cable. But for politicians it threatened the complete absence of sport from the screens of terrestrial channel viewers and these were their voters. Thus a number of important issues around access to historic viewing 'rights' were raised, particularly around sports events seen as important in cementing national unity and identity, which were to be denied to certain groups in society, who would thus be excluded from national culture. The politics to some extent overcame the paradoxes involved, for people had become accustomed to 'free' sport on TV, rather than expecting similar access to the latest films, drama or theatrical shows. But for politicians the constraint on traditional access to national sports events demanded action.

Even under the New Right Conservative government led by John Major, intervention came as part of the brief of the Department of National Heritage established in 1992. The Ministry quickly confirmed a core of eight key sports events, seen as being an important element in traditional national identity, which were to be protected and accessible on terrestrial TV. These special events had been identified in April 1991 as: the Olympic Games; the football World Cup Finals; the FA Cup Final; the Scottish FA Cup Final; cricket Test matches in England; Wimbledon tennis finals; and horse racing at the Derby and Grand National. While this list is subject to review by the successor Ministry of Culture, Media and Sport, as in 1998, there is no suggestion that it will markedly diminish, and every prospect that the protected list will increase.

From a Conservative Party point of view, state intervention went against the deregulation of most other media activities, but was justified to secure access to nationally important sports events. These were considered significant in heritage terms as contributing to national identity and communal solidarity and hence worthy of specific protection. Reformist New Labour has continued this position, though perhaps more motivated by egalitarian aspects of access, which would otherwise be denied to large numbers of citizens. So, justifying a need to intervene where markets, albeit in sports events, threaten to increase social exclusion and diminish access for large sections of population.

Access, as these two cases show, takes a variety of forms but is likely to be a continuing feature of leisure policy intervention under New Labour. Quite how extensive is their concern with leisure policy will only be established over time, but it may historically be seen as less of a legitimate area for government intervention as a result of the lasting ideological impacts of the New Right era. For leisure managers, however, politics and policy are likely to continue as an important context within which activities in the commercial sector and even more importantly, the public and voluntary sectors, are set.

Summary and Conclusions

Leisure is such a diverse and fragmentary category of behaviour, in great part multidimensional, the result of a myriad of very individual choices based on personal circumstances, preferences and even whim, that to consider anything approaching a rationally organised and explicit comprehensive policy must, for most aspects, appear illusory. The politics of post-modernity is about impression management as much as rational policy-making and problem-solving. Policy has become more the management of conflicting pressures and interests than satisfying needs, so definitions of problems and agendas must increasingly be viewed in the context of prevailing political ideologies and electoral priorities.

Certainly, as leisure is such a demand-led category of behaviour, largely facilitated by an anarchic multiplicity of commercial sector concerns and organisations, then the role of the public sector and public policy has diminished. Intellectually and politically, following an era in the 1980s and early 1990s of neo-liberal individualism, a dominant role for the public sector and particularly the state is now seen as inappropriate and perhaps even offensive. So, public policy has tended to retreat and diminish in the face of an ideology in which the individual consumer knows best and the free market most efficiently and effectively responds and provides. In this chapter the role of public leisure policy has been outlined and the focus has been seen to be more narrowly drawn on access and enabling roles within a context of 'safety net' minimal provision aimed at reducing social exclusion and increasing communal inclusivity.

Another continuing theme has been protection of national identity and heritage, in the face of persistent global influences and trends, which will be examined further in the next chapter. Elsewhere, policy initiatives are seen to be those traditional nineteenth-century state concerns of regulation and license of commercial enterprise which may threaten public order or public good. Throughout, access in all its forms has been a continuing theme of social reformist politicians and seems likely to dominate public policy-making alongside commercial regulation, as the context for leisure and sports management, well into the millennium.

Suggested Tasks for Further Study

1. What are the main arguments advanced by each side in the Right to Roam debate? Set out a balance sheet of factors to be considered both for and against the widening of rural access. What real impact do you consider a statutory set of access rights will have on increasing or widening rural recreation opportunities? What constraints remain to limit rural access?
2. Adapt the idea of pressure groups to the conflicts over access to televised sport. Which groups, organisations or companies would you represent in Figure 7.1? How would this debate fit Lukes' three-dimensional approach to power? What would be the likely arguments to be advanced by each side? What has been the longer-term consequence of the competition for televised sport? Who has won and who has lost out in this power struggle?
3. For a readable introduction to all aspects of politics and ideology the books by Heywood (1997 a and b) *Political Ideologies* and *Politics* are suitable starting points. For more specific material related to politics and policy issues in leisure and sports, Henry (1993) *The Politics of Leisure Policy*, or Veal (1994) *Leisure Policy and Planning*, provide more detailed and applied examples. The most accessible discussion of the evolution of the Right to Roam debates and pressure group activity remains the republished classic Shoard (1997) *This Land is Our Land*. There is less material on television sport, but Whannel (1992) *Fields in Vision*, is a useful, if slightly dated, introduction.

References

- Coates D 1995 D103 Unit 15 *Power and the State* The Open University, Milton Keynes
- Haywood L *et al.* 1995 *Understanding Leisure* Stanley Thornes, Cheltenham
- Henry I P 1993 *The Politics of Leisure Policy* Macmillan, Basingstoke
- Heywood A 1997a *Political Ideologies: An Introduction* Macmillan, Basingstoke
- Heywood A 1997b *Politics* Macmillan, Basingstoke
- Lukes S 1974 *Power: A Radical View* Macmillan, Basingstoke
- Shoard M 1997 *This Land is Our Land* Gaia Books, London
- Spink J 1994 *Leisure and the Environment* Butterworth Heinemann, Oxford
- Veal, A J 1994 *Leisure Policy and Planning* Longman, Harlow
- Whannel G 1992 *Fields in Vision; Television Sport and Cultural Transformation* Routledge, London

Chapter 8

Globalisation

Peter Bramham & John Spink
Leeds Metropolitan University

Chapter Content

- Introduction
- The Six Dimensions of Globalisation
- Case Study: F.A. Premier League Football
- Responses to Globalisation
- Global Firms
- Summary and Conclusions
- Suggested Tasks for Further Study
- References

Abstract

This chapter examines the processes of globalisation in relation to ecological, technological, cultural, social, political and economic change. Students are introduced to the three different levels of analysis – the transnational, the national and the local – and are encouraged to apply the debates about 'glocalisation' to a case study of Premiership soccer. Changes in sport and leisure markets have seen the development of global firms with new business and marketing strategies and students have the opportunity to study further case studies in leisure consumption.

Related Chapter

Chapter 2: Commercial Leisure – an International Perspective: Globalisation has opened up new markets and created new challenges for the commercial leisure sector. This, alongside changing developments in the area of technology and cultural identity, bring these two chapters very closely together.

Learning Objectives

- to introduce students to processes of globalisation
- to study the implications of globalisation for both production and consumption of leisure
- to provide a case study of a global firm and to examine its organisational and management practices

Introduction

A generation ago the ugly word 'globalisation' had not been invented, yet today it is a frequently-used term which has penetrated the vocabulary of politicians, policy makers, advertisers and not least of academics. Robertson (1992:133) has argued that globalisation is a general mode of discourse, a way of thinking about the unity of humankind on planet earth. Leisure events such as Live Aid and Band Aid are clear expressions of such unity and global interconnectedness.

In the 1960s and 1970s, previous models of understanding the world focused primarily on continental geography and spatial differentiation. The world was divided into the main compass bearings of North and South, West and East. Polarisation was central to understanding a world in which writers such as Frank (1971) argued that the *North* (USA, Europe) dominated world markets and benefited from trade exchanges which produced a dependency relationship and maintained economic under-development in the *South* (developing countries in Africa, Latin America and South East Asia).

In the Cold War period, there were deep political divisions between liberal democracies in the West and the state-socialist republics of the USSR in the East. This led writers such as Wallerstein (1979) to analyse the world economy in three 'worlds'. The first world of developed nations constituted the industrial core of knowledge, technological innovation, commerce and financial services. The third world was the periphery of the world economy, usually producing raw materials and foodstuffs in an unequal relationship of trade in which all benefits went to the first world. The semi-periphery of the second world was made up of state-socialist command economies, driven by state planning and production targets, which struggled to compete in industrial and manufacturing markets. This global division of labour produced nation states which had to compete within a world-wide capitalist system with market disciplines of productivity, profitability, flexibility, capital accumulation and speculation in currency exchange rates.

During the 1980s and 1990s, there were fundamental changes to these long-term historical characterisations of the world; when the Berlin Wall fell, communism crumbled, parts of great cities in the developed world came to resemble third world slums, and more manufacturing plant migrated to low-wage economies, which all stimulated thinkers to address the concept of globalisation. The term captured the scale and complexity of the radical changes taking place. It encouraged people to think of the variety of transformations and their impacts at local, national and transnational levels. These dramatic changes can be best thought of in six separate dimensions – ecological, technological, cultural, social, political, and economic.

The Six Dimensions of Globalisation

During the past generation, there has been growing awareness of the *ecological* environment and the global impact of human activities upon a fragile, finite and interdependent biosphere. The emergent environmental issues around population growth, depletion and degradation of natural resources, pollution and the contamination of cities, and not least, global climatic changes, have been highlighted by environmentalist ideologies and green politics. The green movement, led by pressure groups such as Friends of the Earth, World Wildlife Fund and Greenpeace, has demanded conservation measures, controls on traffic and environmental pollution, sustainable economic growth and recycling measures. Effective regulation and environmental performance indicators, policed by international agencies, have been seen as the only realistic long-term option. International conferences (Rio 1992; Tokyo 1998) and not least international pollution, floods and famines increasingly drive home the point that we live in one world. International agencies, nation states, regions and individuals need to adhere to the green slogan of *act local, think global.*

Social action groups and political movements have thus tended to transcend the local and to make common cause at a transnational scale. Some of this activity has been facilitated as the past generation has witnessed a revolution in global technology. The very phrase the 'world wide web' signifies a global network that now transcends language communities, regions, nation-states and continents. Bill Gates' Microsoft Corporation and Rupert Murdoch's News International are not only transnational companies, but also carry more global and economic power than national politicians, who head individual nation states only temporarily. Spatial distance no longer inhibits communication flows and information exchanges, as new technological hardware such as computers, with CD-Rom's, tied into cable and satellite networks, compress time and space and permit instant access to world-wide information sites, including tourist destinations and leisure facilities. In addition, mass communications – TVs, videos, newspapers, as well as personal networks of telephone, fax and mobile phones – facilitate what Giddens terms the 'disembedding' of time and space. Global communication companies, such as Vodaphone and BT, are therefore prepared to offer the UK government up to £20 billion for a radio spectrum to be used by the third generation (3G) of phones which can transmit good quality moving pictures and be permanently connected to the Internet. This market is expected to be worth $200 billion and become the biggest consumer market ever. People are no longer tied into local social networks, timetables and cultures, as they were one or two generations ago. Then, individuals were collective bearers of shared rules and regulations in employment, family or public institutions, all contributing to shared consciousness of imagined communities or national identities.

This brings us to the third element of globalisation – that of *cultural* transformation, particularly, the decline of tradition. Exclusive traditional rituals, folk-based routines and regional ideologies have been exposed to the influence of global communications and global markets. Traditional and religious authority no longer commands the same unquestioning loyalty and respect. Cultural values can no longer be contained and constrained within a single nation state. Boundaries become increasingly porous as they experience growing flows of people, culture, information, goods and services. Appadurai (1990) has pointed to disjunctures in global culture because of diverse flows of people, ideas, media as well as finance and technology. Across the world, partly as a result of such migration flows (it is estimated that 80 million people world wide live in a nation state which is not their 'country of birth/origin') and partly because of ubiquitous global communications, local and national cultures have become coloured by transnational cultural flows.

Gilroy (1993) describes these mixtures as cultural hybridity. One should not think solely of the roots of culture as shared ethnic history, distinctive common language, and unique heritage of dates and landscapes but also as the roots and routes of culture leading to the mixing of 'black' and 'white' cultures. (These processes are analysed by Gilroy in *Ain't No Black in the Union Jack* (1987) and *The Black Atlantic* (1993) through the form of popular music – blues, jazz, rock 'n' roll, pop, rap, garage, jungle music and so on.)

Closely linked to cultural changes are *social* transformations taking place which have loosened the constraints of traditional institutions and local communities on individuals. In these 'new times' individuals are forced to choose between a variety of domestic forms. Social networks, particularly within UK households, become more fragmented, flexible and diverse. Marriage and the family are no longer necessarily sequential, as the percentage of single parents increases. Marriage can be deferred into partner relationships and divorce beckons nearly half contemporary marriages. Household patterns become more complex with longevity, mobility, diversity of lifestyles and sexual identities, encouraging some couples to search for stability outside traditional heterosexual relationships. Reshaping the family at global level, there is what Giddens (1999) terms 'a democracy of emotions' as gender relations change and women collectively gain more autonomy from traditional family roles, formerly ascribed to them by traditional cultures. The individual, both male and female, is confronted with greater personal choice in a quest for intimacy in relationships, and for consumption in lifestyle, leisure, diet and exercise regimes.

Another important expression of political change is the growing importance of trans-national institutions and agencies, such as the European Union. Individual nation states have ceded historic legislative and judicial sovereignty with economic, health, social and environmental policies shaped and developed in Brussels and elsewhere. Despite the principle of subsidiarity in the 1992 Maastricht Treaty, which empowered nation states to develop their own independent policies where appropriate, the overall drift of policy-making has been to harmonise policies in separate nation states of the EU to facilitate flows of both capital and labour and consequently to reduce accordingly national autonomy and state sovereignty.

In the UK, the election of 'New' Labour in 1997 has hastened this process, as the previous Conservative governments of both Margaret Thatcher in the 1980s and John Major in the 1990s had a stronger anti-European and more pro-British stance. The other side of this political coin is the decentralisation of power at regional and local levels, clearly symbolised in 1999 by the devolution of power to a Scottish Parliament and Welsh Assembly, as well as the very gradual evolution of a Northern Ireland Assembly as part of the peace process. The nation state is seen to be too small for big policy decisions and too big for small decisions. Consequently, the power and boundaries of the nation state are slowly being redrawn, as both global and local institutions set agendas and win new policy functions and undermine old arrangements. Policy and political impacts become 'decentred' as there is no longer a single focus or location of power; no single political institution or network of organisations which can take control of, or exercise, undisputed authority over all dimensions of decision-making.

There clearly are also *economic* changes at work in changing global patterns of investment, production, distribution and consumption. Developing economies emerged in the Far East in the 1980s and many of the centres of industrial production, technological innovation and financial services shifted towards the 'tigers' of South East Asia. While labour remains rooted in its historical locations, capital becomes footloose and less loyal to regions and nation states, constantly searching for new markets and places which may prove more profitable (see Bauman 1998). Consequently, many regions in the advanced countries became under-developed, with lack of public and private investment, high levels of unemployment and social dislocation, gathering pace in a vicious downward spiral of de-industrialisation and economic decline. These shifts are mediated by dramatic technological changes in mass communication and information systems. This has been most strikingly demonstrated in the development of financial markets and services. With the possibility of instantaneous global flows of information, financial markets in London, Frankfurt, Hong Kong and New York become part of a 24-hour interconnected business network.

It is important to remember the several processes or dimensions of globalisation. There are distinctive and increasing global flows of finance, capital, technology, ideas, culture, information and not least people. But it is essential not to run away with the idea that globalisation is irresistible and inevitable. Although there is much academic debate about globalisation and its changing impact on everyday life, increased flows in one sphere, say in economic life, may not necessarily mean increasing flows in social, political or cultural life. The effects of globalisation are currently uneven in impacts on national states, regions and cities, not to mention the traditional social divisions of class, gender, race and age.

Case Study: F.A. Premier League Football

What sorts of evidence could you provide to suggest that the processes of globalization, explored earlier through their economic, social and technological impacts, have changed the professional game of football in the UK?

Think about the ways in which soccer has changed during the past two decades. What are the key watersheds in your opinion? – Impacts of European and World Cups; Bosman ruling on player contracts; FIFA rule changes to make the game more 'entertaining'; Heysel, Bradford and Hillsborough disasters; ground relocations and redevelopments; televising live games etc.

Think about globalisation specifically in the context of:

- *The production of football* – the players, squad sizes and wages/contracts; the coaches, managers, directors/owners of clubs, sponsorship deals, merchandising and corporate entertainment; their ground developments, diversification and relocations, and emerging new technologies of admission, policing and surveillance; playing styles; impacts on women's football; racism in football.
- *The consumption of football* – changing class, age, gender profiles of spectators, costs of season tickets, admission prices, membership schemes, of fanzines, newspaper coverage, sports tourism, commodification of playing kit and the merchandising of supporter memorabilia.
- *The involvement of media corporations in the game*, such as global satellite/cable TV companies in the transmission of Premiership, national and international matches; the coverage of Italian Seria A football and Spanish and Dutch league games; the role of terrestrial television and radio coverage; the growth of the Internet and official and unofficial websites, and the potential of pay-to-view as widening the disparities between clubs; media ownership of clubs.

Useful information sources

Carling Opta Index
Deloitte and Touche 1998 *Annual Review of Football Finance*
Mintel 1998 *The Football Business*
Kelly J 1997 *The Official Fans' Guide to the FA Premier League* Carlton Books
Rollin J 1998 *Rothman's Football Yearbook* Headline
Johnson M and Williams J 1996 *Football Fan's Guide* Harper Collins

Norman Chester Research Centre http:\www\ncfrc.com
FIFA HomePage: http:\www\fifa.com

Responses to Globalisation

Although the first section of this chapter has mapped out distinctive processes of globalisation, different writers disagree as to the precise significance of these changes. Anthony Giddens (1999) summarises the debate about globalisation as a division into two extreme camps. The first group he calls 'the sceptics' who argue that talk about globalisation is precisely that, 'all talk'. They question the scale of the global flows and suggest little has changed, as for most people, ordinary lives remain untouched. By way of contrast, the second group takes a radical position by suggesting that globalisation is very real and its consequences are to be felt everywhere. In his own analysis Giddens sides strongly with 'the radicals'. But how useful is his analysis to sport and leisure managers and practitioners? Can managers afford to be sceptical and disregard processes of globalisation or do they need to be sensitive to them so as to maximise the potential of changing markets and new opportunities?

One obvious way forward is the need to contextualise the arguments offered. As with most theory, it may well be that there is no single 'best-fit' between organisational structures and their environments. It therefore becomes essential to understand the different contexts of sport and leisure management so as to assess the relevance of the different and conflicting arguments.

One approach would be to argue that the processes of globalisation are more visible in sport than in leisure. Elite and Olympic sports are used by analysts to illustrate the growing commercialisation of sporting spectacles as heroes and heroines are exposed to global media coverage and interest. In sharp contrast, free-time activities can be seen as more traditional and home-based, closely tied to mundane routine, and embedded in local communities. But this is only part of the story. As soon as one starts talking about elites and excellence in sport, the picture becomes more complicated when set against popular or mass participation in sports. Elite performers may operate on a global scale to a global calendar of sporting events, each fueled and sponsored by world-wide media interests, yet participation in sport for ordinary people is very much about involvement with local teams, following local media coverage and visiting local sports centres. Equally, in the world of leisure, elites may travel to distant cities and sites to pursue and realise diverse and exotic leisure tastes, whereas the mass may be more immobile, confined to local facilities and nearby places.

Even the four-fold categorisation in Table 8.1 is too simplistic to help our understanding of sport and leisure or to inform management and planning strategies. Rather than thinking of *either global or local* perhaps one should be aware of *both the global and the local.* To put it starkly, one must be aware of how global processes find their expression in the local and conversely how local processes respond to and modify the impacts of globalisation. Premiership football teams may be full of international stars, managed by 'foreign' managers, and compete for lucrative European Championship honours but they still reflect and express fierce local identities and roots. Clubs like Sunderland, Millwall, Manchester City, Middlesboro or Newcastle retain their appeal whatever their current league form. The case of Charlton Athletic, with its recent history of relocation and sharing different stadia and the fans' campaign to relocate to their traditional home at The Valley, illustrates the importance of local loyalty and community traditions. BSkyB can lodge a bid of nearly £623 million for Manchester United FC but that bid may meet resistance from national government, local fanzines and supporters' groups. Foreign players can pledge their allegiance by feeling 'at home' playing football in England, just as it seems likely that

Table 8.1 Four-fold categorisation in sport and leisure activities

	Sport	*Leisure*
Elite	Global	Global
Mass	Local	Local

individuals throughout the UK, and indeed the world, will be able to watch, in the near future, all the home matches of the team they support via pay-per-view subscriptions. These subscriptions may be collected via the Internet, through credit card payment, received on digital television, and produced by transnational media companies who already hold substantial investments in the clubs themselves, so transforming the *local* game.

The game of rugby league provides stark illustration of the growth of sport as a global commodity. The traditional history of the game celebrates the decision of a handful of Northern clubs to break away from amateur control of rugby union and to establish their own professional code of play. The heartlands of rugby league were rooted in industrial and mining communities in a few northern towns in Cumbria, Yorkshire and Lancashire. But significantly, rugby league as a sport failed to flourish elsewhere. During decades from the 1960s, the game was seen to be inward-looking, male, working-class and anachronistic. Despite weekly winter coverage on BBC Saturday *Grandstand* and the showpiece of the Wembley Challenge Cup Final, rugby league had a relatively low profile. Sides from the southern hemisphere soundly and consistently beat British teams. A gradual revolution in the nature of the game was engineered. This significant transformation (or more accurately the 'Australianisation') of the game occurred; spearheaded by Rupert Murdoch's sports media empire which bought the rights for BSkyB to televise the game. This resulted in a huge injection of capital into rugby league, the emergence of full-time professional players, new styles of coaching, playing and fitness training, and above all, the influx of players and coaches from the southern hemisphere. Local teams were full of global players. There were also changes demanded by the media with new developments in marketing, the formation and branding of new clubs, the complete reorganisation of the game in three leagues, including a Super League which was committed to play fixtures during the summer. New clubs were invited to play Super League, including creating teams in the metropolitan capitals of London and Paris. Franchise arrangements were encouraged to develop the game in the North-east, as Gateshead Thunder started their first season in 1999, with 13 Australian players and their families, imported for the whole summer.

The relationship between global and local processes becomes complex and that tension is captured by the term 'glocalisation'. This concept represents another cultural hybridisation effect of global change as local cultures and identities resist, negotiate with, and mediate global processes. Indeed, one response to globalisation is to celebrate the local, as a unique place or site, which is distinctive from others. In the field of travel and tourism, this has long been the case as cities, for example, present and represent themselves as unique destinations with distinctive local resources of sport, heritage, popular culture, sea/landscape or visitor attractions. During the past decade Sheffield has shed its industrial past and created a substantial infrastructure to re-image itself as a sporting city capable of hosting international sporting events and securing bids to house major elements of the UK Institute for Sport. Glasgow has presented itself as European City of Culture, while Manchester, Birmingham and virtually every provincial centre have attempted to regenerate economy and attract new investment through emphasising local elements of heritage, arts, culture or sports excellence. Local identity is seen by cities as a valuable commodity in a glocalised world threatened by homogeneous placelessness and anonymity.

Global Firms

In the past, economic processes operated within the boundaries of nation states. Companies organised production locally as they depended upon regional resources of capital, raw materials and labour power, as well as support and subsidies from regional and national development agencies. Consequently, economic organisations were rooted in local communities and capitalists, as employers, were committed to develop local workforces, to be involved in local politics and to invest in works' sports and leisure facilities. Cities too were sustained by a regional hinterland of food production linked into local and regional communication networks. Large-scale industrial production and its bureaucratic organisation were tied to particular places. Even when companies were involved in international markets and in investments abroad, their organisational structures and systems of production were self-contained or reproduced as in the host nation, usually managed and supervised by the parent company.

However, when firms operate in or construct global markets, a truly international division of labour takes place and organisations become more flexible and fragmented. Nike provides a good example as an American-owned company that is solely responsible for marketing and advertising strategy on a global scale. Nike's core business is to think globally and to develop global markets for its products. (For a detailed discussion of Nike's advertising image see Goldman R and Papson S 1998 *Nike Culture*, Sage.) To do so it has not only developed a wide variety of niche markets (for example in trainers) but it also uses world sports stars in football (Ronaldo), tennis (Agassi) and basketball (Michael Jordan) to endorse and promote products on a global scale.

Much creative energy is centred on product innovation and product specialisation. Nike trainer shoes no longer simply function as items of footwear for joggers or runners, but are transformed into symbolic commodities which communicate a particular leisure lifestyle – of youth, resistance and *attitude*. To illustrate the processes of glocalisation, the universal Air Jordon baseball trainers became a distinctive part of the uniform of Chicago youth gangs and the 'street credibility' black rap music stars in the early 1990s. To wear items of Nike sportswear becomes part of the local 'cut and mix' culture of youth styles explored in the writings of Dick Hebdige (1979, 1987, 1988). Youth subcultures have just *got to have* particular items of footwear and clothing, listen to distinctive music styles, and go to particular clubs and bars and so on. To provide another example from inner-city UK, sports development officers found it easy to get basketball programmes off the ground, on condition that they provided the correct labelled brand of trainers for kids to borrow in start-up sessions.

Nike is as much concerned with the cultural messages that its products carry as with the new technologies surrounding their production. In an oligopolistic market, Nike is concerned to distinguish itself from competitors such as Reebok, Adidas or Puma. But it is not simply an American company. It is financed by a Japanese bank. Industrial production is subcontracted to companies in the developing world, such as Korea, Thailand, and China. Contracts to produce Nike trainers are short-term, usually on a year by year basis, so that the parent company can shift production from one nation state to another depending on relevant economic and political factors. Bauman (1998) describes these new global firms as absentee landlords mark II – decisions about the livelihoods of communities are decided elsewhere, since footloose capital can choose globally where to invest. If resistance is met in local customs and working practices or severe political regulation through the social wage or heavy taxation, global companies are free to move elsewhere. Unlike the original absentee landlords who were spatially tied to landed estate ownership and local serf populations, the new absentee landlords and their capital are highly mobile, searching for the best sites and suitable populations for capital accumulation and profitability. To sustain their operations global firms must think and act globally.

If Nike represents a firm which continually seeks global markets by promoting design change and innovation, McDonalds represents a global company which maintains and develops its market share world-wide by standardisation. The chain of McDonald's restaurants operates on an assembly-line or Fordist food production regime which guarantees a standard quality of product and fast-food customer service, wherever the purchasing outlet is situated. Ritzer (1998) argues that McDonald's means rationalisation. (For a full debate about the strengths and weakness of the concept of McDonaldisation see Smart B (Ed) 1999 *Resisting McDonaldisation*, Sage.) Staff training, the restaurant ambiance, the menu and prices have been developed to encourage family visits into fast-food eating as, or as part of, a leisure outing. McDonald's most visible global breakthroughs have been in previous state socialist societies which liberalised during the 1990s, for instance, throughout the USSR, China and Asia. The anxieties and uncertainties of purchasing goods and services melt away as the consumer knows exactly what is on offer. These key features of the McDonald's lifeworld: predictability, efficiency, calculation and control also find direct expression in theme parks such as Disney's. The latter offer family holiday experiences which are sanitised and managed by Disney workers or 'cast members', and predictable tours through a stage set representing Main Street, USA as well as visits to Adventure Land, Lilliputian Land, Fantasy Land, Frontier Land and Holiday Land. So much so that academics write about the McDisneyisation of tourism (Ritzer and Liska 1997). In a globalised world the completely authentic becomes much harder to find and the standardisation of tourism systems of production and consumption seems as universal as those of fast-food chains.

Summary and Conclusions

As this chapter has shown, a radical view suggests that processes of globalisation represent a qualitative and quantitative change in every aspect of life in which, in Marx's memorable phrase, 'all that is solid melts into air'. Facilitated by new technologies, but above all driven by the dynamics of economic change, global capitalism has transmitted the disciplinary effects of profit maximisation, marketisation, privatisation, and even Schumpeter's idea of 'creative destruction', to all parts of the globe.

Economic dynamism has brought inevitable social and cultural transformations which have swept away the old constraints of geographical distance and national boundaries. The transcendent changes have invariably produced a cultural climate of challenge and insecurity for traditional values and customs, as discussed earlier in the chapter, and have involved most individuals in growing exposure to risk (Beck 1992) arising from new uncertainties of both citizenship and consumption.

The fundamental global changes discussed have necessarily been expressed locally in every aspect of life and inevitably impact on elements of leisure, whether TV programmes and channels, publishing, the cinema, sport or holidays. The pace of change continues to accelerate, if you think how many of these formerly relatively static aspects of life have been utterly transformed, even during the last decade. Nothing, whether place, nation or sectors of leisure provision, has escaped these profound changes. Particularly in such an area of discretionary spending of time and money as leisure and sport, global forces have come to be the

Summary and Conclusions continued

dominating influence over all our choices. Managers in leisure and sport must therefore have a clear understanding of the scale and scope of forces operating in so radical and globalised an environment in order to respond adequately to the diverse challenges posed by globalisation.

Suggested Tasks for Further Study

1. Investigate the scope, location and business strategies of major transnational leisure companies, e.g. Sony, Nike, Virgin, Disney and McDonalds:
   - What are the main characteristics of these global companies?
   - What are their policies in respect to branding, marketing, staff and customer care?
   - Do companies that provide products differ in their approach from companies that provide services and tourist experiences?
2. Choose one area of leisure to illustrate the processes of globalisation in leisure markets.

   The precise topic is open to individual choice but the most accessible areas in terms of academic research, market analyses and mass media coverage are:
   - sport – the Olympics, national sporting academies and world sports;
   - tourism – regional and national destinations, cities as tourist destinations, leisure forms, events, places as expressions of regional and national cultural identity;
   - mass media – the production and consumption of 'world music', production and distribution of popular culture (e.g. music, films, TV programmes), Hollywood blockbuster movies.
3. Provide a case study of the interactions between local cultures/national identities and transnational processes – the hybridisation of sport – resistance and assimilation in global markets and international organisations.

   Look at cricket in the Caribbean/Australia; baseball in Japan/Dominican Republic; rugby in South Africa/New Zealand; winter sports in Canada; athletics in Cuba/GDR; Gaelic football in Ireland; or examine the 'hybridity' of popular culture – the production and consumption of leisure goods and services in relation to popular music (e.g. youth styles, clothes, clubs and venues, the production consumption and distribution of musical tastes, domestic and world markets).
4. For a readable and breathtaking account of globalisation, Bauman (1998) *Globalization* provides an introduction. For work on comparative leisure policies, the collection by Bramham *et al.* 1993 *Leisure Policies in Europe*, CAB International, offers a useful introduction to leisure in EU countries. Maguire 1999 *Global Sport* provides a broad sociological discussion of local, national and international processes in sport. Goldman R and Papson S 1998 offer an interesting case study of global advertising of leisure goods in *Nike Culture*, Sage, whereas Barker 1999 *Television, Globalization and Cultural Identities* focuses generally on global television.

References

- Appadurai A 1990 'Disjuncture and difference in the global cultural economy' in Appadurai A 1990 *Global Culture: Nationalism, Globalization and Modernity* Sage
- Arundel J and Roche M 1998 'Media Sport and Local Identity: British Rugby League and Sky TV' in Roche M 1998 *Sport, Popular Culture and Identity* Meyer and Meyer Verlag
- Barker C 1999 *Television, Globalization and Cultural Identities* Open University Press
- Bauman Z 1998 *Globalization* Polity Press
- Beck U 1992 *The Risk Society* Sage Press
- Frank G 1971 *Capitalism and Underdevelopment in Latin America* Penguin
- Giddens A *Runaway World* Reith Lectures BBC April 1999 www.bbc.co.uk/reith99
- Gilroy P 1987 *Ain't No Black in the Union Jack* Routledge
- Gilroy P 1993 *The Black Atlantic: modernity and double consciousness* Verso
- Hebdige D 1979 *Subculture* Methuen
- Hebdige D 1987 *Cut 'n Mix* Comedia
- Hebdige D 1988 *Hiding in the Light* Comedia
- Maguire J 1999 *Global Sport: Identities, Societies, Civilisations* Polity Press
- Ritzer G and Liska A 'McDisneyisation and Post Tourism' in Rojek C and Urry J *Touring Cultures. Transformations of Travel and Tourism* Routledge
- Robertson R 1992 *Globalization* Sage
- Smart B (Ed) 1999 *Resisting McDonaldisation* Sage
- Wallerstein I 1974 *The Capitalist World Economy* Cambridge University Press

Section Three

The Management of Leisure and Sport Organisations

This section is a selected insight into the range of areas that influence the operational and strategic management of leisure and sport organisations. The focus is on the leisure and sport management workplace and covers a wide range of relevant and topical areas. The theoretical underpinning includes functional management (service quality, human resource management), the social psychological aspects of the work place (the management of change), and training and development (working in leisure).

Chapter 9 provides an overview of the current state education and training within leisure and sport management. This is done is five sections. The authors, *Sue Minten* and *Chris Wolsey*, draw upon a range of research to provide a structured framework for understanding the nature of work within this sector. Topics include employment trends in the sector, the nature of working in the sector, the match between employers' needs and graduate skills, and a comparison of the work of leisure and sport managers with other types of management.

Chapter 10 relates very closely to chapter nine. The chapter is titled *Human Resource Management in the Leisure Industry*. The authors *Helen Whitrod Brown* and *Angela Green* focus on the principles of human resource management before moving onto how these principles apply to the leisure and sport management context. A main theme running through the chapter is employee development. This is located within the more general theme of training and development. A range of useful techniques and models are also presented which provides a number of helpful prescriptions of how to deal with human resource issues.

Chapter 11 discusses the very topical issue of service quality within the leisure and sport management context. Much of what has been previously discussed is relevant within this chapter. Increased consumer expectations, globalisation, shifts in consumer behaviour, increased accountability and the need to do more with less all have relevance in relation to quality management. The author, *Leigh Robinson*, discusses the phenomenon of quality management with a particular focus on public sector leisure provision. The chapter includes a brief history of this development and the issues that arise out of the quality arena. Quality management is then critiqued within the public sector context identifying the strengths and areas for concern within the sector.

Chapter 12 provides the final chapter and is entitled *The Management of Change in the Leisure and Sport Sector*. The chapter provides an overview of relevant literature and attempts to apply these theories, concepts and practices to the leisure and sport management context. The chapter draws heavily on the generic management literature ranging from prescriptive solutions to complex problems to more critical reviews of the theory and practice of change management. The author, *Jeff Abrams*, uses a range of examples throughout the chapter to relate the theories, concepts and models presented to the leisure and sport management context. Many of the themes explored in the previous chapters are directly relevant to the issues of management of change and many of the drivers for change are highlighted throughout the book (commercialisation, the changing work patterns of leisure professionals, globalisation, public policy, human resource management, quality management).

Chapter 9

Working in Leisure

Sue Minten
The University of Wolverhampton
Chris Wolsey
Leeds Metropolitan University

Chapter Content

Abstract

The leisure industry's future development relies on having a labour force with the correct skills and knowledge. One of the key debates, in this area, is the extent to which the current provision of education and training matches the needs of the industry. However, the concept of matching education and training to the needs of the leisure industry is not as simple as it sounds and can be broken down into further key issues. This chapter will examine each of those issues in order to provide a fundamental understanding of the provision of education and training and how it relates to the needs of the leisure industry.

The first section outlines current employment trends in the leisure industry; this leads into the second section, which briefly discusses whether or not leisure is a glamorous industry to be employed in. The third section provides an overview of the historical development of the leisure manager's job and the skills and competencies needed. This develops into a discussion, in the fourth section, of the nature of leisure management and whether or not it differs to other areas of management.

The fifth section defines education and training, as a foundation to outlining and critically analysing the current structure of education and training provision for the leisure industry. This includes professional and vocational qualifications and HE provision. A specific debate that is examined in the sixth section is whether or not leisure is a graduate profession, this draws on research undertaken by SPRITO and the HE Standing Conference for Leisure, Recreation and Sport commissioned by the Department for Education and Employment (DfEE).

The final section concludes by providing a statement of the current position of the *leisure profession* in terms of status and education and training.

Related Chapters

It would be disingenuous to claim that this chapter is not, in some way, connected to every single chapter and, thus, section within this book. If you read it carefully, *Section One* provides insight into a range of knowledge and personal attributes needed by each of the leisure sectors under review. Similarly, *Section Three* provides insight into the functional skills, abilities, knowledge and understanding needed by both existing and future leisure managers, regardless of whether employed in the public, commercial or voluntary sectors. The key is to keep learning in ways that are instrumental to future personal and career development objectives. All knowledge is transferable when time is taken to think and review the less obvious implications.

Learning Outcomes

- to examine the employment trends in the leisure industry
- to provide an insight into the nature of employment in the leisure industry
- to undertake a critical analysis of the provision of education and training within the leisure industry
- to discuss the employability of graduates in the leisure industry
- to examine the claims of leisure management to be a profession

Introduction

During the past two decades government policy has promoted a belief in the ability of the market to yield the most desirable allocation of resources. This ideological shift has meant a fundamental repositioning of the public, voluntary and commercial leisure sectors. During this time, the nature of leisure provision has become increasingly diverse, particularly within the commercial sector.

The UK worker, typically, works more hours than his/her European counterpart. Those who hypothesised a future of increased leisure time have clearly misjudged the power of technology to replace people in the continual quest for economic growth and global resource sustainability. Paradoxically, the leisure industries are a particularly good exemplar of this trend. If one compares this with a general rise in living standards and disposable incomes, it is not difficult to explain the inexorable rise in leisure provision and thus employment in this increasingly important area of the economy.

Table 9.1 Employment in leisure-related services (thousands)

Service	*1988*	*1989*	*1990*	*1991*	*1992*	*1993*	*1994*	*1995*	*1996*	*1997*	*1998*
Hotel and other accommodation	286	309	318	307	309	319	332	341	331	301	292
Restaurants, cafes, etc.	260	289	308	286	296	305	321	333	341	346	361
Bars, pubs, club	406	433	448	442	400	374	366	400	388	437	430
Travel agencies, tour operators	63	68	72	70	69	69	72	84	84	96	110
Libraries, museums	82	81	77	75	72	76	82	77	77	80	86
Sport and recreation	297	301	313	319	312	317	318	312	315	326	327
Total	1394	1481	1536	1499	1458	1460	1491	1547	1536	1586	1606

Source: Department of Employment 1989–1999: *Employment Gazette/Labour Market Trends*

Leisure Employment

In terms of employment, the leisure sector is more important to the UK economy than industries such as engineering, financial and business services and the chemical, mineral and metals industries. General employment trends show that manufacturing jobs are in decline and are being replaced by service sector jobs such as leisure (DfEE 1998). Table 9.1 shows the trends in employment in leisure-related services since 1988. The table indicates the range of leisure employment areas, indicating a general upward trend for employment in the sector, with the exception of a slight downturn in 1992–93 due to economic recession. Within the upward trend there has been variation between areas, with relatively greater increases in employment such as restaurants, travel and sport compared to other areas of leisure. It is important to note that this data may underestimate employment in the sector, as leisure can be defined more widely than has been presented in Table 9.1. However, due to the fragmented nature of the industry, government employment statistics include elements of leisure employment under a range of headings and it is difficult to tease out exact figures.

The projections for the leisure industry, over the next four years, are for increased leisure spending with particularly high growth in leisure in the home. High growth is also forecasted in overseas holidays, sightseeing, eating out and active sport (*Leisure Forecasts* 1998–99). The resilience of the leisure sector, to the anticipated economic downturn, will determine the impact of such predictions upon leisure employment trends. Whilst home based leisure is a particular characteristic of recession, this may have a differential impact upon employment patterns. Out of home entertainment is often curtailed as consumers look to less expensive forms of leisure until they perceive a future of greater economic stability and prosperity.

A Glamorous Industry?

> *Managerial work in leisure seems to offer many young people the promise of a dream world career.*
> (Bacon and Pitchford 1992:167)

Leisure is often portrayed as a glamorous industry. However, although this may reflect reality for some, the majority of leisure workers are fully aware of the misleading impression such assertions can give. Bacon and Pitchford (1992:174) investigated the actualities of work in the industry and found that much of the work was 'stressful, boring, routine, badly paid and unexciting'. This view is sustained by the Association of Graduate Careers Advisory Services (1997), who highlight the stressful nature of work in this area and the requirement to work long and unsocial hours. Moreover, Davies (1996:249), commenting on the changing employment climate of the sports manager, contends:

> *No longer will they have life-long careers with one organisation . . . They will have short-term contracts, temporary and part-time work with self-funded periods of unemployment and long-term self-provision for their old age.*

However, Bacon and Pitchford (1992) do identify some major satisfiers of employment in the industry. These satisfiers include meeting and working with people, not being confined to an office, the use of leisure facilities while at work and being part of an exciting and generally profitable industry.

As discretionary spend rises, the use of leisure time becomes increasingly sophisticated for the money rich, time poor consumer. As public expectations increase and the market becomes saturated, one of the key differentiators of success will be the people who operate within leisure organisations. There is now a recognition, across all three sectors, of the need to be more 'professional'. In the 1990s, the main distinctions between the public, commercial and voluntary sectors remain intact but are facing a number of both internal and external pressures to reform. Partnership and synergy are the buzzwords of the new millennium. However, whether this signals the rise of a leisure profession is open to debate.

The Leisure Manager: Occupation or Profession?

> *The concept of leisure management is a relatively new one which was rarely heard until the early 1980s when it started to subsume and replace a variety of older terms including sports management, recreational management, countryside management and tourism management . . . Leisure in short is probably the last area of social life which still awaits to feel the full colonising zeal of the professional imperialist.*
>
> (Bacon 1989:2)

The Yates Report (1984:82) viewed a 'profession' as an area that has a recognised body of theoretical knowledge, 'entry being dependant on a substantial period of systematic study, its application in practice, applied study and achievements'. While there are optimistic signs that the leisure industry is continuing to grow, there is only limited empirical evidence available vis-à-vis the knowledge, skills and competencies required by those that work within it. Whilst Davies (1996:251) argues that 'the ingredients for success . . . are axiomatic', the reality is somewhat more complex and subjective.

Clearly, the challenges facing the leisure industry have a direct effect upon organisational development and thus management development in this area. Whilst both factors may drive change forward, it is the symbiotic relationship achieved between the individual, the organisation and the external environment that is critical to future performance. Organisations are abstract entities. As such, it is the people that provide purpose, direction and passion. Management development activities should provide a broad focus for future organisational development. Despite this, commenting on the provision of appropriate courses for recreational managers of the time, McKinney (1984:10) argues:

> *The current disarray in training provision reflects many of the controversial issues which have beset the development, education and training in management over the past 30 years.*

Unfortunately, such arguments have an irrefutable resonance some 15 years later! Whilst the debate now reflects a much greater commercial focus, there is still evidence to suggest that,

> *a characteristic of paid employment in sport and recreation . . . is that a premium is placed on qualities such as personal effectiveness, communication skills, customer care and enthusiasm for a sport, even to the extent that the possession of more formal qualifications is disregarded.*
>
> (Sport and Recreation Industry Lead Body 1989:6)

This point is echoed by more recent evidence. Potter (1993) argues that a proven track record is at least as important as a formal academic background. Moreover, he argues that the commercial sector are even less interested in formal qualifications. Coalter and Potter (1990) found that 38 per cent of those working in the area of sport and recreation had no formal qualifications. This is ironic, as an industry that is fighting for professional status continues to marginalise the role of education within the training function. Paradoxically, this comes against a backdrop of a burgeoning educational and training sector. Clearly, an understanding of the dynamic that exists between the two should, in part, help explain the apparent contradictions.

Understanding the Management of Sport, Recreation and Leisure

There are a plethora of definitions that seek to establish the nature of both 'leisure' and 'management'. The Yates Report (1984:v), using definitions derived from the 1975 Government White Paper *Sport and Recreation* defined recreation as, 'any life enhancing experience that is the outcome of freely chosen activity' and management as, 'the control of resources within an organisation'. However, perhaps surprisingly, there were some major omissions from the study. For instance, the whole area of cultural recreation, whilst being within the remit of the operational definitions provided, was overlooked by the report. Moreover, the explosion in commercial leisure over the past 15 years is not anticipated and given little consideration. The Management Charter Initiative argues that management should seek to be measured against organisational objectives within a cycle of continuous improvement. This assumes, of course, that the objectives are clearly articulated, realistic and achievable. Naturally, objectives are rarely static and reflect the fluidity of the organisation's environment. The role of the manager will vary in this regard, depending upon their place in the organisation's structure and the impact of organisational culture upon approaches to empowerment and decision-making. Whilst Torkildsen (1997) argues that managers should also exhibit leadership qualities, there are managers who provide more of an administrative role, either through personal preference or mitigated by the role expectancies and/or micro-politics of the organisation. We shall take the position that management entails all those activities designed to efficiently mobilise available resources, in order to achieve the explicit/implicit objectives of the organisation. Clearly, such a definition allows a wide interpretation of those who are considered to be engaged in managerial activity.

The juxtaposition of the words 'leisure' and 'management' creates a number of interesting questions. As May and Botterill (1984:20) assert:

> *Why should recreation management be different, has it got such an unusual or unique level of knowledge that general management training does not apply to it? . . . We are kidding ourselves if we believe that recreation management requires such*

a unique body of knowledge that the existing management course cannot meet the demand. In this profession we need generalists from all the fields who can adapt, not specialists.

Thomas (1992) outlines the changing nature of management skills within the public recreation sector. He argues that public sector managers must become more commercial in their outlook. This represents a considerable departure from the founding principles of this important area of leisure provision. It is clear that there is a shift in the type of skills and knowledge required by contemporary leisure managers. The provision of appropriate education and training opportunities is central to this debate.

The Provision for Education and Training

Harrison (1992:4) defines education as something that, 'directly and continuously affects the formation not only of knowledge and abilities, but also of character and of culture, aspirations and achievement'. The Yates Report (1984:v) defined education in relation to training and described it as, 'a much broader process, where the end objective is not usually narrowly identified, and which is not solely orientated towards performance in a particular job'. As such, education is seen as a wider concept than catering for occupational requirements in isolation. Nevertheless, education is seen increasingly as an economic good and as a means of improving employment prospects. An illustration of this is Higher Education (HE) under the influence of the 1987 White Paper *Higher Education: Meeting the Challenge*, which outlined the Thatcher Government's aspirations for HE to serve the economy more effectively by achieving greater commercial and industrial relevance in HE activity. The aim was to ensure undergraduates developed competencies and aptitudes relevant to the workplace, with particular attention to transferable skills. This emphasis remains evident today. The Higher Education Quality Council (1996), stated that HE has an instrumental purpose, with the emphasis on the production of graduates to meet the needs of the economy.

Training has traditionally been seen as the antithesis to education in that it relates directly to work. Yates (1984:v) defined training as, 'a process in which staff are given the opportunity to improve and develop their occupational knowledge and skills', while Reid and Barrington (1996:57) believe that, 'training aims to provide the learner with the knowledge, skills and attitudes necessary to carry out work tasks'. Parker (1984), recognised this debate in his response to the Yates Report and described the structure of leisure education and training as a continuum (Figure 9.1).

Parker's diagram illustrates that only at either end of the continuum can education and training be completely distinguished. Most courses could be placed along the line of the continuum. This illustrates how complicated and fragmented leisure education and training provision is, with many different organisations, both academic and vocational, having a potential input into the learner's choice and opportunities. While there will always be an overlap between education and training it is important to retain the key distinctions. For some, however, there is a perception that the boundaries between the two are becoming irreconcilably blurred. Leisure management provides an important example of this trend.

Figures 9.2 and 9.3 show the range of education and training qualifications, and the providers, available for leisure and illustrates the bewildering array of career pathways a leisure manager could take. It could be argued that this range of pathways creates choice. Conversely, if choice is clouded by confusion, the benefits are more difficult to interpret.

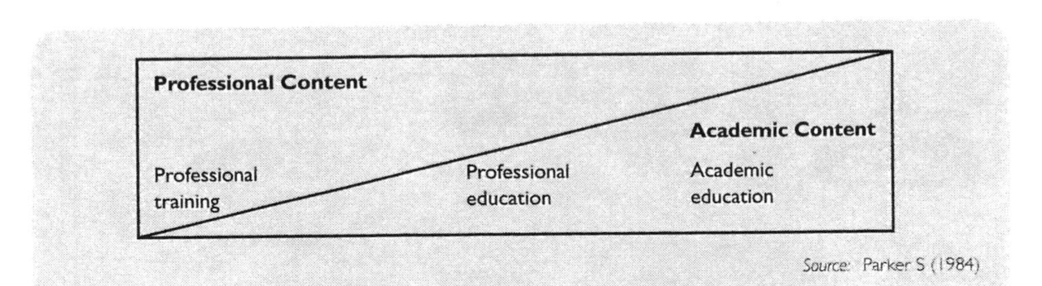

Figure 9.1 The education and training continuum

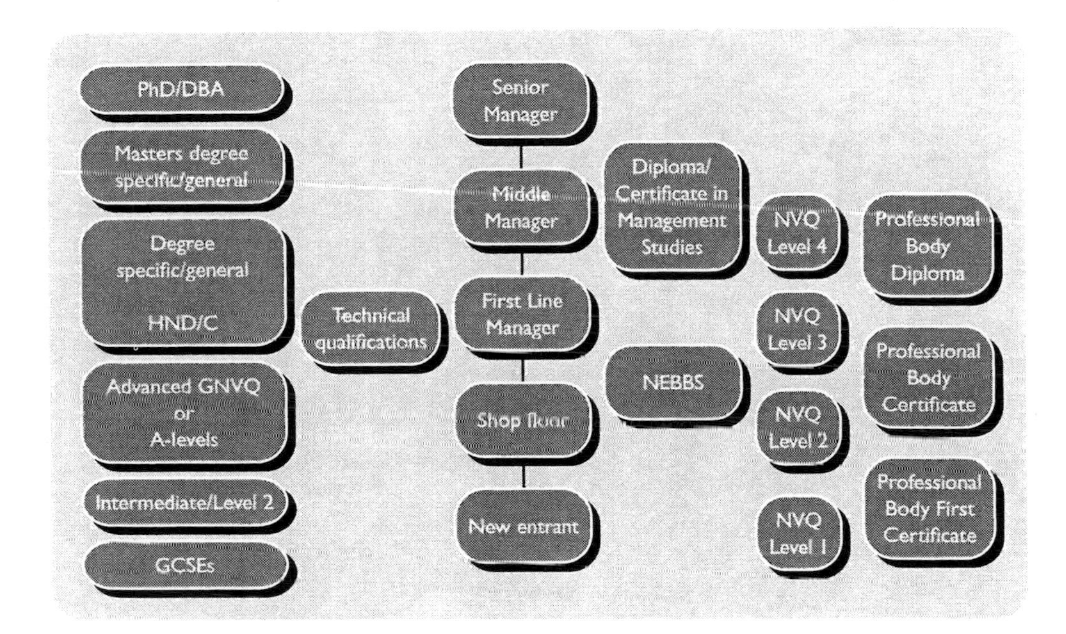

Figure 9.2 The range of academic and vocational qualifications in leisure management

Kitts (1995), in a survey of local authority leisure managers, found that they were confused about the level of qualification appropriate to them. Further compounding this point is the question of equivalence between qualifications and transferability across pathways. It may be possible to theoretically map out these equivalencies, but the crux is how they are actually perceived by employers, education providers and aspiring/practising managers. This is not a new problem as the Yates Report (1984:116) previously raised the issue and as part of its recommendations demanded that, 'it is vital that provision for recreation management development, education and training be viewed as a coherent, planned and collaborative process'. If leisure management is to continue its claim to be a profession then the confusion over the structure of education will need to be addressed.

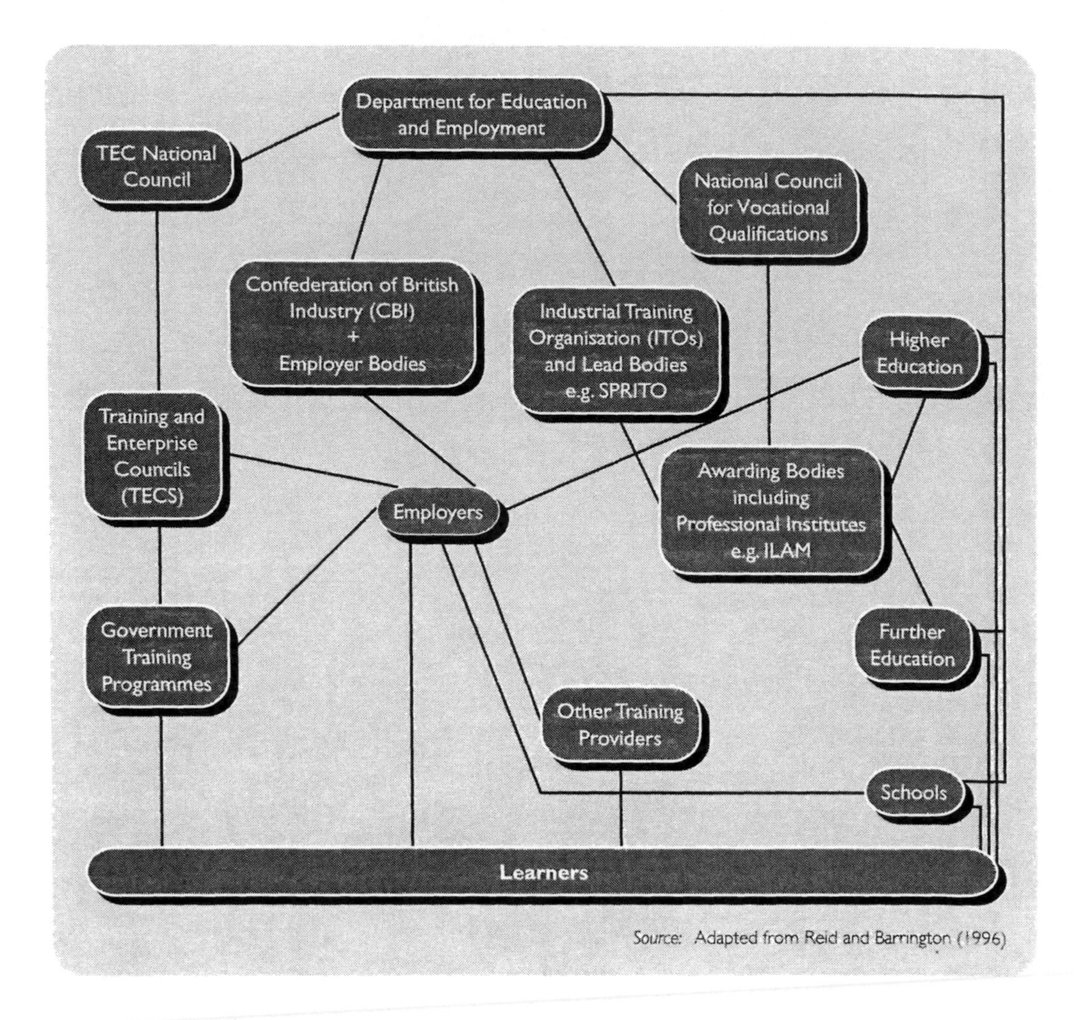

Source: Adapted from Reid and Barrington (1996)

Figure 9.3 The providers of training and education in the UK

A Graduate Profession?

One of the key issues within education and training provision for leisure management is the employability of leisure graduates within the industry. This can be broken down into two fundamental points, as below:

- Is there an oversupply of leisure graduates for the jobs available?
- Do those graduates have the right skills and knowledge?

This section will examine this in the context of the sport and recreation sector of the leisure industry using research commissioned by the DfEE, investigating graduate employability (Hansen, Minten and Taylor 1998).

As already identified, HE has shifted its emphasis towards vocational education. This has not only been caused by government pressure, but also by the creation of a mass higher education system. Slee (1989:63) believes that HE has become a multi-functional activity that addresses three sets of needs, 'the need to safeguard the autonomy of knowledge;

the needs of the state measured by highly qualified manpower; and the needs of the individual'. Therefore, the employability of graduates has become a valid area for debate within HE leisure provision.

The concern for oversupply stems from the fact that the leisure subjects are the fastest expanding and most popular disciplines in HE, particularly sports-related courses (Hansen *et al.* 1998). According to the study, there are currently 160 degrees operating in 80 institutions and 79 postgraduate degrees in 20 institutions. This is likely to be an underestimate as both higher and further education establishments seek to exploit the increasing demand in this area.

Exacerbating this concern is the fact that sport and recreation management has not been considered a traditional graduate profession. Studies in the past have concurred that a degree was not viewed by leisure managers as a particularly relevant qualification (Yates 1984; Veal and Saperstein 1977; Murphy 1980). There is now debate as to whether or not this is still the case. Hansen *et al.* (1998) found that some employers specifically recruited graduates for the benefits they would bring, whilst others saw them as giving no added value to the organisation. The study also found, in common with a similar study by the CNAA (1991), that there was no recognised entry level for graduates. Both reports concluded that this was probably due to a lack of understanding by employers of the nature of degrees and the perception that graduates did not have any 'immediately applicable job related skills' (Hansen *et al.* 1998:4).

This issue is not confined to sport but all sectors of the economy, the DfEE (1998) stated that full-time undergraduate enrolments increased by 70 per cent between 1989 and 1995. One outcome of this expansion has been that there is now no such thing as a graduate level job. Pike, Connor and Jagger (1992) identified that a wider range of employers are taking on graduates, though not into positions that would have been considered graduate jobs in the past. Sport and leisure is a reflection of this trend. The expansion in graduate recruitment in non-traditional jobs may be because of the need for greater knowledge and skills in employees, or may simply reflect the fact that there is a larger pool of graduates available and, therefore, greater competition among applicants.

The second issue is whether or not HE sports courses produce graduates with appropriate vocational attributes (Bacon 1995). Studies on wider graduate employment found that many employers wanted generalist graduates rather than specialists (Government Interdepartment Review 1990; Rigg 1990; Harvey *et al.* 1997). In these studies employers seemed more concerned about the personal qualities of the individual, as opposed to the specific skills they could bring to the organisation. The recent annual review from the Institute of Employment (reported by Howard 1999) reports that only a minority of jobs ask for specific degrees. Softer skills and behavioural characteristics are seen to be more important. Hansen *et al.* (1998) also found this to be the case with many sports employers. They found that the aptitudes needed by graduates were interpersonal and communication skills, self-motivation, the ability to work independently, time management, flexibility, adaptability and the ability to work in a team. It was also identified that for graduates to get a first foothold in the industry they would require technical skills in areas such as first aid, coaching, information technology and, above all else, some experience of working in a service environment.

Hansen *et al.* (1998) found that 82 per cent of the sports graduates surveyed gained employment, 43 per cent in sport jobs, 21 per cent as PE teachers and 36 per cent in other industries. The majority of the other 18 per cent undertook further study. These employment figures compare favourably with the findings from other studies on general graduate employability (Levy and Mackenzie 1996). There was also positive findings on the vocational attributes of sports graduates. The study found that of graduates who gained employment in the sports industry, nearly half felt that they gained all or most of the appropriate knowledge and 44 per cent felt that they had gained all or most of the appropriate skills. Only a small percentage felt that they had not gained any appropriate skills and knowledge. Also of interest was that for those graduates who found employment outside of the industry a quarter felt that they had gained all or most of the appropriate skills whilst 66 per cent felt that they had gained some. This illustrates that sport and recreation courses may enable graduates to develop skills that are transferable across industries.

The main difficulty regarding employability of graduates in the sports industry are the perceptions of students and graduates. First, the study found that graduates do not appreciate the importance/relevance of the graduate skills developed in the degree until they have actually gained employment. Hence, when applying for jobs, graduates are unable to articulate their transferable aptitudes to an employer. This point was supported by sport and recreation employers who felt that graduates do not make it explicit in application forms the skills they have developed.

Second, graduates have a high expectation of the level at which they will gain entry to sport employment, believing they will either obtain a management or trainee management position, which is not usually the case. The study found that most graduates start on the shop floor or in a specialist position such as an assistant sports development officer. The problem is that most graduates become bored and disillusioned when entering at this level. As a consequence, graduates moved jobs several times in their first three years of employment. Not surprisingly, some employers see graduates as disloyal and too highly qualified for a shop floor position. Unless graduates develop vocational competencies during their studies, a catch 22 situation develops in which graduates find it difficult to obtain the requisite levels of experience to facilitate career progression.

The study found that the sector that employed the most graduates were local authorities, supporting a similar report by Coalter and Potter (1990). The increasing provision for sport by the commercial sector is reflected in graduate recruitment with Hansen *et al.* (1998) reporting 32 per cent of the graduates surveyed being employed there, compared to Coalter and Potter's findings of 25 per cent. In this context, Wolsey (1996) presents evidence to suggest that the commercial leisure sector are more likely to provide graduate career structures, within the wider leisure related area of work. Such frameworks have the potential to balance the graduate need for both experience and challenge. Hansen *et al.* (1998) also found graduates were more likely to be employed by larger organisations and this is likely to increase with organisations like Granada, David Lloyd and the Village group developing facilities in sport, health and fitness.

The study concluded that sport and recreation is not yet a graduate profession and suggested many reasons for this. However, the main reason must be that the sector is still immature and has not traditionally been a graduate employer. It will take a period of time for graduates to colonise this profession. The challenge is for the industry and education to work together to ensure that graduates are grounded in the appropriate skills and knowledge, whilst employers make effective use of them.

Summary and Conclusions

> *Leisure managers need to be good advocates. We need to tell, sell and profess our profession . . . 'Real' professionals do not have to rely on structure, but inner strength, insight (inner sight), confidence, competence and calm assurance; none the less, leisure management should assert itself as a leading, different, 21st century profession.* (Torkildsen 1997:14)

Post-modern society is increasingly questioning the role and status of traditional professions. Kerfoot (1998:35) argues that 'Professionals working within leisure . . . are increasingly accountable to their clients ("citizens")'. This reflects a public sector bias to the current discourse surrounding continuing professional development. Despite the above battle cry of Torkildsen (1997), it is clear that it is unrealistic for leisure to claim professional status on the basis of its increasing economic and social importance alone.

This chapter has demonstrated the disparate nature of leisure occupations and the bewildering array of qualifications available to those working within it. The provision of appropriate training and education at different levels of the organisational hierarchy is a complex and dynamic process. For example, Pilkington (1998:23), commenting upon the developing area of health and fitness employment throughout Europe, argues that '. . . although there were areas of good practice in a number of countries, no one nation could say it had all the elements of a professional industry'.

In a seminal paper, Wilensky (1964) argues that all occupations exist on a continuum of professionalisation. The position of any one area varies through time from occupation to semi-professional to professional status. For leisure, one of the key indicators must be the development of a professional association under Royal Charter. However, there are a confusing array of representative bodies in this area.

The Institute of Leisure and Amenity Managers and the Institute of Sport and Recreation Management have histories and membership profiles which are biased towards the public sector. Business in Sport and Leisure, reflects commercial interests whilst the National Training Organisation, SPRITO, have control over the development of occupational standards, in co-operation and partnership with bodies such as the National Coaching Foundation and the British Olympic Committee. The UK Higher Education Standing Conference in Leisure, Recreation and Sport reflects the interests of education. Notwithstanding developments in more specialists areas such as health and fitness, there are those managers, particularly from the commercial sector, who are more likely to align themselves with more established 'professional' bodies such as the Institute of Management or Institute of Marketing. Such heterogeneity belies a coherent and unified leisure profession.

Those working in leisure should not become preoccupied with attaining professional status in the short to medium term. At best, the leisure profession is currently at an embryonic stage. The issues outlined during this chapter are fundamental to the development of a leisure profession in the longer term, although the value of attaining such status is increasingly questionable. What is clear is that the leisure industry, if indeed this actually exists, must work in partnership to achieve the goals and aspirations of tomorrow. Without such co-operation it is difficult to see how the industry will achieve its true potential.

Suggested Tasks for Further Study

1. Interview someone employed in the leisure industry and include the following points:
   - main dissatisfiers of their job
   - main satisfiers of their job
   - main areas of knowledge needed
   - main skills needed
   - what qualifications they have obtained.
2. Collect ten job advertisements for jobs in one sector of the leisure industry and identify the main attributes that the organisations ask for.
3. Undertake a self-analysis of the skills and qualifications that you possess.
4. Identify an area of leisure employment that you would be interested in working in. Find out the skills and qualifications needed to gain employment in that area of work. Using the results from task 3 draw up an action plan of how you would gain any remaining relevant attributes.
5. Visit the ILAM website on careers in the leisure industry: www.ilam.org.uk.

References

- Association of Graduate Careers Advisory Services 1997 *Graduate Careers Information: Leisure Management* AGCAS, Manchester
- Bacon W 1989 'The Professionalisation of Leisure Management' in White J (Ed) 1989 *The Leisure Industry: Leisure, Labour and Lifestyles: International Comparisons* Volume 10 LSA Conference Papers No.41 LSA Publications, Brighton
- Bacon W and Pitchford A 1992 'Managerial Work in Leisure: A Deconstruction' in Sugden J and Knox A (Eds) *Leisure in the 1990s: Rolling Back the Welfare State* Publication No.46, LSA Publications, Brighton
- Bacon W 1995 *Accreditation: Key Issues and Questions for ILAM* Paper presented at ILAM National Education and Training Conference, Stoke 9–10 November 1995
- CNAA 1991 *Review of Sport, Recreation and Leisure Degree Courses* Council for National Academic Awards, London
- Coalter F and Potter J 1990 *A Study of 1985 Graduates from Sport, Recreation and Leisure Studies* Sports Council, London
- Davies I 1996 *The Successful Sports Manager: Ins and Outs* Proceedings of the Fourth European Congress on Sport Management, Montpellier pp.249–253
- Department for Education and Employment 1988 *Labour Market and Skill Trends 1998–1999* DfEE Publications
- Hansen A, Minten S and Taylor P 1998 *Graduate Recruitment and Development in the Sport and Recreation Industry* DfEE/SPRITO/UK Standing Conference for Leisure, Recreation and Sport
- Harrison R 1992 *Employee Development* Institute of Personnel Management London
- Harvey L, Moon S and Geall V 1997 *Graduates Work: Organisational Change and Student Attributes* Centre for Research into Quality, University of Central England, Birmingham
- Howard S 1999 'It's not what you know, it's how you behave that counts' in *The Sunday Times* 24 January 1999 p.7.24
- Kerfoot R 1998 'Gulf Course' *The Leisure Manager* November 1998 pp.35–37

- Kitts C 1995 'Managing Change and Changing Managers' in Leslie D (Ed) *Tourism and Leisure: Towards the Millennium* Vol 2 Tourism and Leisure – Perspectives on Provision, LSA, Brighton
- Leisure Industries Research Centre 1998 *Leisure Forecasts 1998–2002* Leisure Industries Research Centre
- Levy M and MacKenzie K 1996 *The Class of '92* Scottish Graduates Careers Partnership, University of Glasgow
- *Management Charter Initiative* Institute of Management's 'Leader' Series candidate guidelines circa 1995
- May and Botterill 1984 'An American Perspective' in Mckinney G R (Ed) 1984 *op. cit.*
- Mckinney G R (Ed) 1984 *Yates and After: The Management of Recreation Management and Training* Leisure Studies Association November 1984
- Murphy W 1980 *Recreation Managers: Current Practitioners in Local Government and Industry* The Centre for Leisure Studies, University of Salford
- Parker S 1984 'The Core of Leisure Studies' in McKinney G R (Ed) 1984 *op. cit.*
- Pike G, Connor H and Jagger N 1992 *The IMS Graduate Review Report 232 Review of Post-graduate Education* IMS, Bristol
- Pilkington A 1999 'Cultural Exchange' in *Health Club Management* January 1999 p.23
- Potter J 1993 *A Guide to Jobs and Qualifications in Sport and Recreation* John Potter Publications in association with ILAM
- Reid M, A and Barrington H, 1996 *Training Interventions: Managing Employee Development* (4th Ed) Institute of Personnel Management, London
- Rigg M, Elias P, White M and Johnson S 1990 *An overview of the demand for graduates* HMSO, London
- Slee P 1989 'A Consensus Framework' in Ball C and Eggins H (Eds) *Higher Education into the 1990s: New Dimensions* Open University Press, Milton Keynes
- Sport and Recreation Lead Body 1989 *Mapping Sport and Recreation* 7 June 1989
- Thomas 1992 *ILAM 1992 Conference Report, Leisure Under New Management* Harrogate International Conference Centre ILAM Services Ltd, 29 June–1 July 1992
- Torkildsen G 1997 'Who Needs Leisure Managers?' in Collins M F and Cooper I S 1997 *Leisure Management: Issues and Applications* CAB International, Wallingford, Oxon
- Veal A and Saperstein H 1977 *Recreation Managers in Britain: A Survey* working paper 56 CURS, Birmingham
- Wilensky H L 1964 'The professionalization of everyone' in *American Journal of Sociology* Vol.LXX No.2 September 1964
- Wolsey C 1995 'From Theory to Practice and Back Again: An Investigation into the Development of Recreation Management Courses within Higher Education' in Fleming S, Talbot M, Tomlinson A 1995 *Policy and Politics in Sport, Physical Education and Leisure* LSA Publication, No.55 pp.325–350
- Wolsey C 1996 'The Changing Nature of Employment for the Leisure Graduate' paper given to the Leisure, Time and Space in a Transitory Society Conference Leisure Studies Association, Wageningen, The Netherlands, 4–12 September 1996
- Yates A 1984 *Recreation Management Training Committee: Final Report* HMSO, London

Chapter 10

Human Resource Management in the Leisure Industry

Helen Whitrod Brown & Angela Green
Leeds Metropolitan University

Chapter Content

- Introduction
- HRM Philosophy
- HRM Functions
- Leisure Industry Context
- Employee Development (ED)
- Training and Development
- Theoretical Approaches to Training
- Training in the Leisure Industry
- Skills/Competence Development
- Continuing Professional Development (CPD)
- The Learning Environment
- Summary and Conclusions
- Suggested Tasks for Further Study
- References

Abstract

The chapter begins with an overview of Human Resource Management (HRM) to introduce the reader to the guiding principles. The leisure industry is examined in relation to the topic area and the main features of Employee Development (ED) outlined. The focus then turns towards a more detailed discussion of training and development and its relevance to HRM in the context of the leisure industry. An analysis of current practice drawn from interviews with practitioners directs the reader's attention to the most pertinent issues facing the industry, its managers and its employees.

Related Chapters

Chapter 1: The Public Sector, Best Value and Local Authority Sports Development: HRM models can be contrasted with the realities of working within a public sector sports development department. Definitions of HRM can be contrasted with the attitudes of employees. These include a lack of motivation, the perception of limited career development opportunities, a less than supportive management hierarchy and a system of control that stifles individual autonomy and creativity.

Chapter 6: Strategy, Competition and the Commercial Leisure Markets: The rhetoric espoused by prescriptive HRM approaches, can be compared with the section in chapter six which takes a strategic look at the competitive advantages of a highly motivated workforce.

Learning Outcomes

- to provide a clear understanding of the guiding principles of HRM
- to identify the functional areas of HRM
- to explore training and development as it relates to theory and current practice in the leisure industry

Introduction

Any organisation serious about success should embrace the principles and practice of HRM. This involves linking the organisation's business goals to operational practice in a clear, well planned and appropriate way in an effort to meet the needs of the business and the employees. Employee Development is one of five key functional areas of HRM and the area analysed in more detail in this chapter. Training and development are central aspects of Employee Development which are currently receiving much attention nationally. The leisure industry is beginning to recognise and respond to the HRM philosophy and much of this can be seen in training and development initiatives.

In support of the theory discussed in this chapter four leisure organisations who are directly involved in training and development have been investigated and examples of good practice highlighted.

HRM Philosophy

HRM as a concept continues to cause debate amongst both theorists and practitioners making it difficult to find a common definition. As a starting point for the reader Bratton and Golds (1994:5) interpretation of HRM is perhaps the most useful:

> *That part of the management process that specialises in the management of people in work organisations. HRM emphasises that the employees are the primary resource for gaining sustainable competitive advantage, that human resources activities need to be integrated with the corporate strategy, and that human resource specialists help organisational controllers to meet both efficiency and equity objectives.*

The difficulty in finding a concise yet comprehensive definition may be related to its history. HRM is a relatively new concept that was born in the 1980s and largely attributable to the writings of American academics such as Beer *et al.* (1984) and Fornbrun *et al.* (1984)

who proposed it as an alternative model to personnel management. The personnel management model had mainly focused on the welfare of employees and support to management in terms of recruitment, administration, training, industrial (employee) relations and employment law (Armstrong 1995; Guest 1990). HRM on the other hand sought to provide a much more strategic approach to managing people. Where personnel management had provided a workforce-centred approach, HRM proposed a resource-centred approach which placed the emphasis on the demands of the employer rather than the employee (Armstrong 1995). Many writers however have questioned whether HRM is in fact a new management paradigm. Lowry (1990:8) believes that it is not a new theoretical concept at all, but that 'HRM is just the continuing process of personnel management – it is not different'. Armstrong (1995:51) quotes an earlier work (1987) in which he reports that 'HRM is regarded by some personnel managers as just a set of initials or old wine in new bottles'.

In order to more fully understand the philosophy of HRM it is worth considering its main features:

- HRM is initiated by senior management.
- Line management are centrally involved in the delivery of HRM strategies.
- HRM policies outline the inter-relationship between the overall business strategies and goals and the human resources.
- HRM strategies are used to reinforce organisational culture.
- With HRM, the focus shifts from management–trade union relations to management–employee relations; from collectivism to individualism.
- HRM stresses the importance of winning the commitment of employees to its organisational goals, missions and values.
- Employees are seen as assets rather than as costs.

HRM Functions

Bratton and Gold (1994), Armstrong (1995) and others have categorised HRM activities into a number of functional areas. Figure 10.1 identifies the common key areas. There are numerous authors who give detailed analysis of the functional areas highlighted in Figure 10.1. These include Thompson and Mabey (1994), Armstrong (1995) and Bratton and Gold (1994). Currently Critten (1994) is the only one who refers specifically to the leisure industry although others have included chapters on HRM in their books (Torkildsen (1992); Henry (1990); Edginton and Williams (1978) and ILAM (1995)).

Leisure Industry Context

HRM has been recognised and adopted with varying degrees of success by the leisure industry, although Critten (1994:94) does report that the industry '. . . is more characterised by personnel management than the HRM approach'. This may partly explain the findings of the 1998 Annual Remuneration Survey for the leisure industry which reports that the industry 'faces a shortage of skilled, motivated staff, who are discouraged by the rates of pay, working conditions and perceived lack of career opportunities' (Salmon 1998:7). Clearly in a service sector industry the employees' quality of working life will be paramount to excellent service delivery together with a shared understanding of the organisation's mission. Commitment to excellent HRM practice, at both the strategic and operational level, will be key in any determination to improve. The five functional areas of HRM outlined in Figure 10.1 provide a useful starting point from which better practice could emerge.

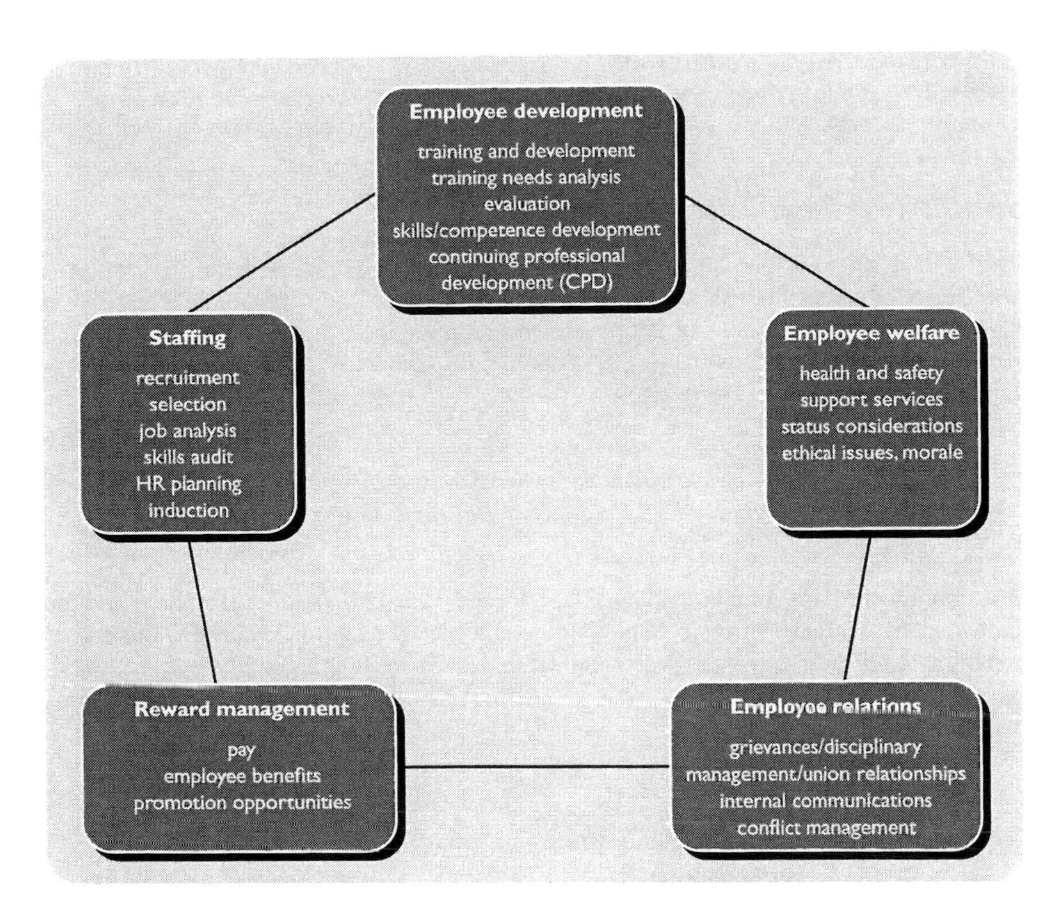

Figure 10.1 The five functional areas of HRM

A commitment to HRM may also give an organisation a competitive advantage which in an increasingly consumer-led economy could be a critical success factor in a highly competitive and volatile service industry. As John Oxley (1998) the Director of Health and Fitness for Sport and Leisure Management Limited (SLM) explains:

> *We no longer compete against the leisure centre down the road – the market has grown beyond that. Our competitors include David Lloyd, Esporta, Livingwell, Fitness First to name but a few. As the club market becomes saturated so too does the labour market. The actual amount of quality labour that is available is dwindling as a consequence. Our focus has to be towards making a much greater commitment to the whole philosophy of HRM and integrating that into our training and development. It is through our staff that we will maintain our competitive strengths.*

HRM may also reap further rewards for an organisation in the form of reduced absenteeism and turnover leading to savings in training new staff. Quality of output may also be enhanced. When the CBI (1998) reports that for the leisure industry £11 billion was lost as a result of absenteeism in one year alone and that the highest levels are to be found in the public sector, ways of reducing this figure have to be considered.

HRM, then, has a critical role to play in the success of any organisation whatever its size, age, turnover or sector status. For the leisure industry in particular staff are the greatest and often most costly resource, frequently undervalued and underinvested in. With appropriate, well-timed and planned investment they may become their most valuable asset. As Bill Morris of the Transport and General Worker's Union (TGWU) observes:

paying and treating workers badly is a false economy. A successful business understands that a well trained, well rewarded and respected workforce will itself attract more business. (Morris in *Leisure Manager* March 1998:10)

Employee Development (ED)

The pivotal role that Employee Development plays in the strategic success of HRM is confirmed by such theorists as Stewart and McGoldrick (1996) and Bratton and Gold (1994). Earlier the key areas of Employee Development were identified as: training and development; training needs analysis; evaluation; skills/competence development; and CPD. Furthermore Armstrong (1995) states:

> *Employee Development, often referred to as human resource development (HRD), is about the provision of learning, development and training opportunities in order to improve individual, team and organisational performance.*
> (Armstrong 1995:489)

A commitment to investing in Employee Development can benefit an organisation and the individual in a number of ways. Some of the main benefits that may accrue to the organisation as a result of Employee Development initiatives are highlighted below:

- competitive advantage
- decreased turnover
- reduced absenteeism
- reduced redundancy/recruitment/training costs
- increased productivity/quality output
- reduction in accidents/complaints
- increased staff motivation
- fosters proactivity rather than reactivity
- creates an attitude more receptive to change
- encourages a learning culture
- encourages multi-skilling
- facilitates national recognition for good practice – Investor in People (IIP)/QUEST

Similarly the individual may benefit in the following ways:

- confidence to do the job and do it well
- increased commitment to the organisational goals/mission
- planned career development opportunities
- environment conducive to learning
- empowerment
- increased education, training and development opportunities
- lifelong learning can be learner-managed
- increased job satisfaction and motivation
- fewer errors or complaints
- updated knowledge and skills

Having outlined the main features and benefits of Employee Development the focus will turn to a more detailed exploration of the key aspects of training and development. To supplement this section the following texts are worthy of study: Thomson (1998 ch.6); Armstrong (1995 ch.33); Attwood and Dimmock (1996 ch.8); Critten (1995 ch.6); and Thomason (1988 ch.11).

Training and Development

There is a tendency to refer to training and development as interrelated which they clearly are in HRM terms. However it would be useful here to explore the differences in order to understand that for all leisure organisations there is often a legal requirement to 'train' staff (health and safety etc.), but there is no such stipulation to 'develop'. This perhaps has been one reason it has taken the industry time to appreciate the need to offer both as part of an HRM strategy and thus create a successful business.

Truelove (1995:291) defines the differences between training and development as follows:

> *Training endeavours to impart knowledge, skills and attitudes necessary to perform job-related tasks. Its aim is to improve job performance in a direct way . . . Development is a process whereby individuals learn through experience to be more effective. It aims to help people utilise the skills and knowledge that education and training have given them – not only in their current jobs, but also in future posts. It embodies concepts such as psychological growth, greater maturity and increased confidence.*

According to Thomson (1998:121):

> *. . . most people are clear what they mean by 'training'. Training is usually directed towards acquiring specific skills, knowledge or competencies related to a job or task . . . It involves changing or improving behaviour through learning to achieve effective performance.*

All of the industry practitioners interviewed for this chapter had very clear views of what training meant to their organisation. John Oxley from SLM identified training as including 'essential skills and knowledge' and that its purpose was 'to deliver to the bottom line, in other words it is concerned with the relationship between training spend and organisational profit'. Of development he states:

> *it is much deeper and more individual. Opportunities need to be identified through coaching rather than training and our industry needs to invest time in an individuals potential value to the company. We shouldn't be frightened of giving people the opportunity to show off. We need to identify abilities and create opportunities for development.*

Kevin Collinge (1998) the Chief Executive of Kirklees Stadium Development Limited (KSDL) noted that training relates to a 'specific job role'. The relationship between training and development was also clearly articulated by David Bradley from CRAGRATS Training Ltd., he said:

> *Training is about skills, it is often practically based and the necessary first step in development. Development is about an individual's ability to grow, change and succeed. It holds more risks. It is ongoing and involves aspirations, motives and direction; the chance to move on and up.*

He also noted that in the leisure industry there has historically been a tendency to 'train to deliver but not develop'.

The following section takes a training focus which more accurately reflects the current practice across the industry. However, the developmental aspect of training is highlighted and the importance of moving towards integrating training and development policy and practice as part of an HRM strategy for the future success of the industry is noted.

Theoretical Approaches to Training

A number of approaches or theoretical methods have been used to explain how the training is addressed within organisations. However, the format of the majority of these models tends to remain very similar. Each of them appears to focus on four key activities. Figure 10.2 provides an example of the four stage systematic model of training which is perhaps the most simplest.

The model provides a continuous cycle to describe how training is managed and can, as Martin and Jackson (1997) highlight, be linked to the Investor in People initiative. In order to achieve the award, organisations have to satisfy the four key principles of Commitment, Planning, Action and Evaluation, which are demonstrated by the model. IIP can also help to integrate training with development in support of a cohesive HRM strategy.

Stage one – training needs analysis

Training is all too often thought about in response to a problem or crisis, such as change in staff, introduction of a new machine or piece of equipment or a surge of customer complaints. Quite often management respond by sending people off on a training course – this is certainly not the answer. If an organisation strategically plans for the future, it may help to circumvent this type of reactive situation. In doing so an organisation must evaluate its training needs in a logical and planned manner. A training needs analysis is a method of auditing existing performance, predicting future change and comparing these with the desired level of performance and skills required for the development of the organisation and the individuals within it.

In today's world, change is paramount. It occurs both inside and outside of organisations and affects the employees that work within them. Those that are affected by change must adapt and learn the new skills and knowledge needed to accommodate such

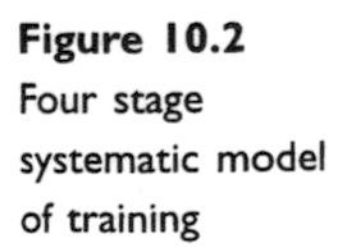

Figure 10.2 Four stage systematic model of training

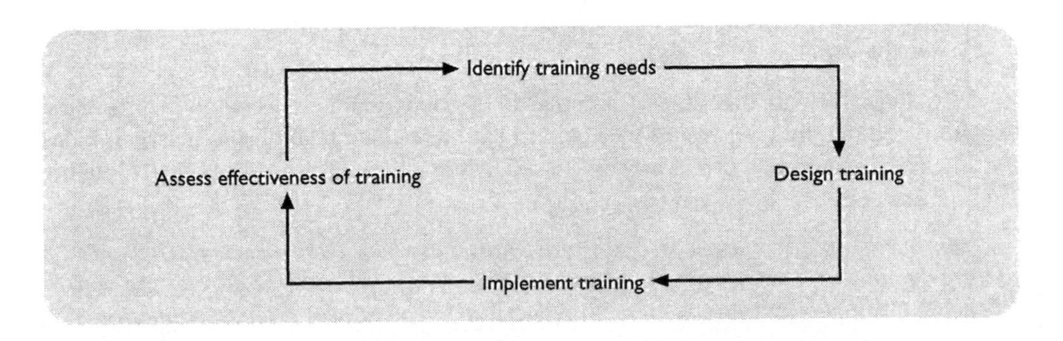

Political: CCT, Best Value, government intervention, IIP, NVQs
Economic: restructuring, downsizing
Social: women managers, management skills training, holistic health approach
Technological: computerised booking systems, SWIPE card technology, virtual reality, online health and fitness – Internet
Legal: Health and Safety, worktime directives, Children's Act
Environmental: conservation, recycling

Figure 10.3 External changes that may result in a requirement for training

changes. Many training needs arise as a result of changes that are not only within the organisation itself, but also external to it. A number of such external changes are highlighted in Figure 10.3 which also shows how training needs arise as a result of external factors, but training needs also arise internally. When a new member of staff is appointed, there is a need to provide induction training into the company and their specific role within it. Employees who are promoted or redeployed within the organisation may also require additional training to support their development. Furthermore, staff who have returned to the organisation after a period away for maternity or illness may also require updating in new procedures, practices or equipment.

It can, therefore, be said that training is required at three levels. First, at the organisational level; second, at the job or occupational level; and finally at the level of the individual employee. It is this last level which avails itself most readily to the development aspect of Employee Development.

According to Armstrong (1995) there are four methods of analysing training needs:

- analysis of business and human resource plans
- job analysis
- analysis of performance reviews
- training surveys

For the leisure industry it is also important to undertake a training needs analysis from the customer's perspective. This may take the form of an evaluation of customer comments and complaints. Critical though, is not to look at training in isolation but to ensure that the needs analysis of the individual employee also identifies the personal and professional development aspect.

John Oxley (1998) has this to say in relation to the training and development needs of SLM health and fitness club managers:

> *When we became a separate division within SLM we analysed our business plans and current performance and quickly identified a particular skill shortage common to all our health and fitness club managers which we needed to address immediately. In consultation with training providers we decided the approach we should take was on a much more personal level in terms of recognising that individuals learn differently. We have decided to undertake an evaluation of the individual using a self-perception inventory and match this to an individual training programme which includes the identified common skill areas required for their jobs. In this way the training will be much more effective as it is based on an evaluation of an individual's particular learning style and the particular developmental stage they are at as well as the organisation and job requirements.*

Stage two – methods of training

The leisure industry is faced with a plethora of training and development products that appear to cover anything and everything that an employee could ever want to learn. Managers are offered videos, books, workshops, business games and a whole host of products that vary in terms of cost and delivery. Some organisations prefer to develop their own in-house training programmes rather than pay for external consultants and training agencies, and others prefer to adopt a mixed approach. Choice of method is often dependent on whether the organisation has a training department, financial costs and time involved and the nature of the training need itself. Other influences on the method chosen may also relate to the organisation's recognition of the need to develop as well as train staff. For example a secondment or workshop approach is more likely to provide an integrated training and development experience for the employee. Figure 10.4 highlights a range of the current methods available.

Whilst the above figure identifies an overwhelming range of external methods of training, Thomson (1998) points out that there are often criticisms levelled at these. One such claim is that because the courses often take place outside the work environment, it is difficult to apply the learning to the employees' own specific job, role, or workplace. An example of this could be where an employer sends a pool attendant on a pool plant operator's course. Critics may argue that the training would be more meaningful if the pool attendant were to learn about the pool plant operation in the swimming pool in which (s)he worked. Furthermore, since many courses provided by external agencies do not offer assessment, it is often difficult to assess their worth other than in a permanent change in the behaviour of the employee – almost impossible to measure long term.

This does not, however, mean that all external training courses are a bad thing – on the contrary, many provide the perfect solution to an organisation's training needs. An example of industry good practice comes from SLM whose staff training and development methods emerged out of a recognition that historically the industry had been guilty of 'simply booking courses and seminars "off the shelf" and sending staff away for a couple of days or a week'. In John Oxley's experience often such courses were not 100 per cent relevant for either the staff or their organisation. SLM made a policy decision that ensured the training reflected the organisation's goals, missions and values:

Figure 10.4
Training methods

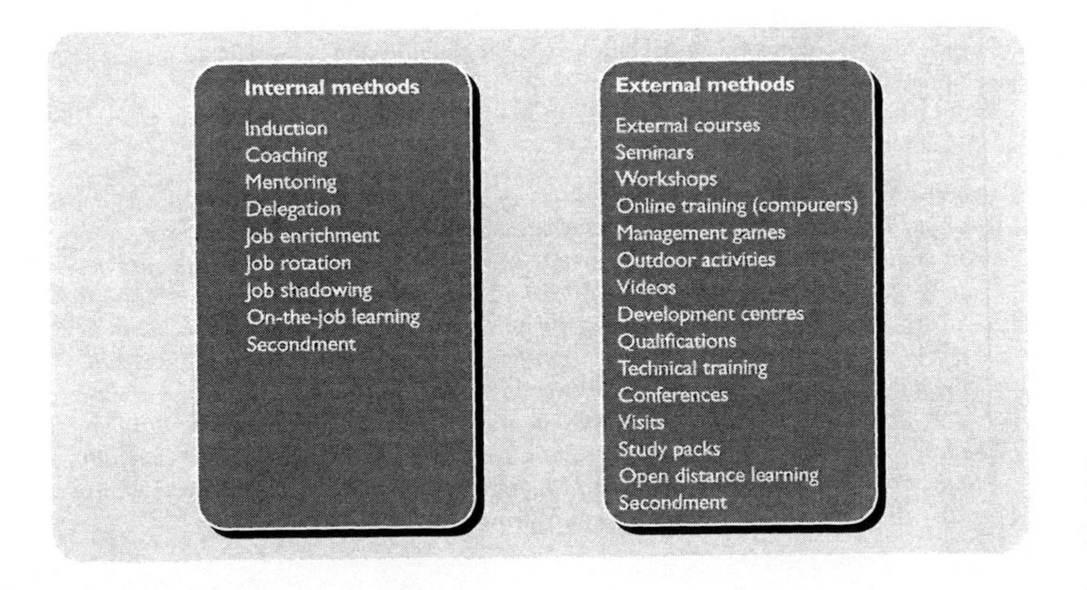

> *whatever training we do needs to be bespoke to the company and its brand and therefore, we needed to identify people within the market place who were prepared to work with us and design and deliver relevant and appropriate training. We sought strategic alliances with companies who understand our business, its goals, the particular philosophy of our brand and the specific needs of our employees. We have successfully worked with Forza Fitness to strengthen our brand, Marins for our instructor training, Bodyline for management training and independent from this we encourage our managers to visit other leisure facilities and explore models of good practice.* (Oxley 1998)

SLM have worked hard to ensure they achieve a balanced training programme reflecting individual and organisational needs and cogniscant of their overall business goals. Such a model is indicative of an HRM approach to managing people.

Clearly an holistic approach at the design and planning stage is critical and a further example of good practice can be seen from the training provision provided for the McAlpine Stadium staff prior to its opening by CRAGRATS Training Ltd. The senior managers from both organisations share the same beliefs and ideals about training and developing staff and this was reflected in the end product which involved all the stadium staff, including the chief executive, in wearing the same T-shirts and doing the same practical activities. This included role play and working with trained actors to produce a video recording of what working at the McAlpine Stadium meant to them, individually. As Kevin Collinge (1999) points out:

> *this was about customer care, about passing on our business aspirations and philosophy and creating a common vision, about empowering people to explore their motives for working here. It was a bonding process but vital for our business and gave us the opportunity to bring everyone together in an unthreatening environment – the actors helped there. We would certainly repeat this sort of training again.*

With regard to the many internal methods of training outlined in Figure 10.4 the most notable criticism relates to work shadowing where, if workers shadow other workers, there is a likelihood that bad habits or short cuts to performance may be transferred. The training received is also dependent on the organisational environment and the quality and enthusiasm of the expert training the new recruit.

Stage three – training delivery/implementation

Once the training programme has been designed taking into account the needs of the employee, the training methods available and the resources available to the organisation, it is time to move on to the implementation stage. At this stage it is paramount that all parties involved agree the objectives for the training and clarify why the training is being undertaken. Without such an agreement the learner is less likely to be motivated and the trainer will be unclear about the direction the training is to take. It is also important to set timescales with respect to 'how long' and 'when' training will take place at this stage. The methods by which the training will be evaluated must also be identified here.

Stage four – evaluation

The preceding sections have demonstrated that there is a wide choice of training and development methods available that can be undertaken both within and outside the organisation. Careful planning must be undertaken to ensure that the delivery of the chosen method meets the specific individual or organisational goals. In order to ensure that these objectives are being met it is essential that organisations evaluate their chosen approaches. Martin and Jackson (1997:82) provide a comprehensive list of reasons why an evaluation of training and development should take place:

- justifying the expense
- providing feedback to the trainer
- providing feedback on techniques
- establishing whether the needs and objectives of the training have been met
- improving future programmes
- identifying further needs
- providing data for justifying further expenditure
- helping top management to understand the broad costs and benefits of developing people

While the reasons given above appear to more than justify the need for evaluation, it seems that in practice, particularly in the leisure industry, evaluation is given a low priority. Reasons often given for failing to evaluate are that: 'the beneficial effects of training are obvious'; 'only rigorous and scientific evaluation is worthwhile – such approaches are difficult or impossible to implement in real-life situations'; 'trainers lack the knowledge, skills and incentives to evaluate'; 'end of course reaction sheets are sufficient and their contents demonstrate that training is effective'; and, 'evaluation will use scarce resources needed for the prime tasks of training' (Truelove 1995:124).

Further reasons for the failure to focus on evaluation include the fact that many of the benefits of training are intangible. Development activities in particular may not become obvious immediately following the course. The growth of an individual may take a longer period of time. Furthermore, training is often set without clear objectives therefore making it difficult to set criteria on which to evaluate.

Despite these difficulties, there is certainly a trend today towards organisations being more accountable. The government's introduction of Best Value, the use of quality systems and the IIP initiative have all led to organisations having to justify and rationalise their operations and expenditure.

Evaluation is the fourth IIP principle and organisations wishing to achieve the award have to demonstrate that the outcomes of training and, significantly, development are evaluated at individual, team and organisation levels. They must also evaluate whether their development actions have achieved their objectives.

Evaluation can therefore be seen as a method of determining whether the training and development was worthwhile in terms of cost benefit.

Hamblin (1974) suggests that there are five levels at which evaluation can take place:

1. reactions
2. learning
3. job behaviour
4. organisational unit
5. ultimate value

The five levels are seen as links in a chain where training results in reactions, which lead to learning, which may lead to changes in job behaviour. This will impact on the organisational unit and lead to changes in the achievement of the ultimate goals.

Martin and Jackson (1997) adopt Hamblin's levels of evaluation and provide a useful table that illustrates the methods of evaluation that may be undertaken at each stage. Table 10.1 shows that the easiest levels to evaluate are 1 and 2 and that the process becomes increasingly more difficult as level 5 is reached. The reason for this difficulty is that at level 5 it is harder to establish cause and effect. The overall departmental or organisational effects may be down to a large number of staff therefore making it difficult to single out the individual worker's improved behaviour. This is perhaps why at level 5 evaluation is treated in a more general manner.

On the whole leisure and sport organisations do not evaluate much beyond levels 1–2. The predominant method for evaluation purposes are end of course questionnaires. Clearly if the industry is to progress and fully embrace the HRM philosophy it will need

Table 10.1 Hamblin's levels of evaluation

Level	***The levels***	***Methods of evaluation***
1	Reactions of trainees to the content and methods of training, to the trainer, and to other factors perceived as relevant. What the trainee thought about the training.	Discussion. Interview. Questionnaires. Recommendations of trainees. Desire for further training.
2	Learning attained during the learning period. Did the trainees learn what was intended?	*Behaviour*: Objectives attained. *Knowledge and understanding*. *Skills*: Examinations and other tests. Analysis by observation of demonstrated skill. Evidence of skills applied. Projects or assignments. *Attitude*: Questionnaires.
3	Job behaviour in the work environment at the end of the training period. Did the learning get transferred to the job?	Production rate. Customer complaints. Discuss with manager/subordinates/peers. Activity sampling. Self-recording of specific incidents. Evidence of competence. Appraisal.
4	Effect on the department. Has the training helped the department's performance?	Minutes of meetings. Deadlines met. Stress indicators. Quality indicators. Interview other managers and superiors.
5	*The Ultimate Level*. Has the training affected the ultimate wellbeing of the organisation in terms of business objectives?	Standing of the training officer. Growth. Quality indicators. Stress indicators. Achievement of business goals and targets.

Source: Martin and Jackson (1997:83).

to redress this imbalance and focus more overtly on the fourth stage of the systematic model of training – *Evaluation.*

Training in the Leisure Industry

At the time of writing there were no national statistics available that related specifically to training initiatives in the leisure industry, although research by Bacon (1991), ILAM (1992) and the TGWU (1996) have provided an insight into current working practices whilst others have taken a training needs based approach (SPRITO/SCLRS 1996). However the *Labour Market Quarterly Report* for Spring 1996 gives an indication of the trends across all the labour market sectors for the UK. It reports three million employees of working age (13.8 per cent of the employed population) were said to have received training 'related to a current or future job' in the four weeks prior to the summer 1995 official survey, compared with 1.8 million (which is well below ten per cent) in 1984. The 1996–97 *Labour Market and Skills Trends Report* analysed training in more detail and concluded that most training was of a short duration and of those receiving training 46 per cent reported having training for under one week, 12 per cent for one week to six months, four per cent for six months to one year, 11 per cent for one to three years and seven per cent for over three years. More alarming still, 20 per cent of businesses failed to plan or provide for training or development within their organisations. Employee Development is about creating a sustainable advantage for an organisation by investing in its staff and their training and development. The above statistics clearly show that the investment in training is generally short term and unrelated to longer-term organisational and individual development needs. Stephen Studd (1996), the Chief Executive of SPRITO, is very clear about the contribution training makes to an organisation's performance:

> *The reason why the industry must press ahead and focus on its training and skills are clear. And it is not just to bow to government pressure. Plans to improve the nation's export potential and competitiveness are irrelevant to many areas of the sport and leisure field. More pertinent is survival. Whether your organisational objective is profit, or developing excellence in sport, or personal and social development, we share a dependence on the people we employ. The coach, the instructor, the manager, the receptionist, the lifeguard, the playleader have a crucial upfront role in delivering and selling our services. With changing customer preferences and higher expectations, with greater competition for people's time and money, with increasing technology and innovation, with increasing emphasis on health and safety and the demands of legislation, we have to keep the skills of our workforce up to date.* (Studd 1996:156)

One reason for the lack of investment in training or development by the industry may be successive governments' failure to form a co-ordinated national training policy between the key players – unions, employers and government departments. But organisations must also take some of the blame, often preferring to circumvent training and development costs by directly recruiting skilled workers. This practice continues today and is reflected in the job advertisements placed in the *ILAM Weekly Appointments Service* and *Leisure Opportunities* Classified. Most state candidate requirements in the way of skills, knowledge, experience and qualifications. Phrases such as 'All applicants must possess . . .', 'You will need to excel in . . .', 'You must be able to demonstrate . . .', 'experience essential', are all frequently in evidence and usually followed by a daunting list of skills, qualifications, abilities or knowledge requirements which the applicant must evidence.

On a more positive note some organisations are clearly marketing the fact that they recognise the value to their organisation of providing sustainable training and development opportunities.

There is evidence that investment in Employee Development has paid off for some leisure organisations. Scottish and Newcastle report in *Leisure Opportunities*:

> *The year on year increase in trading profits of pubs with a high level of NVQs is on average 10.5 per cent more than those with low NVQ activity. Added to this, staff turnover has reduced by 50 per cent and more employees are moving from behind the bar into management.* (*Leisure Opportunities* 1998:8)

Staff training and development in relation to vocational/competence based schemes has obviously played an important part in the overall success for Scottish and Newcastle and it is to this area of Employee Development that the discussion now turns.

Skills/Competence Development

The move towards a competence-based approach to training could be attributable to developments that began in the 1980s when the then Conservative government established Training and Enterprise Councils (TECs). These had a primary remit from government to improve and support training and education regionally, raise the profile of training nationally and provide 'pump prime' funding for vocational training. This move towards vocational training was further cemented and enhanced to include 'development' in the 1990 Government White Paper *Employment for the 1990s*. Other initiatives that have help to raise the profile of an integrated approach to training and development include Modern Apprenticeships, S/NVQs, National Standards, ISO9000, Investor in People (IIP), QUEST, CCT and most recently, Best Value and Foundation Degrees.

According to Critten (1994) IIP has certainly led to an improvement in training and development for those leisure organisations who have involved themselves in the initiative. The IIP award was designed to make organisations committed to training and development, help organisations structure training and development and to link organisational needs to individual needs; all features of an HRM approach.

The organisations that Critten explored, Butlins South Coast World, Torquay Leisure Hotel Group and Pleasureland each embodied the principals of Employee Development in their approach to attain the IIP award. All of these organisations had developed a training and development policy as part of their HRM strategy which clearly linked to the organisation's overall corporate goals. This type of approach is an excellent model for any organisation wishing to embrace the philosophy of the HRM paradigm.

For public sector leisure providers training and development initiatives are more often than not government led. Currently competence-based approaches such as NVQ qualifications and Modern Apprenticeships are part funded by government offering local authorities the opportunity to increase their resources to support training initiatives. Ian Kendal of Kirklees Metropolitan Borough Council (MBC) recognises that they operate within a much more constrained environment than commercial operators but believes it is vital for long-term success to recognise individuals' training and development needs. NVQs are the vehicle through which this happens. Kirklees is an NVQ assessment centre for Sport and Recreation and employees are encouraged to undertake job-specific NVQs at the appropriate level. In this way, staff can train, develop and progress accordingly through a nationally recognised scheme. Similar schemes are in operation in a number of local authorities within the UK.

Continuing Professional Development (CPD)

The most significant recent development has been the establishment of a network of National Training Organisations (NTOs) across British industry to initiate, help implement, support and advise on all matters relating to education and training policy and practice. SPRITO is the recognised Specialist Industry Training Organisation for Sport, Playwork, Recreation, Outdoor Education and Development Training, Fitness and Exercise. In its Strategic Plan SPRITO (1998) sets out its vision for 'human and skill development' and 'organisation and sector development' which includes initiating a programme of research, development, implementation and support in order to give the industry a shared strategic focus. This co-ordinated approach will seek to:

- Develop a framework of education, training, qualifications and opportunity to support the lifetime learning and development of all individuals working in its field.
- Link mainstream government programmes with specialist industry provision to ensure quality, accessibility, appropriateness and continuous improvement for organisations and individuals (SPRITO Strategic Plan 1998:9).

The philosophy of HRM is clearly embedded in the approach to training and development advocated by SPRITO (1998) in an effort to 'build a unified and cohesive industry equipped for the 21st century' (SPRITO Strategic Plan 1998:10).

There is evidence that the industry itself is recognising the value of opting into this new training and development culture:

> *As we continue to search for ideas to differentiate our clubs, we all realise that the 'added value' in what we can offer is our people. Staff, at all levels, are demanding that their training and development needs are met, so the answer is to train, train, train!* (Dicker 1996)

> *. . . we must continue to invest in staff training and development . . . The leisure sector, unfortunately, has a reputation for low pay, low skill and high turnover. We in Whitbread are committed to changing this image because we know we'll only succeed in the new millennium if we are able to attract the right people to join our industry and ensure more of them stay with us to pursue their careers.*
> (Thomas 1999:38)

Both training and development are seen as key features of Employee Development for these organisations. However, investment which is based on the Four Stage Systematic Model of Training, or similar, will not in itself be enough to ensure success. Critically important is an understanding of learning and fostering a 'learning environment' as a prerequisite to any training and development activity. As John Oxley (1998) explains:

> *We need to identify abilities and create opportunities for development. We should seek to understand how individuals learn and what motivates them and then create the right environment for people to motivate themselves – as an organisation we are becoming much better at that.*

The Learning Environment

In 1987 the Institute of Personnel Management (now Institute of Personnel and Development) published a code of practice in support of learning. It had the following aims:

- To broaden all senior managers' views about learning and training.
- To help them firmly anchor their learning activity in the organisation's business activities.
- To emphasise that learning within the organisation must be managed on a continuous basis. (cited in Cumming 1993:200)

This recognises that managers responsible for training and development need to be empowered through their own education, training and development opportunities to provide better and more appropriate training and development for their staff. As Gilpin (1996:10) suggests:

> *Managers need to take responsibility for developing their understanding of how human beings work, how they think, how they have acquired their beliefs (empowering and limiting ones), how they will become motivated and turned off, how they succeed and why they fail to learn.*

Tackling the issue of 'training the trainers' is a step closer to success but there are other factors which will need to be addressed. A cultural change may have to take place within the organisation to create an environment conducive to learning. The starting point would be in recognising barriers to learning and where they exist in the organisation. Some organisations inadvertently set people up to fail through misunderstandings and misconceptions in relation to learning. Setting a challenge, creating a competitive environment or giving unrealistic targets and performance levels could be perceived as threatening and demotivating by some or conversely a real motivator by others. According to Thomson (1998):

> *some adults who have had bad experiences of learning as children have a number of barriers to overcome when it comes to learning as an adult, they see the whole process as one that will lead them to fail.* (Thomson 1998:122)

She goes on to suggest that such employees need to be re-motivated to consider learning again or such barriers will remain to adversely interfere with training. In an industry that employs a high percentage of school leavers and young people, 'bad experiences of learning' may not be too far removed and individual need should thus be identified from day one and incorporated into the induction and subsequent training and development provision.

Gilpin (1996) advocates:

> *leaders must have the skills to create a safe environment to experiment. They must lead by example and demonstrate by their own success the tangible benefits of committing to learning.* (Gilpin 1996:10)

David Bradley (1998) of CRAGRATS Training Ltd continues:

> *If you don't change management attitudes at the same time then training will never progress to incorporate the development aspect. There are too many 'suits' in some organisations. Our aim is clear: we use a very powerful medium through which to bring about behavioural changes and encourage a learning culture.*

The training provided by CRAGRATS for the McAlpine Stadium referred to earlier provided a risk-free environment for experimentation. Employees were encouraged to try out tactics or behaviours that were new and evaluate their effectiveness.

Summary and Conclusions

This chapter has explored a range of theories and practices that are available to leisure managers in their quest to maximise the contribution that employees can make to the overall business success.

It has highlighted the key role that HRM can play in meeting the challenges facing the industry today and demonstrates the important role ED plays in this process. It has demonstrated how an integrated approach to training and development can assist in improving both employee and organisational goals and argued that training in itself will not meet the long-term business goals of an organisation – it is too immediate and often reactive and does not achieve career or personal development needs. Training has to be considered alongside development within a conducive learning environment for sustainable success and economic benefit.

Furthermore, the leisure industry examples that are provided help to illustrate that there appears to be an encouraging trend towards investment in employees. However, despite this reassurance the picture is not as rosy as one would hope. It appears that whilst promising efforts are being made most leisure organisations are failing to complete the Four Stage Systematic Model of Training. The key problem appears to be at the fourth stage, where there is certainly little regard for evaluation.

If the industry fails to engage with this important process it will find it difficult to justify the benefits of training and development. As a direct consequence employee development and the philosophy of HRM will remain low on the agenda of many leisure organisations. If the industry is to succeed and achieve competitive advantage through its employees this situation should be reversed and HRM given increased salience.

Suggested Tasks for Further Study

1. Identify a training activity you have taken part in. What were the objectives of the activity? In your opinion were these objectives met? How was the activity evaluated? Assume you have been given the task of measuring the effectiveness of the activity – what evaluation methods would you choose to adopt and why?

2. Find out about training and development within your own organisation. Do you have a specific department or person responsible for it? Is there a written policy for training and development? How does this link to other policies within the organisation.

3. How are training needs identified within your department/organisation? How would you improve the effectiveness of this process?

4. Identify the training and development methods that are undertaken within your own organisation. Use Figure 10.4 to assist you. Do you feel these are adequate? If you were to improve the effectiveness of training and development what would you change and why?

References

- Armstrong M 1987 'Human Resource Management: a case of the emperor's new clothes' *Personnel Management* August pp.30–35
- Armstrong M 1995 *A Handbook of Personnel Management Practice* (5th Ed) Kogan Page
- Attwood M and Dimmock S 1996 *Personnel Management* (3rd Ed) Macmillan Press Ltd, Hampshire
- Bacon B 1991 'Working in Leisure: delight or drudgery' *Leisure Management* May 1991
- Beer M, Spector B, Lawrence P, Quinn Mills D and Walton R 1984 *Managing Human Assets* The Free Press, New York
- Bratton J and Gold J 1994 *Human Resource Management, theory and practice* Macmillan Press, London
- Cowling A G and Mailer C J B 1981 *Managing Human Resources* Edward Arnold, London
- Critten P 1994 *Human Resource Management in the Leisure Industry* Longman, Harlow
- Cumming M W 1993 *The Theory and Practice of Personnel Management* (7th Ed) Butterworth-Heinemann, Oxford
- Dicker L 1996 'Taking Issue with IIP' *Health Club Management* November 1996
- Edginton L R and Williams J G 1978 *Productive Management of Leisure Service Organisations* John Wiley, Canada
- Festa P 1997 'Half Equals More' *Leisure Opportunities* 15–28 September 1997 No.192
- Fornbrun C J, Tichy N M and Devanna M A 1984 *Strategic Human Resource Management* John Wiley, New York
- Gilling J 1994 'Giving Instructions' *Leisure Opportunities* No.130
- Gilpin A 1996 'Training Takes Root' *Leisure Opportunities* No.153 19 February 1996
- Government White Paper 1990 *Employment for the 1990s* HMSO
- Guest D 1990 'Human Resource Management and the American Dream' *Journal of Management Studies* Vol.27 No.4
- Hamblin A C 1974 *Evaluation and Control of Training* McGraw-Hill, Maidenhead
- Henry I P 1990 *Management and Planning in the Leisure Industry* Macmillan Press, Hampshire
- Honey P and Mumford A 1992 *The Manual of Learning Styles* Ardingly House, Berkshire
- ILAM Survey 1992 'How Stressed are Leisure Managers?' *Leisure Management* October 1992
- ILAM 1995 *Guide to Good Practice in Leisure Management* Buswell J Section 3 Human Resource Management, Critten P and Neyndorff C
- IPM News 1993 'A satisfactory record of learning' *Personnel Management Plus* Vol.4 No.9 September 1993 p.36
- Ives J 1998 'People Power' *The Leisure Manager* September 1998 Vol.16 No.9 pp.27–28
- Kerfoot R 1998 'Gulf Courses' *The Leisure Manager* November 1998
- Kolb D *Labour Market and Skill Trends* 1996–97 Department for Education and Employment
- *Labour Market Quarterly Report* 1996 Skills and Enterprise Network Publication Department for Education and Employment, Spring
- *Leisure Opportunities* 1–13 September 1998, No.216, p.8
- Lowry 1990 *Personnel Management Plus* December, p.8
- Martin M and Jackson T 1997 *Personnel Practice* Institute of Personnel and Development, London
- Megginson D, Joy-Matthews J and Banfield P 1993 *Human Resource Development Fast Track MBA Series* Kogan Page, London
- Molander C (Ed) 1987 *Personnel Management – a Practical Introduction* Chartwell-Bratt Ltd
- Morris B 1998 'Adding Value' *The Leisure Manager* Vol.16, No.3 March 1998 p.10

- Robbins S 1978 *Personnel: the Management of Human Resources* Prentice Hall, New Jersey
- Salmon J 1998 'Rich Get Richer and Managers Stay Much the Same' *Leisure Opportunities* 20 July–2 August 1998 Issue 213 p.7
- SPRITO/SCLRS 1997 *Graduate Recruitment and Development in the Sport and Recreation Industry* DEE
- SPRITO 1998 *A National Strategic Plan for the Industry* p.10 SPRITO
- Storey J 1989 *New Perspectives on Human Resource Management* Routledge, London
- Stewart J and McGoldrick J 1996 *Human Resource Development* Institute of Management Foundation Pitman, London
- Studd S 1996 'The Training Challenge' *Leisure Opportunities* 29 April–12 May 1996, No.156
- Studd S 1999 'On the Record' *The Leisure Manager* February 1999 Vol.17 No.2 pp.31–32
- Thomas D 1999 'Raising the Capital' *Leisure Management* January 1999 Vol.19 No.1 p.38
- Thomason G 1988 *A Textbook of Human Resource Management* IPM, London
- Thomson R and Mabey C 1994 *Developing Human Resources* Butterworth-Heinemann, Oxford
- Thomson R 1993 *Managing People* Institute of Management Foundation, Butterworth-Heinemann, Oxford
- Thomson R 1998 *People Management* Orion Business, London
- Torkildsen G 1999 *Leisure and Recreation Management* (4th Ed) E and FN Spon, London
- Transport and General Workers' Union 1996 *The Leisure Manager* September 1998 Vol.16 No.9 pp.27–29
- Truelove S 1995 *Handbook of Training and Development* (2nd Ed) Blackwell, Oxford
- Turok F 1998 'People Power' *The Leisure Manager* September 1998 Vol.16 No.9 pp.27–29

Chapter 11

Service Quality and the Public Leisure Industry

Leigh Robinson

Loughborough University of Technology

Chapter Content

Abstract

This chapter aims to discuss the phenomenon of quality management and its applicability to the public leisure industry. It provides a brief history of the development of the quality movement and considers the appropriateness of the concept within the current public leisure context. The chapter will also consider the relevance of prominent definitions of quality and will outline a framework for the management of service quality. Within this, it will evaluate the merits of the main quality programmes available to public leisure providers.

Related Chapters

Chapter 1: The Public Sector, Best Value and Local Authority Sports Development: An awareness of the changes that have faced the public leisure sector is essential in order to understand the advantages and disadvantages of different approaches ▷

to quality management. Chapter one should be read prior to this chapter if the reader does not have an in-depth knowledge of the contemporary public leisure context.

Chapter 7: Access and Leisure Policy: The antecedents of Leisure Policy can be compared with the explosion of 'quality' initiatives during the last 5–10 years. In what ways are quality assurance schemes linked to the factors impacting upon public policy during the same period?

Learning Outcomes

- to provide an understanding of the key concepts of quality and quality management
- to encourage an assessment of the appropriateness of this concept in contemporary public leisure management
- to develop an awareness of how to implement quality management within a leisure organisation

Introduction

In 1980 a programme called *If Japan Can, Why Can't We?* was broadcast in America during which it became apparent that an American, W Edwards Deming, had been responsible for the culture of management that had transformed the struggling Japanese economy to one that was synonymous with quality. Through a series of lectures on quality control and management responsibility, Deming advocated a philosophy or vision of a 'constancy of purpose' that resulted in the movement away from quality inspection to a management culture encouraging quality in all of its operations.

Deming's work in Japan was continued by Joseph Juran who emphasised the role of communication, management and people in the pursuit of quality. In doing so he was responsible for bringing together a number of unconnected quality approaches formulating an integrated management philosophy. The quality movement gained world-wide momentum through the further work of people such as Philip Crosby, John Oakland and Tom Peters, eventually spreading to all sectors of industry.

The management of service quality within commercial leisure organisations is relatively straightforward and reflects the management of quality within other commercial service industries. It is also apparent that this management culture and its associated techniques have been adopted by non-commercial organisations and there is evidence to suggest that quality management has been of paramount importance in the management of some public leisure organisations (Robinson 1999). This chapter focuses on quality management within the public leisure industry and the principles discussed will be illustrated by the quality management practices of six UK local authority leisure services, established by research carried out by Robinson (1999).

The expansion of quality management into local government began in the late 1980s, gaining momentum in the early 1990s. This occurred for three main reasons. First, the foundations of quality management were laid by the work of Clarke and Stewart (1987) and the Local Government Training Board (1987) who promoted the need for local authorities to become customer focused and concerned with 'quality'. Second, legislative and resource constraints imposed by central government policy initiatives were intended to develop a local government concern with effectiveness as well as efficiency, and this fostered a concern with quality. Finally, as customer expectations of quality were met in other areas, it was inevitable that attention would turn to public services and public service providers were faced with a demand by the public for quality services, alongside increasing financial constraints and financial accountability. In response, they looked to the commercial service sector to learn the management principles and techniques that led to the financial success of commercial leisure organisations. The key success factor that was considered to be transferable to public sector management was a concern with providing an experience that was considered, by customers, to be of high quality, which led to the adoption of quality management techniques such as quality programmes.

Why Quality Management?

There is little doubt that the quality movement has spread to all parts of the leisure industry and that customers and managers of all types of leisure facilities are concerned with the quality of the delivered service. The research carried out by Robinson (1999) showed that quality management appears to have become the way forward for public leisure services and the reasons for this are presented in Figure 11.1. From this it is apparent that there are a variety of factors that, in isolation and in interaction, have brought about the presence of quality management within the public leisure industry.

The research showed that the factors within the operating context of public leisure services, required them to be increasingly competitive. This need to become more competitive in the management of their service was a result of the increasing customer expectations of service quality and increasing competition and serves as a justification for the popularity of quality programmes over this period.

For public leisure providers, competition not only comes from local alternatives, but also from leisure providers abroad. In addition, those that provide leisure opportunities have to compete with all other claims on the discretionary income in customers' pockets and in their discussion of quality within the public leisure service, Sheppard and Studd (1994:1) considered that the very nature of leisure makes a customer focus important as:

> *In an age when there are increasing demands on our time and new and exceptional opportunities on offer, people can and are becoming increasingly discerning about how to spend both their precious time and disposable income.*

The opportunity for choice, which differentiates leisure from most other public services, alongside the requirement to generate revenue, reinforces the need for local authority leisure providers to be customer focused in their service delivery. Customers can choose whether to make use of the local authority service, they can choose which leisure service to use

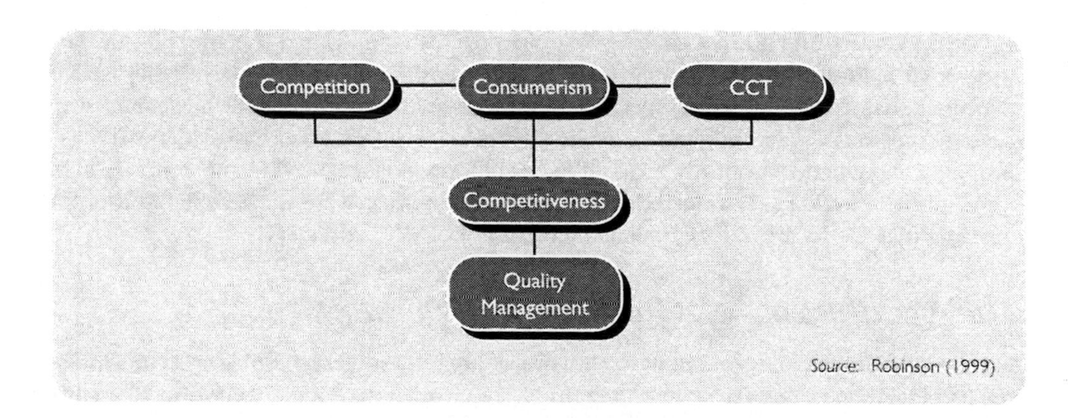

Figure 11.1 The rationale for quality management within public leisure services

and they can change their habits at any time. In response to this, public leisure providers have responded in a manner that reflects commercial provision and adopted quality management techniques to retain customers.

Most importantly, however, public leisure providers began to use quality management as a result of government legislation, primarily in the form of Compulsory Competitive Tendering (CCT). CCT meant that local authority leisure providers had to become more competitive in their operations in order to win CCT contracts and meet the revenue requirements of CCT specifications, which require competitiveness. Research carried out by Robinson (1999) established how, leisure professionals, having identified this need to become competitive, determined that first, quality management and quality programmes were the vehicle for improving organisational competitiveness and second, that they increased the competitiveness of the local authority when bidding for contracts. Consequently they ensured that quality programmes were included within CCT contracts.

The influence of government legislation is likely to continue with the introduction of Best Value. Based on the principles of accountability, transparency, continuous improvement and ownership (The Scottish Office 1997) the underlying rationale for Best Value is, once again, quality management and a customer focus. A central commitment to quality management is inherent in Best Value which is seen as being 'not just about economy and efficiency, but also about effectiveness and the quality of local services' (Armstrong 1997:2). As an agenda for quality, Best Value will become increasingly prominent within local authorities as it replaces CCT in the new millennium.

Quality management assists with competitiveness in a number of ways. The need to be competitive requires a commercial approach to management in order to manage the efficiency and effectiveness of the service. The role of quality management in bringing about this approach can be seen in Table 11.1 where the requirements of quality management and, in particular, quality programmes, have led to the use of many commercial management techniques. Not only does quality management facilitate a customer-oriented approach to meet the demands of consumerism, it also facilitates the development of a commercial culture of management required to meet increasing competition and CCT.

Quality management, however, is not the only vehicle available for bringing about this culture change within local authority leisure services. The use of techniques such as strategic planning, marketing and financial reporting will assist with the management and organisation and increase revenue. Why, therefore, have local authority leisure providers chosen quality management over other management practices as the tool for addressing the changing leisure context?

The findings of the research suggested that this was because quality management can meet the demands of all of the key factors influencing the leisure context. The customer focus inherent within quality management allowed the increasing customer expectations to be addressed and the need to be competitive was managed by the holistic and integrative nature of quality management which has the capacity to address all aspects of operations. It was, however, the unique role of quality management in dealing with the demands of CCT that made it an obvious choice for public leisure providers. The use of quality management not only enabled local authority leisure providers to compete with other leisure providers, but accredited quality programmes were an acceptable tool for ensuring that the local authority maintained control of CCT contracts.

The Vocabulary of Quality Management

The spread of quality management to all types of organisations and industry sectors indicates its perceived value as a management tool. The general acceptance of the word quality

Table 11.1 The commercial nature of public leisure services management

Region of authority	*Professional management techniques*	*Standards and measures of performance*	*Emphasis on output controls*	*Stress on disciplined resource use*
Yorkshire	Quality management Planning and marketing PRP scheme Financial management	Standards associated with quality programme Customer comments cards User forums and surveys Customer contract with service standards Financial PIs	ISO9002 to assure quality Monthly income and expenditure analysis Investor in People Staff training	Use of quality programmes to assist with efficiency Strict financial planning and budgeting
Lincolnshire	Quality management Planning and marketing Staff review scheme Well qualified staff	Standards associated with quality programme Customer comment scheme Measures of effectiveness Financial PIs	ISO9002 to assure quality Monthly income and expenditure analysis Investor in People Staff training	Use of quality programmes to assist with efficiency Strict financial planning and budgeting
Norfolk	Quality management Planning Appraisal Scheme PRP scheme Well qualified staff	Standards associated with quality programme 2,500 customer comments cards per annum User and non-user surveys Customer contract with service standards Measures of effectiveness Financial PIs	ISO9002 to assure quality Monthly income and expenditure analysis Investor in People Staff training	Use of quality programmes to assist with efficiency Strict financial planning and budgeting Staff levels at minimum
Cheshire	Quality management Development plans Well qualified staff	Customer contract with service standards 1,000 customer comments cards per annum 'Are you being served?' Suggestion schemes User surveys Financial PIs	Monthly income and expenditure analysis Staff training	Strict financial planning and budgeting
Derbyshire	Quality management Planning Employee reviews PRP scheme Well qualified staff	Standards associated with quality programme Suggestion schemes User surveys Financial PIs	Monthly income and expenditure analysis Investor in People Staff training	Use of quality programmes to assist with efficiency Strict financial planning and budgeting Staff levels at minimum
Northumberland	Quality management Planning Performance indicators Staff surveys Well qualified staff	Financial and quality PIs Standards associated with quality programme	ISO9002 to assure quality Monthly income and expenditure analysis Investor in People	Use of quality programmes to assist with efficiency Strict financial planning and budgeting

into management has not, however, extended to a generally accepted definition of what is meant by quality. This has led to an over abundance of definitions of quality that have been identified and discussed by Davidson and Bailey (1995). Their review of the literature on 'quality' provided a detailed consideration of the main definitions of quality and identified the logical progression in their development from the manufacturing to the service sector.

From this review it is apparent that definitions of quality have evolved around several key themes, however, it is the definition of Clarke (1992:23) that is considered to be an appropriate definition of quality for the leisure industry:

> *Quality is how consistently the product or service delivered, meets or exceeds the customer's expectations and needs.*

The strength of this definition is that first, there is an awareness that meeting expectations can provide an acceptable level of quality. Second, both expectations and needs must be addressed and, finally, there must be a consistency of delivery which is a key criteria for the assessment of service quality (Parasuraman, Zeithaml and Berry 1985).

Having defined quality it is useful to identify the three other commonly used terms of quality management. These are quality control, quality assurance and quality programmes. Quality control has been defined as:

> *the operational techniques and activities that are used to fulfil requirements for quality* (BS4778 1987:1)

which in leisure terms encompasses such activities as testing chlorine levels and inspection visits of catering outlets and toilets for cleanliness. One stage further in the quality process is quality assurance which is:

> *all of those planned and systematic actions necessary to provide confidence that a product or service will satisfy given requirements for quality* (BS4778 1987)

This incorporates organisational processes from mechanical items such as thermostats on heating systems, to staff training and development. The 'confidence' brought about by quality assurance also decreases the need for quality inspectors as quality is built in to the service delivery. Finally, quality programmes are considered by Sanderson (1992) to be a combination of working practices and appropriate procedures that ensure that the provision of quality is built in to the organisation's activity.

Although the literature is full of definitions of the quality vocabulary, it is more important to define quality in terms that are meaningful for individual organisations. An indication of what is considered to be 'quality' is important as this provides the direction for quality management and quality programmes (Robinson and Wolsey 1996). It also provides a benchmark for the measurement of quality and Stabler (1996) commented that without an agreed definition of quality its assessment would be impossible as the terms used in the definition should highlight what is important when aiming to deliver a quality service. This therefore needs to be directly relevant to the organisation seeking to deliver quality services.

For example, in one local authority quality is defined as:

> *producing standards of service in our facilities which mean that customers will be encouraged to return to use our facilities.*

For this local authority, quality was used as a technique for retaining customers and as a result management activities were all geared to meeting the *standards of service* referred to above. Another local authority defines quality in a similar manner, for a similar purpose. In this local authority, quality is defined as:

providing certain standards which the customer will appreciate which means that they will make repeat visits.

In a third local authority, quality was defined as:

the best possible service at the lowest cost.

For this authority and two others, quality had to be delivered within budget constraints indicating a strong awareness of the financial difficulties affecting public leisure services management.

A Framework for Quality Management

Based on research originally carried out by Gaster (1995), the principles outlined below provide a framework for the management of service quality within the leisure industry. The holistic nature of this framework suggests that a quality strategy can be guided more effectively by a framework, incorporating the following features:

- The identification of key interest groups.
- The establishment of quality objectives.
- The management of the characteristics of service quality defined in certain key dimensions.
- Understanding of the gap between expectations and experience of a service – the 'satisfaction' gap, than by quality control initiatives.

Table 11.2 shows how the local authorities included in the research have used the framework to manage service quality. The framework allows flexibility in dealing with the changing leisure context as it requires leisure providers to consult with key interest groups in order to understand and manage the customer satisfaction gap. This overcomes a tendency to consider the development of a quality strategy to be a one-off exercise.

The identification of key interest groups

The framework, although simplistic in theory, is complex in operation. The need to firstly identify key interest groups is fundamental to the provision of a quality service as it is the expectations of these key groups that establishes what is an acceptable level of service quality. Leisure services are all affected, to some degree, by a myriad of customer groups. Public leisure providers need to consider the needs and expectations of direct and indirect customers, staff, politicians, professionals and citizens. Meeting the often conflicting requirements of all of these groups is not only impossible, but often unnecessary (Robinson 1997) and for public leisure professionals, the changing environment within which they operate requires the priority of the paying customer and of politicians and staff.

The establishment of objectives for quality

Having identified the needs of key groups, the second stage in developing a quality strategy is to establish the objectives of the strategy. There are numerous texts available on objective setting and therefore the process to be followed will not be considered further. It is important, however, that leisure providers ensure that the objectives for the quality

Table 11.2 The framework for quality management in public leisure services

Region	*Key interest group*	*Objectives for quality management*	*Management of the characteristics of service quality*	*Understanding the 'gap'*
Yorkshire	Paying customers	Service standards outlined in a customer contract. Objectives associated with ISO9002 and Investor in People.	ISO9002 Investor in People Customer care	Customer comment cards User surveys User forums
Lincolnshire	Paying customers Leisure Client function	100 per cent contract compliance. Objectives associated with ISO9002 and Investor in People.	ISO9002 Investor in People TQM Customer care	Customer comments scheme User surveys
Norfolk	Paying customers	Customer satisfaction rating of a minimum of 90 per cent. Service standards outlined in a customer contract. Objectives associated with ISO9002 and Investor in People.	ISO9002 Investor in People Charter Mark TQM British Quality Foundation	Minimum of 2,500 customer comment cards Customer forums User and non-user surveys
Cheshire	Paying customers	Service standards outlined in a customer contract.	Charter Mark Customer care	Minimum of 1,000 customer comment cards per annum 'Are you being served' meetings User surveys
Derbyshire	Paying customers	99 per cent contract compliance. Objectives associated with ISO9002 and Investor in People.	ISO9002 Investor in People Customer care	Complaints and suggestions scheme User surveys
Northumberland	Paying customers	100 per cent contract compliance. Objectives associated with ISO9002 and Investor in People.	TQM Investor in People ISO9002	Compliments, suggestions and complaints scheme Focus groups

Table 11.3 Characteristics of public service quality

Criteria	*Definition*
Reliability	Consistency of performance and dependability.
Responsiveness	Willingness of staff to provide service and timing of service.
Competence	Possession of the required skills and knowledge to perform the service.
Access	Approachability and ease of contact.
Courtesy	Politeness, respect and friendliness of contact personnel.
Communication and voice	Keeping customers informed and allowing customers to contribute to service specifications.
Credibility	Trustworthiness, honesty and believability.
Security	Freedom from danger, unnecessary risk and doubt.
Customer oriented	Knowing customer requirements and giving customer individualised attention.
Tangibles	Physical evidence of the service.

Source: Curry and Monaghan (1995) Parasuraman *et al.* (1985) and Skelcher (1992)

strategy are meaningful, realistic, obtainable and measurable in order to assist with the management of the quality of the service.

The management of the characteristics of service quality

The third principle of the framework for quality management was established by the work of Parasuraman, Zeithaml and Berry (1985) who identified a number of factors that customers use when evaluating service quality. Subsequent research by Skelcher (1992) and Curry and Monaghan (1994) tailored these for the local government context. It has been argued that the characteristics outlined in Table 11.3 need to be provided at a standard that is considered acceptable to the key customer groups and if this does not occur the quality of the service will be perceived to be poor.

These criteria provide the operating principles for the substantive content of quality management which is the use of quality programmes. This is because quality programmes have been developed to assist with the management of the above criteria, at a level that is perceived to be of a high quality.

Quality Programmes and Public Leisure Facilities

There are two types of quality programme, those that are externally developed and assessed and those that are developed in-house and are not assessed. The first group of programmes is developed, prescribed and assessed by external awarding bodies. Externally awarded programmes are considered to have advantages in terms of external recognition and validation and have been used to meet the monitoring and quality assurance requirements of CCT in the public sector. It is also possible to argue that these programmes have an additional advantage in that they provide a structured means of focusing on the quality of operations as they require a full assessment of the relevant organisational systems.

The objectives of each programme are clearly defined, by the awarding body, providing a direction for quality management and these programmes often include measures of success. They have, however, a tendency to be inflexible, requiring adherence to a formatted structure and are relatively costly to gain and maintain. The main externally awarded programmes available to leisure providers are ISO9002, Investor in People (IIP), the Charter Mark and, more recently, QUEST.

ISO9002

Originally developed by the British Standards Institute for the manufacturing industry, ISO9002 sets out how an organisation should establish, document and maintain an effective quality management system. All operations undertaken by the organisation must be identified and procedures need to be developed for ensuring the consistency of these. This means drawing up work instructions for staff who are carrying out these operations and setting associated standards. The manual must also outline a set of corrective actions for dealing with problems. Registration is gained when the auditors have carried out a detailed check to ensure that the organisation successfully operates the quality system laid out in the manual. Once registered, the systems must continue to be followed as there are bi-annual inspections for as long as registration is maintained.

One obvious strength of this quality programme is that it requires organisations to identify all operations, to write procedures for these operations and then to set associated performance standards. This is invaluable in managing the quality of the specified service and has a role to play in ensuring that operations like staff training and satisfaction measurement are carried out. ISO9002 assists with the reliability of the leisure service by ensuring that the operations of the local authority are carried out in a consistent and standardised manner. Customers can expect the service to be consistent from day-to-day and between service deliverers within the local authority. The incorporation of staff training and development activities into the work instructions helps to ensure that staff are competent and accessible. The main role ISO9002 has to play in the management of the characteristics of service quality, outlined in Table 11.3, is, however, the management of security and tangibles. Maintenance programmes, cleaning schedules and staff rotas all lend themselves to being incorporated into the quality manual as it is easy to draw up work instructions for these processes and relatively easy to set acceptable standards.

ISO9002 has an inherent weakness in that although it requires the systems incorporated into the manual to meet set standards, these standards are not evaluated by the auditors. Therefore, it is possible to successfully obtain registration of ISO9002 without setting standards that guarantee a quality service, or indeed setting standards that are acceptable to customers. If there is a requirement to obtain registration, i.e. for CCT purposes, there is the option of setting standards which are easy to achieve in order to obtain registration. Thus, registration of ISO9002 in these cases will be no indication of the provision of a quality service.

Investor in people

The Investor in People (IIP) initiative is based on a national standard of action and excellence in the continued development of the human resources of the organisation. Any organisation reaching the recognised standard in these four criteria receives the investors award and is classified as an 'Investor in People':

- *Commitment* from management to develop all employees in order to achieve business objectives.
- *Regular planning and review* of training and development needs for all employees.

- *Action* to train and develop individuals on recruitment and throughout employment.
- *Evaluation* of the organisation's investment in training and development to assess achievement and to improve future effectiveness.

(Employment Department Group 1994)

There are several potential advantages of IIP in an industry that relies on staff to deliver services of a high quality and IIP is the most commonly used accredited programme within the leisure industry. Critten (1994) discusses evidence from the Employment Department which shows that this quality programme led to accredited organisations demonstrating improved profitability and a more committed and adaptable workforce. Evidence from the Institute of Manpower (1994) shows that organisations involved with Investor in People are significantly more advanced in their human resource and business planning than those without IIP. Robinson (1998) found that local authority leisure providers felt that IIP increased staff involvement and morale.

From this, the role of IIP in managing service quality is evident. Although it is impossible to guarantee an appropriate response from staff, a good training and development programme, linked to the objectives of the organisation, is likely to increase the quality of the customer/staff interaction by improving morale, ensuring knowledge and skills and increasing communication. As a result IIP can make a significant contribution to the management of quality by improving staff responsiveness, competence and credibility.

The time and financial commitment required to resource IIP is a disadvantage for many smaller organisations, however, it can be argued that employers should have these resources available as a matter of course. It can also be argued that IIP is awarded to organisations that demonstrate little other than good practice in the management of people and the need for a quality programme to encourage organisations to carry out such management practice is concerning. In addition, there is some disadvantage to making Investor in People an achievement in that organisations who are sceptical of the value of IIP may ignore the human resources aspects of their organisation.

The Charter Mark

The Charter Mark scheme is an integral part of the Citizen's Charter and has the objective of recognising and rewarding excellence in the delivery of public services. As a result, it is only available to public leisure providers and contenders are required to outline how they meet these nine criteria devised by the Charter Mark Board:

- *Standards*: standards of service delivery must be set, monitored and published.
- *Information and openness*: full and understandable information must be made available about the running of services.
- *Choice and consultation*: providers must consult with users and should provide choice where possible.
- *Courtesy and helpfulness*: users can expect a convenient, courteous and helpful service from identifiable staff.
- *Putting things right*: services must have a complaints procedure leading to an apology, an explanation and a remedy.
- *Value for money*: services should be run in an efficient and economical manner.
- *Customer satisfaction*: providers need to be able to demonstrate customer satisfaction.
- *Measurable improvements in the quality of service*: providers must be able to demonstrate continuous improvements in services.

- *Innovative enhancements*: Improvements must be made to services without any extra costs to users.

The Charter Mark is different from other externally assessed quality programmes as only 100 awards are made each year and this external recognition of service quality is by far the most significant reason for the use of this programme (Robinson 1998). The importance of this may be explained by the fact that the Charter Mark is only open to public services and therefore has a direct relevance to public leisure providers as a benchmark of service quality.

The strengths of the Charter Mark are the need for local authorities to address the desires of customers through consultation and to provide services that are convenient to users and to provide information in an understandable form. The Charter Mark has also forced local authority leisure services to become more accountable by requiring the publishing of performance standards. It is inherently customer-oriented and also assists with the management of the characteristics of responsiveness and communication and voice.

There are three main weaknesses of the Charter Mark. First, the criteria for success were developed by the government without consultation with the users or providers of public services. There has also been a tendency to concentrate on economy and efficiency, rather than effectiveness (Pollit 1994; Gaster 1992) and finally, there has been little serious attempt to ensure equality of access.

QUEST

QUEST is the leisure specific quality programme which aims to:

> *define industry standards and good practice, and encourages their application and development in a customer focused management framework,*
>
> (Associated Quality Services 1996:1)

by encouraging managers of leisure facilities to consider their operations from the customer's point of view. Launched in September 1996, QUEST has been supported and promoted by a wide range of industry representative organisations, which includes the four home country Sports Council's who have endorsed and financed the drive for the initiative.

It is too soon to assess the impact of QUEST upon the public leisure industry, however, in theory, it should be a significant improvement on the above quality programmes as it aims to address all aspects of the organisation. The assessment of this programme focuses on operations within:

- facilities operation
- customer relations
- staffing
- service development and improvement

and requires managers to address all aspects of their operations and their customer satisfaction.

At the time of writing, however, the industry's uptake of QUEST was far below expectations, leading Sport England to commission an investigation into its poor performance. Although the results of this investigation will not be known for some time, this performance is likely to be for two main reasons. First, QUEST was launched ten years after ISO9002 and seven years after IIP and the Charter Mark. As a result, it is likely that organisations concerned with obtaining external accreditation of their service quality will have done so via these earlier initiatives. Second, the self-assessment pack which is an integral part of the programme provides a comprehensive guide to strengths and weaknesses within facility operations, thus removing the need for an external audit. Both of these factors are likely to have led to the low uptake of what can be considered the most appropriate quality programme for the leisure industry.

The second group of quality programmes to be discussed is considered to offer a more flexible and tailored approach to quality management. Quality programmes developed within the organisation have no required format and can be developed and extended in line with the organisation's aims, direction and, most importantly, resources. Although these programmes are likely to be based on published initiatives, they lack external validation which may lead to a minimalist approach to quality management. The successful use of in-house programmes requires an organisation-wide commitment to quality, particularly from senior management, and the development of a culture of quality. The main two internally developed programmes are Total Quality Management (TQM) and customer care initiatives.

Total Quality Management

Total Quality Management is considered to be distinctive as a quality programme and is differentiated by its focus on the organisation as a whole, rather than addressing specific operations within the organisation. It is defined as:

> *an approach to improving the competitiveness, effectiveness and flexibility of a whole organisation. For an organisation to be truly effective, each part of it must work properly together towards the same goals, recognising that each person and each activity affects and in turn is affected by others.* (Oakland 1993:22–23)

On a more cynical note, Dickson (1994:3) has referred to TQM as 'a complex statement of the blindingly obvious', however, the attainment of an organisational quality culture has been advocated as the way forward for all organisations facing competition in the 1990s.

TQM is often considered to be more than a quality programme and is promoted as a management philosophy, encompassing these aspects of the organisation:

- A customer orientation, both internal and external, throughout the organisation.
- Clear and appropriate organisational objectives.
- The commitment and involvement of all staff led from the top of the organisation.
- A commitment to seek to improve continuously the operations of the organisation.
- The use of systems and procedures to assure quality.
- The regular monitoring, measure and feedback of all operations.
- The education and training of all staff to ensure that they have the necessary knowledge and skills for the quality philosophy.

If TQM successfully addresses the aspects of the organisation outlined above, it is clear that this programme will allow the comprehensive management of service quality. The commitment and involvement of staff through communication, education and training assists with the service characteristics of reliability, responsiveness, competence, access, courtesy and credibility and thus goes further than IIP in managing the quality of staff. The use of systems and procedures to ensure quality assists with the reliability, security and tangibles of the service in the same manner as ISO9002. Finally, the customer orientation of

TQM, like that of the Charter Mark and customer care programmes, ensures that customers are the focus of the organisation which inevitably leads to the delivery of good service quality.

It is possible to argue, however, that Total Quality Management has several disadvantages which means the possibility of achieving it in leisure services can be contested. First, as this initiative is developed in-house, it means different things to different people and this has ensured that there is no consistent approach to TQM, nor can there be any guaranteed outcomes. In addition, this means that comparison between organisations is inevitably difficult, if not impossible, given the differing approaches to quality that have been called TQM. Second, Haywood-Farmer and Nollet (1994) noted that TQM is no 'quick fix' programme and its implementation needs to be viewed in terms of years, rather than months. This often leads to staff disillusionment and demotivation, particularly if an organisational change of priorities requires the introduction of new initiatives. Finally, the success of TQM is dependent upon a variety of principles, such as the need for clearly expressed objectives and associated performance indicators, which will present barriers to the attainment of TQM, particularly in public leisure services (Robinson 1997).

Customer care

The increasing frequency of customer care initiatives was the first indication that the quality movement was beginning to emerge within leisure services. The concern with the customer brought about by the consumer movement led leisure providers to embark upon a series of activities that have been incorporated into customer care programmes. Customer care programmes are non-assessed and encompass activities which ensure that the customer is the focus of the organisation. Concentrating on communication with customers, these quality programmes incorporate comments/complaints/suggestion schemes, customer questionnaires and user panels. In addition, they include staff training to support the customer focus.

The underlying principle of a successful customer care programme is that the quality of the service is as the customer defines it, thus highlighting its role in the management of customer satisfaction. The advantages of customer care programmes are increased customer satisfaction and thus increased revenue and motivated staff. They are also developed to suit the specific needs of the local authority and can be managed within the resources that are available to the leisure organisation.

The disadvantages of the customer care approach to quality are twofold. First, there is a danger that leisure providers will take a minimalist approach to customer care, considering customer care training for staff to be adequate to ensure the provision of quality services. Consideration of the characteristics of service quality, presented in Table 11.3 above, indicates that this approach would not be enough for the management of service quality. Second, effective management of one aspect of customer care may set up unrealistic customer expectations of the service to be delivered, as customer care programmes do not help with the quality of the tangibles of the service.

The Role of Quality Programmes in Managing Public Leisure Services

It has been argued by Gaster (1992) and Skelcher (1992) that quality programmes can assist with the management of the parts of the leisure service that can be specified, standardised and are primarily within management control. As a result, their role in the management of quality is apparent as many of the characteristics of quality outlined above require

Table 11.4 The role of quality programmes in the management of service quality

Programme	*Characteristics of service quality managed by the programme*
ISO9002	Reliability, competence, access, security and tangibles.
Investor in People	Responsiveness, competence, credibility.
Charter Mark	Responsiveness, communication and voice, customer orientated.
QUEST	All aspects of the service.
Total Quality Management	All aspects of the service.
Customer care programmes	Responsiveness, competence, communication and voice, customer orientated.

the specification of standardised features and characteristics. The potential role of quality programmes in the management of the aforementioned characteristics of service quality is presented in Table 11.4.

The customer satisfaction gap

The final dimension to be considered in the framework of quality management is how the customer satisfaction gap is identified, understood and managed. This refers to the gap between customer satisfaction with the level of service quality and the actual service quality that is delivered. Gaster (1992) considered this dimension to cover the attitudes, behaviour, impressions and expectations of customers. For many leisure providers this is likely to present the biggest problem in managing quality as it requires the acknowledgement and management of the differences between customer expectations and service performance.

The main issue to be addressed by public leisure providers in the management of customer satisfaction is the need to measure the quality of their operations. Stabler (1996) has argued that without a measurement of service quality, the management of the gap between the quality of service expected and that delivered will be difficult. This is because customer satisfaction is inherently subjective, influenced by timing and circumstances and reacts to external influences. As it never remains constant it therefore needs to be measured to be assessed.

The various methods of measuring service quality have been discussed by Robinson (1997) and Robinson and Wolsey (1996), however, there is a tendency for key measures to be financial and more specifically expenditure based. As a result, leisure organisations must consult with customers to establish first, expectations of service quality and second, standards of actual performance. In addition, public leisure providers must not rely on one measure of service quality. Customers need to be directed to comment on all aspects of the service to ensure that the complete service is being assessed. Reliance on one measure of satisfaction is likely to provide an inadequate picture of service quality.

It is possible, however, to argue that the assessment of customer satisfaction only establishes the size of the customer satisfaction gap, this then needs to be managed. This is the purpose of quality programmes as given their roles in managing the aspects of service quality, identified by Curry and Monaghan (1994), Parasuraman *et al.* (1985) and Skelcher (1992), their value in managing the customer satisfaction gap is evident.

Summary and Conclusions

This chapter has shown the value of quality management within public leisure services and as a result suggests that quality management and its associated techniques are a valuable management tool for leisure managers. Indeed, the presented research carried out by Robinson (1999) suggests that quality management is the vital key to the successful management of public leisure services into the millennium. Although this chapter focused primarily on public leisure services, the principles and evidence presented within are equally, if not more so, applicable to the commercial sector as commercial organisations rely on customer satisfaction to survive. As a result, the outlined framework for quality management will provide a means of ensuring services of high quality within all leisure organisations.

Suggested Tasks for Further Study

1. Compare and evaluate the quality management strategies adopted by one commercial leisure organisation and one public leisure organisation.
2. Evaluate the relevance of the framework for quality management within voluntary organisations.
3. Identify the role of quality management within the context of 'Best Value'.
4. Evaluate the concept of the 'public service orientation' for local authority leisure services.

References

- Associated Quality Services 1996 *QUEST* Publicity material, Sports Council, London
- BS4778 1987 *Quality Vocabulary: Part 1, International Terms* British Standards Institute, London
- Clark F 1992 'Quality and service in the public sector' *Public Finance and Accountancy* 23 October pp.24–26
- Clarke M and Stewart J 1987 'The Public Service Orientation' *Local Government Policy Making* Vol.13 No.4 March pp.34–40
- Critten P 1994 *Human Resource Management in the Leisure Industry* Longman, Harlow
- Curry A and Monaghan C 1994 'Service quality in local authorities: BS5750/ISO9000: friend or foe?' *Local Government Policy Making* Vol.21 No.4 pp.43–50
- Dale B G 1994 *Managing Quality* Prentice Hall, London
- Davidson C and Bailey S J 1995 *Quality: A literature review and analytical framework* Discussion paper 26, Dept. of Economics, Caledonian University, Glasgow
- Dickson T 1994 'In search of excellence – TQM is about to gain a higher profile' *The Financial Times* 2 February 1994 p.3
- Employment Department Group 1994 *Investor in People: can employers afford not to participate?* Briefing paper Issue 3 May 1994
- Gaster L 1992 'Quality in service delivery: competition for resources or more effective use of resources?' *Local Government Policy Making* Vol.19 No.1 July pp.55–64

- Gaster L 1995 *Quality in public services: manager's choices* Open University Press, Buckingham
- Haywood-Farmer J and Nollet J 1994 'Professional service firms and Total Quality Management: A good fit?' *International Journal of Service Industry Management* Vol.5 No.3 pp.5–13
- Institute of Manpower Studies 1994 in Employment Department Group 1994 *How do employers benefit from becoming Investor in People?* Briefing paper. Issue 9 May 1994
- Local Government Training Board 1987 *Getting closer to the public* LGTB, Luton
- Oakland J S 1993 *Total Quality Management* Butterworth-Heinmann, Oxford
- Parasuraman A, Zeithaml V and Berry L 1985 'A conceptual model of service quality and its implications for future research' *Journal of Marketing* Vol.49 Fall pp.41–50
- Pollitt C 1994 'The Citizen's Charter. A preliminary analysis' *Public Money and Management* April–June, pp.9–14
- Robinson L 1997 'Barriers to Total Quality Management in public leisure services' *Managing Leisure: An International Journal* Vol.2 No.1 January pp.17–28
- Robinson L 1998 'Chapter 14: Quality management in public leisure services' in Collins M F and Cooper I S 1998 *Leisure management: issues and applications* CAB International, Oxon
- Robinson L 1999 *The management of service quality within public leisure services* Unpublished Doctorate, Loughborough University
- Robinson L and Wolsey C 1996 'Considerations in Developing the Public Service Orientation' *Local Government Policy Making* Vol.23 No.1 July pp.65–70
- Sanderson I 1992 *Management of quality in local government* Longman, Harlow
- Sheppard M and Studd S 1994 *Quality in perspective* Sports Council, London
- Skelcher C 1992 *Managing for service quality* Longman, Harlow
- Stabler M 1996 'The emerging new worlds of leisure quality: does it matter and can it be measured?' in Collins M (Ed) *Leisure in different worlds Vol.2 Leisure in industrial and post-industrial societies* pp.249–268, Leisure Studies Association, Eastbourne
- Wille E 1992 *Quality: achieving excellence* Century Business, London

Chapter 12

The Management of Change in the Leisure and Sport Management Sector

Jeff Abrams
Leeds Metropolitan University

Chapter Content

- Introduction
- Understanding Organisational Change
- Key Variables for Change
- Some Research Considerations
- The Process and Models of Organisational Change
- Effective Change: Popular Prescriptions for Success and Failure
- Summary and Conclusions
- Suggested Tasks for Further Study
- References

Abstract

This chapter provides an overview of relevant literature in the area of managing change and applies this to the leisure and sport management context. Models and theories are discussed and reviewed. This includes a range of theoretical perspectives; some which are prescriptive and recipe driven and some which are theoretical. Examples of the impact of these theories and models are presented throughout the chapter. The first section of the chapter deals with the basics of understanding organisational change. Key variables for change are discussed in the next section which is followed by a series of models, theories and practices relating to change management from various traditions and viewpoints. Conclusions are drawn from the above discussion points followed by a number of further activities and tasks.

Related Chapters

Chapter 1: The UK Public Sector: the theory and practice of change management can explain many of the changes experienced within the public leisure sector.

Chapter 3: The UK Voluntary Sector: The need for the voluntary leisure sector to become more businesslike and more accountable raises certain challenges for the sector. Again the theory and practice of change management may help to explain some of these problems and challenges.

Chapter 6: Competitor Strategy: The debates about the extent to which managers shape the nature of change and strategy as opposed to the markets and external forces brings these two chapters closely together. Often the unassailable assumptions held by strategic planners are that they can anticipate and control the external environment. This may not always be the case as outlined in the chapter on managing change.

Learning Objectives

- to provide a framework for understanding organisational change in the leisure and sport management context
- to present processes and models and theories for change
- to identify prescriptions for effective change management as well as why things go wrong
- to relate the theory to leisure and sport management practice through the use of examples

Introduction

The leisure industry is diverse and it is difficult to make broad generalisations that will apply in all cases. It is fairly safe ground to say, however, that leisure providers are experiencing significant changes at the moment and will continue to do so into the future. Whether it is about responding to government policy in the case of the public sector, or the need to become more professionalised in the voluntary sector, change will be a key preoccupation for leisure providers. This chapter sets out to identify a range of models and theories, which may be useful in addressing organisational change within the leisure industry. In order to achieve this objective a brief review of relevant generic management literature will be presented followed by a range of relevant examples.

It is hoped that the reader will be able to make the connections between the two.

Understanding Organisational Change

To understand organisations it is important to remember that the organisation will be viewed differently by different interest groups. In addition, organisations are often made up of coalitions of competing interest groups (see Salaman 1981; Mouzelis 1985) looking to protect their respective interests.

The work of Argyris and Shon (1978) is particularly relevant here. They suggest that in order to accurately assess the internal workings of organisations you need to be clear on the difference between espoused theory and theory in use. Espoused theory relates to what people say and theory in use is what people do. They concentrated on managers in their study and found a mismatch between espoused theory and theory in use. The interesting point of this work relates to the fact that managers were not aware of this mismatch. From a leisure and sport manager's perspective this is an important point which is often not fully considered during a period of significant transformational change. In order to address this issue leisure and sport managers need to consider the impact of their change management process on key stakeholders.

Wilson (1992) makes an interesting distinction between planned and emergent change. He suggests that planned change is about the uncritical acceptance of the managerial role and is primarily about convincing others of the utility of reorganisation. Emergent change is about powerful factions in organisations trying to get what they want out of the change process (see Hickson *et al.* 1986).

It is important to accept that all organisations change over time and it is the degree and pace of change which is significant. There are interesting assumptions about the best way to change, which tend to be cultural bound to the UK and the USA. The dominant British and American perspectives are based on sweeping, usually unassailable, assumptions that change is best left to senior management. The onus for change, therefore, lies solely with management. This is challenged by the Swedish approach based on the Law of Co-determination. In this context change becomes the responsibility of a wider forum to include works supervisors, junior and middle managers.

The Japanese emphasise teamwork, responsibility and autonomy. They also have national culture, which is less likely to challenge legitimate authority. The American and British perspectives on change take little account of context in which needs, values and beliefs are formed (or manipulated). Social psychology emphasising success in persuasion and negotiation is most important to the above.

Organisation development (OD) approaches are one way of addressing these issues. Sociological perspectives would take subordination and control as its prevailing themes (Salaman 1981; Mouzelis 1985). The ideas of managerial hegemony (managers as powerful interest groups), managerialism (managers using their power for the promotion of self interest reinforced by the divide between managers, owners and subordinates), power and politics are all relevant here. For example, Barlow (1989) describes many western human resource strategies for change as being little more than symbolic affairs in which dominant power groups define reality in their own interests. This is reinforced by Feldman (1989). According to Feldman planned changes involving the development of decentralised, flexible and innovative firms in the west are largely at the expense of the individual worker's autonomy. The dominant theory in use, therefore, is concerned with planned change through managers trained (or not) in specific techniques who develop specific skills to see change through.

The model below attempts to provide a broad framework for understanding the structure and variables that impact or most significant change processes. Each situation a leisure and sport manager faces, however, will be different, so therefore the balance and weight of these variables will also shift according to the particular circumstances.

Key Variables for Change

Outer context: the external environment

- *Socio-political*: This includes changing consumer tastes and expectations as well as macro political interventions in the form of government legislation. Examples of this are the implementation of Compulsory Competitive Tendering and Best Value in the public sector.

- *Economic*: This includes economic trends and the impact of these trends on leisure and sport providers. Issues such as disposal income and the nature of employment are relevant here.
- *Legal*: The legal responsibilities of leisure and sport providers are continually assessed. The regulatory framework within which leisure and sport managers operate will often shape the decision-making process during periods of significant change.
- *Technological*: Technological change has an impact both on consumer taste and expectations but also on the changing nature of work.
- *Business competitive environment of the organisation*: The competitive environment will shape the markets that leisure and sport organisations trade in and ultimately whether the organisation succeeds or fails. Change is often driven by the need to stay in touch with competitors in order to survive.

The organisation response to change driven by external factors is the key to success or otherwise. The next part of the model addresses the internal dynamics of organisations. It is the fit between the internal response to change and the external factors which is the key to successful change management. It is extremely difficult, however, to accurately account for all of the possible external factors leisure and sport managers need to consider during periods of significant change. The model at least provides a framework which could be the starting point for identifying how internal processes, systems and behaviour responds to external forces.

Inner context: the internal organisation dynamics

- *Leadership*: It goes without saying that leadership during periods of significant change is critical to the success of that change. It is often the leaders in the organisation who initiate and drive change. The approach adopted and the style of management alongside this will influence the implementation of change. This also influences the degree of resistance or compliance and the internal health of any organisation.
- *Organisation structure*: Structures are often the first thing that changes in an organisation when faced with external pressure. The prescription in the late 1990s through to the present suggests that organisations need to be leaner with fewer managerial levels, less people at all levels and generally more efficient all round. This leads to a situation where there are fewer people having to be more flexible in their work patterns and, at the same time, to provide a higher quality of service or product to keep up with the competitive environment. Here again there are interesting challenges for leisure and sport managers.
- *Organisational culture*: The organisational culture relates to the values and beliefs held by the majority of the people working in an organisation. This is shaped by the history of the organisation, its people and primarily its leaders. It is thought that the leader's role is to articulate the values required in the organisation and to reinforce what is acceptable behaviour. As in all issues of human dynamics this is not as easy as it may first appear. In most organisations there are sub-cultures which have their own set of values and behaviour patterns which may, or may not, be consistent with that of more senior people. Again, this becomes an important issue with regard to resistance, power and control during periods of significant change.

- *Personalities and people*: This area is very closely aligned to the issue of culture, behaviour and control. Being sensitive to the needs, skills and informal networks is also important. It is thought that change is now becoming a way of life in most leisure and sport organisations, creating a range of responses. These include:
  - enthusiasm
  - neutrality
  - hostility
  - behavioural
  - attitudinal
  - compliance
  - resistance
- *Political processes*: through which ideas for change must proceed.

The timing, pace and historical context for change are also relevant.

Some Research Considerations

According to Wilson (1992), if the theory of change demands that evidence is collected about the history, socio-economic context and the inter-play of organisational power plays over time, then the method should be in-depth and longitudinal. If the context is thought to be less important than the attributes of individual managers then individual attributes (such as personality, leadership qualities, etc.) become the focus of the study.

Cross sectional studies

- *Voluntarism*: the cognitive actions of managers as a means to understand change.
- *Determinism*: forces of economics, environment and context (determinism) as a means to understand change (Wilson 1992).

> *The power of the economics of the market versus the power of managers to effect change has become one of the key theories of debate at the moment. This leads to a fundamental question – can managers plan strategically for change?*
>
> (Wilson 1992)

According to Wilson (1992:48), to understand the implementation of change is to place the management (and in the extreme, perhaps, the manipulation) of individuals at centre stage. Wilson (1992) goes on to state that in order to understand the process of change, it is necessary to critically examine the context, the antecedents and the movement and history of changes, keeping at the same time an analytical eye on the organisation's theories-in-use which inform such analysis. In other words, leisure and sport managers need to be sensitive to the history of the organisation as well as the personal histories of the people within the organisation during periods of significant change. This is particularly the case with people who can inform the change process or who will be affected by it. This awareness may help to reduce resistance to change and improve the decision-making process.

Hickson *et al.* (1986) identify the examination of context as a huge undertaking which requires a synthesis of understanding of the environment, the characteristics of strategic decision-making processes and the characterisation of transformation and change in specific organisations.

Wilson (1992) is very critical of much of the theory and practice of change. He suggests that much of this is recipe-driven at best. In the worst cases theories of change rest upon few theoretical foundations, rely as much upon emotional feel as upon rigorous analysis. Leisure and sport managers are often looking for practical solutions to problems rather than theoretical explanations. Nonetheless, a sound grasp of the research into managing change and the resulting theory can help to inform the choice of action a leisure and sport manager decides to take.

Structural functionalism: The search for generalised laws of change – for example Taylorism or Human Relations Theories – which set out to find the answer to how to improve organisational effectiveness. In doing this both of these theories, and many more like them, identified key factors that lead to success. In the case of Taylorism it was managerial control that was the key and in the case of Human Relations Theory it was the role of the group in task performance that was the key. This leads to change being achieved through a set of specified managerial skills (inter-personal, team building, self-development and management competencies), which are based on underpinning assumptions. Again in the case of Taylorism it is the idea that workers need to be controlled and in the case of Human Relations Theory it is the need to work with and through groups.

The irrational school of change management

- March and Simon (1958) *Bounded Rationality*
- Lindblom (1959) *Incrementalism*
- Quinn (1982) *Logical Incrementalism*

The above represent how organisational transitions are made through the decision-making process which is less about rational, informed strategy and more about step-by-step approaches. These ideas challenge the ability of organisations to plan strategically and suggest that in reality there is a bit of planning and more than a bit of reacting to the forces of change. Often it is the external forces which drive change. A good example of this is the implementation of Compulsory Competitive Tendering and Best Value in the UK public leisure sector. This could not really be planned for in any meaningful way. Leisure providers in this sector could only react to the change when it became clear that it was going to be implemented. It is often the case that elaborate strategies are produced by leisure and sport providers which are obsolete before the ink is dry due to the changes in the external environment.

March and Olson (1976) extend the above ideas by describing organised anarchy as there being little connection between rational decision-making and actual choice of decision. This, they argue, is driven by organisational politics. March and Simon (1958) state that the change process could become more linear and more rational if better information were available. This assumes, however, that information once available is shared within the leisure and sport organisation. This may not always be the case. This issue is explored below.

Michels (in Mouzelis 1984) Describes organisation oligarchy as the situation where powerful individuals or groups withhold or distort information to serve their interests. As a consequence of this, organisations can never truly be democratic. Wilson (1992) identifies the political perspective on change that argues, even where the knowledge base is optimised, processes of strategic change would still be predominantly shaped, and outcomes largely determined, by the exercise of power and influence.

There is a general theme in the literature supporting the view that an approach which provides opportunities for individual accounts of situations, which is interpretative, and which considers power and influence as most appropriate.

The Process and Models of Organisational Change

The models and prescriptions for managing change outlined below provide useful processes for managing and understanding change in the leisure and sport management context. Again these are models which need to be considered alongside the theoretical points raised in previous sections of this chapter.

Change process: steps

- diagnosing problems and solutions
- identifying resistance to change
- developing a strategy of implementation that allocates responsibility and deals with planned change

Resource dependence theorists (Aldrich and Pfeffer 1976)

Organisations are unable to sustain resources sufficient for survival. They become dependent on external resources which creates uncertainty. Many leisure and sport providers may find themselves in this situation. Examples include the dependency of National Governing Bodies of Sport in the UK, on grants from the UK Sports Council, or the public sector leisure provider who is dependent primarily on block grants from government to support their provision.

Institutional theorists (Dimaggio and Powell 1983)

Change to conform to expectations: corporate fitness is an example of this.

Adaptive approaches: culture (see Meek 1988; Kanter 1983; Deal and Kennedy 1982)

Emphasises organisational culture as a source of commitment and resistance to change. Slack (1991) suggests that you need to look at organisational change from more than one perspective to understand the complexities of change. Slack supports the ideas of Tolbert (1985:3) who states:

> *Organisational phenomena are much too complex to be described adequately by any single theoretical approach. Current research on organisations could benefit greatly if researchers were to pay closer attention to specifying the points of intersection of different theoretical perspectives and to combining these perspectives to provide more complete explanations of the behaviours they study.*

This quotation is based on contingency theory, which states that there is no one best way to solve organisational problems. Instead, in order to assess change, researchers and leisure and sport managers need to address the different contingencies faced by the organisation. We have already highlighted some of these considerations above and they include the external environment, technology, inter-personal relationships, power and politics, resources, to name a few. Contingency theory advocates the need to create the best fit between the key variables and the organisation.

Other areas for consideration include whether the change was managed. There is an assumption that all change is managed. This is sometimes not the case with organisations drifting from one crisis to another. The current knowledge and skill base of the transformational leaders is a critical consideration during periods of significant change. The links between strategy, planning and implementation for change is also key. It is important to note that if there is a general consensus that change is required then implementation is considered less problematic. The problem arises when objectives between groups in leisure and sport organisations are in conflict, leading to a more powerful group imposing decisions on the less powerful group. This in turn leads to tensions within the organisation, which need to be managed. The effectiveness of change will be directly related to the strategy pursued and the quality of the change managers' skills.

Other areas of importance relate to the sources, timing and pace of change.

Change approaches

Approaches to organisational change tend to come under one of the following headings:

- *Behavioural approaches* – these include the interpersonal, social psychological and organisational development techniques, which will be outlined below.
- *Structural approaches* – which include organisational design, structure, environmental linkages based on systems theory.
- *Cultural approaches* – which considers organisational climate, ideologies and prevailing beliefs (culture) as pre-eminent.
- *Resource dependence approaches* – organisations are unable to sustain resources sufficient for survival and become deponent on external resources. This is prevalent in the voluntary leisure sector.
- *Panacea school of change approaches* – identifies key variables for successful change. A universal view of effective change management is then adopted. The most successful authors in this area are Peters and Waterman. It is interesting to note that the work of Peters and Waterman has been widely criticised for being empirically and theoretically weak.
- *Models for change approaches* – Kurt Lewin's Force Field model is perhaps the most noted of these approaches. The model consists of three basic elements:
  1. Unfreeze the existing organisation practices (for example this can be done by creating dissatisfaction with the present state)
  2. Change the existing practices
  3. Refreeze the organisation in the new approaches for a period of stability.

Elms (1968) suggests that the management of change within an organisation requires the manager to deal with and understand two major concepts, those of attitudes and behaviour. Attitudes are what one believes, how one feels and behaviour is what one does.

Heider (1946) coined the term 'cognitive consistency', which began to relate these two variables. The human mind, according to Heider, has a strong need for consistency and attitudes may be generally changed in order to eliminate some inconsistency. Cognitive consistency is therefore the state where no inner psychological tensions exist for the individual and there is no need to change one's mind about anything. The difficulty for individuals within organisations faced with significant change relates to what Festinger (1957) describes as 'cognitive dissonance'. This is the state of psychological discomfort or tension when faced with change. The individual is motivated to achieve consonance to reduce the feeling of psychological discomfort. This manifests itself in a number of ways. Individuals can either conform to the change process and rationalise this choice, can look to influence the change process in a way that is consistent with their psychological needs (this is always quite difficult to achieve in practice), or they can look to leave the organisation which is dependant on the fluidity of the employment situation. Alternatively, they may entrench against, attempt to ignore or resist the change. Schon (1971) takes the view

Table 12.1 Dunphy and Stace contingency model for change

	Simple change	*Transformational change*
Collaborate	When the organisation is in fit with its environment but only needs fine tuning. Time is available. Key interest groups favour the change.	When the organisation is out of fit. There is little time. Key interest groups support radical change.
Coerce	When the organisation is in fit with the environment but needs fine tuning. Key interest groups oppose the change.	When the organisation is out of fit. There is little time. Key interest groups oppose change, but change is central for survival.

that organisation members resist change and are dynamically conservative in nature. As a consequence the response by managers when faced with significant change is exhortation. It has been pointed out by Wellens (1975) that academic behavioural scientists and experienced managers have come to the view that exhortation is not usually an effective instrument for producing change, yet it is still the technique most frequently advocated both within organisations and the public generally. Wellens (1975) advocates a model based on an attitude behaviour loop. He argues that it is necessary to penetrate change at the behavioural stage, in other words, to change what people are doing and the ways they behave towards each other, rather than to attempt to change what people are thinking or believing. Dunphy and Stace (1988) more recently provide a change model based on contingency theory, which incorporates both of the above ideas (see Table 12.1).

Kurt Lewin's planned change strategy

We have already discussed briefly Kurt Lewin's model for organisational change. It is worth exploring this approach a little further as it provides a useful framework for identifying forces for and against change.

Force Field Analysis as we know consists of three processes which are outlined below:

- unfreezing or status quo
- the change to be effected
- refreezing or consolidation of new state

Lewin provides a list of prescriptions which are useful for the leisure and sport manager to consider when faced with the responsibility for implementing change.

Forces for change:

- new personnel
- changing markets
- shorter product life cycles
- changing attitudes towards work
- internationalisation
- global markets
- social transformations
- increased competition
- new technology

Forces against change:

From individuals:

- fear of failure
- loss of status
- inertia
- fear of unknown

From organisations:

- strength of culture (this can work both ways)
- rigidity of structure
- lack of resources
- strongly-held beliefs

Effective Change: Popular Prescriptions for Success and Failure

Pettigrew and Whip (1991) suggest that you can observe the way higher performing firms manage change from their lesser performing counterparts and you can observe the actions of higher performing organisations. They define five central factors, which help to explain these differences.

- environmental assessment
- leading change
- linking strategic to operational changes
- human resource as assets and liabilities
- coherence in the management of change

Nadler (in Mabey and Mayon-White 1993) provides a model based on systems theory which includes: inputs (environment, resources) history (transformation process) and outputs. He goes on to suggest that the organisational arrangements generally consist of structures, processes, systems, set against motivation performance, task accomplishment. The basic hypothesis of this model is to achieve effective change through congruence of the major components or variables affected by change.

Problems with implementing change are also highlighted by Nadler (1993) and include:

- resistance
- organisation control linked to stability
- power and political difficulties

Nadler (1993) goes on to describe effective change. He suggests there are several criteria to consider:

- the organisation is moved from the current state to the future state
- the functioning of the organisation in the future state meets expectations, i.e. works as planned
- the transition is accomplished without undue cost to the organisation
- action steps to motivate for change include:
  creating dissatisfaction with the present state, one way of achieving this is through the use of information linked to performance
  participation reduces resistance to change
  reward desired behaviour
  develop and communicate a clear image of the future

Beer, Eisentat and Spector (in Mabey, Mayon-White 1993) are interested in why change programmes don't produce change. The fundamental flaw in change programmes relates to the basic assumption that the starting point is with knowledge and attitudes of individuals. Change in attitudes leads to change in behaviour. They argue that this is back to front. Change in behaviour is shaped by the organisational roles that people play. The most effective way to change behaviour is to put people into a new organisational context, which imposes new roles, responsibilities and relationships on them. This forces new attitudes and behaviour on people. They suggest that there are three interrelated factors, which lead to effective change:

- co-ordination
- commitment
- competencies

The problem is that organisations usually address one or two of the above but not all three. They prescribe six steps to effective change:

- Mobilise commitment to change through joint diagnosis of the problems.
- Develop a shared vision of how to organise and manage for competitiveness.
- Foster consensus for the new vision, competence to enact and cohesion to move it along. Strong transformational leadership is critical.
- Spread revitalisation to all concerned without pushing it from the top.
- Institutionalise revitalisation through formal policies, systems and structures.
- Monitor and adjust strategies in response to problems in the revitalisation process. According to this prescription organisations must continually evaluate their behaviour – they must *learn how to learn.*

The above points present a somewhat one-dimensional view and do not wholly account for the political realities experienced in most leisure and sport organisations, since they appear to not recognise some of the contingencies which are so powerfully represented in other models of organisational change.

Pugh (in Mabey and Mayon-White 1993) begins to address the political realities in his change model, which is based on four substantive principles and six rules. The principles are:

- Organisations are organisms: change must be approached carefully, with the implications for the various groupings thought out and the participants convinced that it is worthwhile from their point of view.
- Organisations are occupational and political systems as well as rational resource-allocation ones: change thus affects the ways of working, number of jobs, career prospects, motivation, the political systems, and the power and prestige of groups.
- All members of an organisation operate simultaneously in three systems – the rational, the occupational and the political.
- Change is most likely to be acceptable and effective in those people whose groups are successful but who are experiencing tension or failure in some particular part of their work. They will have confidence in their ability and motivation to change. The next group of individuals most likely to change is the successful, while the least likely to change are the unsuccessful.

Pugh's six rules for managing change successfully are as follows:

1. The need for change should be carefully established.
2. The change should not only be thought out, but thought through. In order to achieve this the likely impact of the change on key stakeholders needs to be considered, e.g. by systematically addressing the following issues:
   - Will the change alter job content?
   - Will it introduce new and/or unknown tasks?
   - Will it disrupt established methods of working (and for how long)?
   - Will it rearrange group relationships (or remove some)?
   - Will it reduce autonomy or authority? Whose?
   - Will it be perceived to lead to lower status? Whose?
   - Will/can it be established with full explanation and discussion?
3. The change should be through formal discussion to obtain feedback and participation from stakeholders.
4. Those concerned should be positively encouraged to state their objectives.
5. The change agents should themselves be prepared to change: otherwise, rigidity and resistance can be the result.
6. The change should be monitored and reinforced.

Pfeffer (1981) provides a list of suggested key guidance points for consideration when implementing change:

- Decide on the goals, and what it is intended to accomplish.
- Diagnose patterns of dependence and interdependence. What individuals are influential and important in achieving the goal?
- What are their points of view likely to be? How will they feel about the proposed change?
- What are the power bases? Which is more influential in the decision?
- What are the bases of influence? What bases of influence can be developed to gain more control over the situation?
- Which strategies and tactics for exercising power seem most appropriate?
- Based on the above, choose the appropriate course of action for approaching the change.

Summary and Conclusions

It is clear that there is no one best theory or approach to organisation change that will be applicable in all situations. There are many impinging variables that will need to be considered in any set of circumstances. These have been highlighted through the literature presented in the chapter. It is also important to state that the literature in the field of organisation change is quite extensive. The information provided in this chapter represents a small sample of such literature. There are no easy answers, prescriptions or quick fixes when dealing with the complexities of significant organisational change. Contingency theory, which advocates a best fit approach, may go some way to helping leisure and sport managers to diagnose problems and identify appropriate strategies when faced with the difficult task of managing change.

Suggested Tasks for Further Study

Identify a leisure and sport organisation that has gone through a recent significant change.

1. Plot out the process of change that the organisation has gone through.
2. Identify the main drivers for change. Was it internal? Was it external? Was it poor performance?
3. Identify whether there was resistance to the change. Where was the resistance? Was it overt or more subtle? How was resistance managed?
4. Who were the winners in the change? Who were the losers?
5. Was the change for the better?
6. Was the implementation of change successful? How do you know that the implementation was successful?
7. What leadership and decision-making processes were apparent? Were key stakeholders involved during the change process?
8. How could the change process have been improved? Justify your response here by using theories outlined in the chapter.

References

- Aldrich H E and Pfeffer J 1976 'Environments of organizations' *Annual Review of Sociology* 2 pp.79–105
- Argyris C and Schon D 1978 *Organisational Learning. A Theory of Action Perspective Reading* Addison Wesley, Mass
- Barlow G 1989 'Deficiencies and the perpetuation of power: latent functions in management appraisal' *Journal of Management Studies* 26 pp.499–517
- Beer M, Eistenstat R A and Spector B 1993 in Chris Mabey and Bill Mayon-White (Eds) *Managing Change* Open University Press, Milton Keynes pp.99–107
- Deal T E and Kennedy A A 1982 *Corporate Cultures* Penguin Business
- Dimaggio P and Powell W 1983 'The iron cage revisited: institutional isomorphism and collective rationality in organizational fields' *American Sociological Review* 48 pp.147–160
- Dunphy D C and Stace D A 1988 'Transformational and coercive strategies for planned organizational change' *Organisational Studies* 9(3) pp.317–325
- Elms A C 1968 'Role Playing, Incentive and Dissonance' *Psychological Bulletin* Vol.68
- Festinger L 1957 *A Theory of Cognitive Dissonance* Stanford University Press, California
- Hickson D J, Butler R J, Cray D, Mallory G and Wilson D C 1986 *Top Decisions: Decision Making in Organizations* Blackwell, Oxford
- Kanter R M 1983 *The Change Masters: Corporate Entrepreneurs at Work* Counterpoint, New York
- Lewin K 1951 *Field Theory in Social Science* Harper and Row, New York
- Meek V L 1988 'Organizational Culture: Origins and Weaknesses' *Organization Studies* 9 pp.453–473
- Mouzelis N 1984 *Organization and Bureaucracy* Routledge, London
- Nadler 1993 in Chris Mabey and Bill Mayon-White (Eds) *Managing Change* Open University Press, Milton Keynes pp.85–98
- Peters T J and Waterman R H 1982 *In Search of Excellence* Harper and Row, New York

- Petergrew A and Whipp R 1991 *Managing Change for Competitive Success* Blackwell, Oxford
- Pfeffer J 1981 *Power in Organizations* Pitman, London
- Pugh 1993 in Chris Mabey and Bill Mayon-White (Eds) *Managing Change* Open University Press, Milton Keynes pp.108–112
- Quinn J B 1980 *Strategies for Change: Logical Incrementalism* Irwin
- Salaman G 1981 *Class and the Corporation* Fontana, London
- Schon D A C 1983 *The Reflective Practitioner. How Professionals Think in Action* Basic Books, New York
- Slack T 1992 'Understanding change in national sports organizations: an integration of critical perspectives' *Journal of Sport Management* 6 pp.114–132
- Tolbert P 1985 'Resource dependence and institutional environments: sources of administrative structure in institutions of higher education' *Administrative Science Quarterly*
- Wellens J 1975 *Attitudes and Behaviour Industrial and Commercial Training*
- Wilson D 1992 *A Strategy of Change: concepts and controversies in the management of change* Routledge, London

Index